*The Art and Life of Clarence Major*

# The Art and Life of Clarence Major

KEITH E. BYERMAN

THE UNIVERSITY OF GEORGIA PRESS

ATHENS AND LONDON

A Sarah Mills Hodge Fund Publication

This publication is made possible in part through a grant from the
Hodge Foundation in memory of its founder, Sarah Mills Hodge, who
devoted her life to the relief and education of African Americans
in Savannah, Georgia.

Set in Minion Pro by Graphic Composition, Inc., Bogart, Georgia.
Manufactured by Sheridan Books

The paper in this book meets the guidelines for permanence
and durability of the Committee on Production Guidelines for
Book Longevity of the Council on Library Resources.

Printed in the United States of America

16   15   14   13   12   C   5   4   3   2   1

Library of Congress Cataloging-in-Publication Data

Byerman, Keith Eldon, 1948–
     The art and life of Clarence Major / Keith E. Byerman.
        p. cm.
     Includes bibliographical references and index.
     ISBN 978-0-8203-3055-6 (cloth : alk. paper)
     — ISBN 0-8203-3055-8 (cloth : alk. paper)
     1. Major, Clarence. I. Title.
     PS3563.A39Z55 2012
     813'.54—dc23
     [B]        2011047041

British Library Cataloging-in-Publication Data available

# Contents

# Illustrations

PLATES

(following page 132)

# Acknowledgments

I want to express my appreciation to the library staffs at the Archie Givens Sr. Collection at the University of Minnesota and the Harry Ransom Center at the University of Texas for their invaluable assistance with archival materials. The University Research Committee of Indiana State University provided grants to cover both research expenses and some of the costs of printing images. Colleagues at various conferences offered insightful comments as I worked through ideas that became part of this project. Kit Kincade was infinitely patient and thoughtful as I tried to make sense of some of the puzzles and quandaries that go along with writing biography. But my greatest appreciation goes to Clarence Major, who opened his home and his memory banks to provide me with facts, names, and stories that were not available from any other source, and who allowed me to reprint the various images that appear herein. He has been consistently forthcoming, gracious, and encouraging throughout the years it has taken to complete this book.

*The Art and Life of Clarence Major*

# Performing Transgression, Seeking Community

Clarence Major is an artistic renaissance man; he is a painter, fiction writer, poet, essayist, editor, anthologist, lexicographer, and memoirist. For the first three of these, he must be considered a professional. He has pursued them since childhood and has won awards in all three. He has been part of twenty-eight group exhibitions, has had fifteen one-man shows, and has published fourteen collections of poetry and nine works of fiction. Although he has never achieved the fame of other writers of his generation, such as Toni Morrison or Ernest Gaines, he has a substantial reputation among those interested in experimentation in the arts. He is a technician, working and reworking problems in composition in his various arts. He also thinks across genres, such that a poem or novel is fractured or layered like a modern painting or a painting hints at character or narrative.

His life is experimental as well, stabbing out in various directions and toward numerous identities. He has been married four times, has had many jobs, primarily in academia, has established a wide array of contacts throughout the world, has been connected to a number of the avant-garde movements of the last fifty years, and has challenged many of the social and racial conventions of U.S. society. Together, these suggest a man seeking different paths for himself, never content with what is assumed about him or expected of him. He tries out different roles, moves into different circles. At the same time, his is also a very American story of childhood in the rural South and coming-of-age in the urban North, of initiative and persistence in pursuit of a distinctive self and unique career. After a childhood in a broken, abusive Georgia home and a scrambling life as a bohemian artist, he has settled into life as a distinguished author and painter with a beautiful home in the California suburbs. It is the story of this life and career that I wish to tell.

When I was considering what shape this book would take, I had a conversation with Joe Weixlmann, who was then editor of *African American Review*, about writing a life of Clarence Major. He seemed the logical person to talk to; after all, the journal had done two special issues on Major, and Weixlmann's areas of expertise are African American literature and contemporary fiction, especially its experimental forms. He warned me that although Major is an intriguing subject, he could also be reticent and distant if he were offended or felt intruded upon. I am grateful that my experience has been very different; he has been responsive to all my questions, both in person and in e-mail correspondence. He has provided names, dates, and explanations, even in matters where he had concealed information in his own autobiographical statements. Sometimes he would reveal things only when I posed very pointed questions. For example, early in my research I was initially confused when comparing the dates of his first two marriages and divorces with the birthdates of his children. Reluctant to raise what might be a sensitive subject, I cautiously asked him directly about the discrepancies. Not offended at all, he very straightforwardly explained that the first two children he had with Olympia Leak were born while he was still married to Joyce Sparrow. Similarly, he has suggested a number of places holding material by and about him and has opened his house (and garage) so that I could see his paintings. He has sent photographs of family members and made copies of works that are not available anywhere else. His cooperation has made it much easier to tell a detailed story of his life and career.

Why has my experience differed so much from Weixlmann's prediction? I think it very much has to do with what I see as the central theme of Major's life and career. It is a story of paradox. On the one hand, he has defined both his life and his art as transgressive of conventions. On the other hand, he has sought approval from and connections to those who could appreciate who he is and what he does. Moreover, he is perfectly willing to operate within the mainstream culture as long as his individuality is not compromised. The very publication of this book validates his significance as a person and an artist. Thus, he has been willing to provide what I needed to write it.

The dialectical pattern I am talking about can be found throughout his life and career. From early in life, he seems to have had an outsider sensibility. As a child, he received attention for his writing and drawing rather than for the athletic skills most African American boys were trying to develop in that part of Chicago. In high school, he wrote an unperformable symphony, a television script, and a collection of poems, all of which he tried to get produced or published. When he studied drawing at the Art Institute of Chicago, it was the work of Van Gogh that he admired; he continues into the present to identify that ultimate outsider as his artistic model. When he returned after his time in the air force, he went to clubs uptown in Chicago that were patronized by the bohemian crowd rather than those in his South Side neighborhood. He published a little magazine that included work by Henry Miller and Lawrence Ferlinghetti. His first two marriages were disasters, in part because he was trying unsuccessfully to settle into a middle-class career. His first novel was published by a press that specialized in erotica. He never completed college, at least not in the usual sense, though he received both bachelor's and doctoral degrees. He persistently has argued that his art defies conventions, even when that unconventionality is not readily apparent.

At the same time, he has sought audiences to approve his efforts. His mother seems to have been a doting parent who filled her house with his youthful paintings. He sent his television script to the producer of a network drama series. He sent letters along with poems and stories not only to editors of little magazines but also to prominent figures such as William Carlos Williams, Ralph Ellison, Isaac Bashevis Singer, and Sheri Martinelli. He participated in various groups, such as the black artists' group Umbra, the Fiction Collective, and PEN and was willing to use his networks to get his work published and to get jobs. In other words, he combined the romantic notion of the bohemian, outsider artist with maneuvers necessary to garner attention for himself and his art.

In developing this theme, I am not especially interested in linking it tightly to performance theory or to notions of transgression as articulated by postcolonial or gay studies. I am also not making use of a psychoanalytical model, though notions of desire, deprivation, and anxieties about family dynamics are clearly present. Instead, I believe it makes the most sense to follow the model of Major's own art, in which the self is not one thing or locked into one pattern and in which the art is constantly undergoing revision. In this sense, both self and art are endless experiments in performance, in which some inner drive or impulse engages with the materiality of the world and seeks to gain the approval of whoever is watching or can be enticed to watch. At various times, Major has described his interest in his chosen arts—painting, fiction, poetry—as technical; he identifies problems and seeks interesting ways to solve them. I would suggest that his way of living out his life has been similar; by rejecting (mostly) a conventional life, he generated a set of problems for himself. How does a black man who does not take race as his principal identity, an artist who deliberately defies mainstream rules, a social and cultural critic who wants to be admired by the world he attacks, and a creator who refuses to commit to one expressive form make his way in the world? The task I have set for myself is to follow the multiple layers of problems and solutions in both the work and the life, to consider the successes and the failures.

In the larger sense, while I have focused, especially in the early chapters, on biography, it is the art that holds greater significance. Major has largely avoided the debates about what constitutes African American art and literature by insisting on his own themes and methods, found in whatever sources he came across and could use. He follows in the grand tradition of U.S. artists who find it more important to follow their own path than to accept the road already opened by others. It is also the case, of course, that such artists are also hustlers who have to persuade (or manipulate) others to accept their vision of the way forward. In this case, as in so many, especially in the modern period, that has happened by creating or joining communities of outsiders, those who share a certain view of conventional aesthetic practice.

The case I wish to make is that the patterns of Major's life helped to determine the patterns of his art. The same combination of attention to others and performance of self-assurance (even if it was a facade) enabled him to attract woman after woman and to get his work published by literary magazines and small presses; it also helped him in entering networks that could lead to employment or publication.

Ultimately, of course, it is the quality of the work that matters. Major's independence made it possible for him to do things differently, to make art that is distinctive. Because he never has taken race as his primary identity, he had the freedom to create from a variety of places in himself. His willingness to take chances on everything, something learned in childhood, has made him one of the most resourceful of modern artists. This book aims to show how that came about.

The final issue to be raised in this introduction is the most fundamental: Why spend so much time and effort on an artist who is so little known and who has received relatively little critical attention? The answer, I believe, has to do with the nature of that neglect. Clarence Major has refused to live his life or express his vision in the terms that U.S. society and U.S. culture have found acceptable. For almost all of his life, he has largely ignored the dominant racial formation that seeks to define black masculinity in very specific ways. To oversimplify, the black man is expected to be either a beast or an imitation white man. In either case, his life is determined by social expectations and rules. Likewise, African American art has largely been shaped and evaluated in racial terms. The very category "Black literature" implies a fundamental difference from other American writing. A debate that began with the poetry of Phillis Wheatley continues to this day.

Clarence Major has been diligent in trying to remain outside these definitions. By this I do not mean that he has ignored them; his work shows an acute awareness of the nuances of racial discourse and social practice. It is rather that he does not think or act primarily in terms of them. Similarly, he has consistently argued that the primary responsibility of the artist is to the art. That requires an understanding of the traditions and materials of the expressive form, regardless of where those come from. One must master technique by practicing it. Major's career reveals that he neither embraces nor rejects blackness as an aspect of art. The only relevant question is whether it is useful for the work at hand.

This way of leading his life and doing his work means that he cannot be easily placed by critics or others, so he is simply ignored by most, despite the complexity and productivity he has consistently demonstrated. The point of this book, then, is to see how he went about the business of living and working as much as possible on his own terms in a society and culture that demanded acceptance of certain principles in order to succeed. How does a person so independent minded and creative survive and even thrive under such conditions? It is a story that needs to be told not only because Clarence Major has led a very interesting life and produced very interesting art but also because it reveals a great deal about the limits and possibilities of contemporary culture.

# CHAPTER ONE

# Breaking Boundaries: A Family History

The history of Clarence Major's family on both sides is a variation of the American racial family romance. It is a story of
blacks and whites, men and women, who jointly create a network of relationships that has to be reconstructed through personal testimony as much as official documentation. It is also a
story with gaps because African Americans, for a number of
reasons, are less likely to appear in public records, newspaper
reports, or historical or genealogical accounts. Tracing the connections often requires following genetic lines rather than legal
ones and family stories rather than birth and death certificates
and census records. It involves uncovering secrets and decep-
tions that were either socially convenient or absolutely necessary for survival. Some of them have been maintained to this
day. In this sense the transgression of boundaries that has been
the trademark of Major's artistic career is in his blood.

The paternal line can be traced as back as far as Ned Major, a
slave on the John Major plantation in Chatham County, North
Carolina. He was married to a slave named Peggy, who was
born around 1820 in South Carolina. Since Chatham County
was on the state border, it is possible that they were from neigh-
boring plantations. Ned and Peggy had several children, including a son also named Ned, born around 1845. After the Civil
War, the son settled in Smiths Station, Alabama, and was married to a former slave named Dellia. One of their children was
George, Clarence Major's grandfather, born in 1883. He moved

to eastern Georgia as a young man, where he met and eventually married Anna Lankford Bowling Jackson. To this point, the genealogy is rather conventional, with all the individuals presumably African American; the only noteworthy point is that it is possible to trace a black family back into the antebellum period.[1]

Anna Lankford Bowling Jackson's string of family names suggests complications now introduced into the family narrative, especially since none of them belongs to any men in her life. Jackson was the surname of a foster parent, Edith, who raised Anna in her very early childhood. Lankford is the surname of her birth mother, Rebecca, who was white. Rebecca was born in 1858 to Curtis Caldwell Lankford and Nancy McCarty. Curtis was born in 1827 in Jackson County, Georgia, and served as a private in the Confederate Army. This family line, being white, can be traced back several generations in Georgia and before that to Ireland and England. Nancy McCarty Lankford's family tree is similar. After the birth of Anna, Rebecca filed suit against a white man, William Bowling, claiming that he was the father of the child. In fact, according to family lore, the father was Stephen Bowling, a local black man. The suit would appear to be a device to save Stephen from lynching. Rebecca gave the infant to Edith Jackson, a local black woman, with the putative stipulation that it not be fed from the same breast as Edith's own infant. Later, Stephen's mother, Harriet Bowling, adopted Anna, which is how she acquired that part of her name. Anna had nine children before she married George Major and six with him, including Clarence Major Sr., born 10 July 1910 in Atlanta at Grady Hospital. At various times she was both a domestic servant and a traveling preacher. She was divorced from George Major by the time Clarence Jr. was born ("Licking Stamps," 175–76).[2]

Little is recorded of the life of Clarence Sr. He seldom appears in public records, such as census reports, and even then his name is usually misspelled as "Majors." Moreover, he was reluctant to talk about his life to his wife and children. He seems to have lived virtually all of his life in Atlanta, owning various businesses, both legal and illegal. He had a particular dislike for manual labor, though that was the most regular work available for black men in the city. He much preferred to own or operate small businesses, even though these often failed (*Come by Here*).

The maternal line cannot be so fully traced back (in terms of African American ancestry); it can be followed to one set of great-great-grandparents, about whom nothing other than names are known. Sarah

FIGURE 1.
Major's great-great-grandmother

FIGURE 2. Anna Bowling Major

and Joe Dupree lived in Georgia, presumably as slaves. Their daughter, Lucy Dupree, was married three times, last to Bell Brawner. They had a child, Ada Mae Brawner, born in Lexington, Georgia, on 29 June 1886, the descendent, according to Major, of Cherokees as well as African Americans. Ada married Henry Huff, a prominent black man in Oglethorpe County. He owned property and was a successful contractor, designing and constructing both public and private buildings. It is logical to assume that both his daughter and grandson found him an important model for their creative endeavors. According to Major, Huff was the son of a white man, Judge Hill, of Wilkes County, Georgia, and a black mother, Luvenia; he was born 12 July 1868 ("Licking Stamps," 176; *Come by Here*, 45–50).

Major's mother, Inez, was born in Lexington, Georgia, on 24 April 1918. She was the legal daughter of Huff, but family history claims that her biological father was Edgar Corrie Maxwell, a local white man. The relationship that produced Inez apparently occurred before Edgar married his second wife, Sarah, in 1920 (his first wife, Susie, died in 1913), but several years after Ada had married Henry Huff. The Maxwell family line can be traced back at least as far as Revolutionary soldier Robert Maxwell.

The childhood of Inez, who was the youngest of six children in the Huff household, has been recorded in what might be considered a postmodern memoir, in that Clarence Jr. actually writes the narrative based on conversations he had with his mother; he tells the story primarily in chronological order, though he often juxtaposes memories about the same event or person from different time periods. Moreover, some of the names have been changed, apparently out of regard for members of families still living. From *Come by Here* (2002), we learn of the complexities of being a light-skinned black child in a racially binary society. Inez was treated so badly by black children that her parents sent her away to school, first in Atlanta and then in Athens. Moreover, since Lexington was a small town, it was inevitable that she would encounter her biological father, who was a cotton farmer in the area. Though he never acknowledged his paternity, he always spoke to her by name and gave her small gifts of money. She is careful in the narrative not to address any possible tensions that might have existed between her two fathers or between her legal parents, except to note that the affair that led to her birth occurred when the Huffs were separated. Thus, she is part of a long southern tradition of paternally unrecognized biracial children whose very existence was a challenge to both black and white family and social structures.

FIGURE 3. Ada Huff

FIGURE 4. William Henry Huff

## INEZ AND CLARENCE

Inez met Clarence Sr. while she was still a high-school student in Athens. He was approximately eight years older and, though his mother, Anna, lived in her hometown of Lexington, Inez was not acquainted with the family. She later met Anna, who had returned after several years working as a part-time preacher. Anna was at this point divorced from George Major, who was her third husband. She was the cook for Edgar Maxwell, Inez's biological uncle, and this connection enabled Inez to see Clarence on a regular basis, as he would drive from Atlanta to visit his mother.

After graduating high school, Inez moved to Atlanta to live with her brother and his wife. Clarence would regularly visit her there; she speaks of him as a pleasant companion, though he was reluctant to talk about his source of income. Finally, he admitted that he ran a gambling establishment, which explained his money but created moral problems for her. She was certain that her parents would not approve of such a man, yet she found herself irresistibly attracted to him. Moreover, by late 1935, he showed remarkable confidence in their future together, going so far as to rent a house on McGruder Street and pointing out rings for their wedding. He did not, however, formally propose. Instead, he one day simply announced that they were going to get a marriage license. A few days later, they were married at the house in a private ceremony. Inez did not inform her family until after the ceremony. His sister Minnie moved in with them, and Inez took a job as an elevator operator at a hotel because it was work open to "yellow" women.

Problems developed early in the marriage, as Clarence spent long periods of time, both day and night, at his gambling business; during this period she also learned that he was an important figure in the numbers racket in Atlanta. After Minnie left to live with her boyfriend, Inez became lonely and depressed. She decided to return to Lexington, where she discovered that she was pregnant. Clarence and his mother came to see her, and she was convinced to return to Atlanta with him, but this was only the first incident in a situation that steadily deteriorated. After her return, he did seem to reform; he moved them to a house closer to family and sold the gambling establishment. He also spent somewhat more time at home, though he would often leave dressed in a suit in the morning and not return until night. She was not privy to how he spent his time. She also returned to

FIGURE 5. Clarence Major Sr.

FIGURE 6. Clarence Major Jr., age four

FIGURE 7. Inez in Chicago, 1946

work, though the doctor warned her that this might create problems with the pregnancy. She finally quit about two months before the birth.

Clarence Major Jr. was thus born into a very fluid family life that remained unstable throughout his childhood. His birth, on 31 December 1936, was in the "colored" wing of Grady Hospital in Atlanta. The delivery was difficult, but there were no serious complications. When Inez returned home, her mother came to visit, and her sisters, Saffrey and Brenna, moved into a house across the street. At two months, the baby developed an inflammation that was finally treated by grafting some of her skin onto his face. Clarence Sr. was generally indifferent to the situation, though he was willing to show off his son to friends. Shortly after the infant was brought home, Inez became pregnant again. During this time, Clarence Sr. started a restaurant and gambling business in Savannah that was initially successful but ultimately failed because, according to his brother, Clarence could not control his own gambling habit (*Come by Here*, 89). He returned with little money and began again his abuse and neglect of Inez. Serena Mae was born on 19 February 1938, also at Grady Hospital. Soon after this, Inez took up dressmaking as a way of stabilizing the family income. Occurrences of domestic abuse increased as Clarence felt the pressure of family responsibility. On multiple occasions, Inez returned with the children to her family in Lexington, only to move back to Atlanta and her husband.

After they had moved into their third house, she decided to enroll Clarence Jr. in a preschool. Serena cried so much that the teacher agreed to take them both. A few weeks later, a note was sent home asking Inez to come to the school. Miss Bellamy, the instructor, wished to point out to her Clarence's distinction in drawing: he always put four wheels on cars and trucks, something that none of the other children was capable of doing (*Come by Here*, 115). This was the first of many occasions when his artistic talent was commented on by teachers.

## MOVING TO CHICAGO

Continuing to experience unhappiness and abuse in her marriage, Inez was offered an opportunity to visit relatives in Chicago, and Clarence agreed to pay her way. She took the children to stay with her mother in Lexington and left for several weeks. She returned, but after more abuse she decided to leave permanently and did so in 1942, again leaving the children with her mother. Her plan was to save enough money after about a year to bring her son and daughter to live with her in Chicago. Much of *Come by Here* is devoted to her experiences in the city working variously as a waitress, retail clerk, and seamstress. Because of her light skin, she held some jobs that were open only to white women, and she was able to avoid riding in the Jim Crow train cars when she would return to Georgia to visit her family. She claims not to have been "passing," in the sense of pretending to be something that she was not, but rather to be allowing others to make their own judgments about her identity. The statement is somewhat disingenuous, since she knew the rules for employment and travel, but it helps to establish the importance of performance in the family narrative.

One effect of this separation was to alienate the children from her, such that she recalls young Clarence not wanting to speak to her when she came to Lexington. In addition, for a time, their father took them back to Atlanta to live with him. The crisis came when she was served with divorce papers claiming that she had abandoned her husband and children. She made every effort, through the assistance of a cousin who was an attorney, to demonstrate her responsibility for the children. Nonetheless, it was another two years before she brought them to Chicago. The precipitating event was a call from her mother-in-law in 1946 saying that one of Clarence Sr.'s sisters had beaten Clarence Jr. for bringing a stray dog onto the property. Though she did not yet have sufficient savings to establish the home she wished for her family, Inez immediately sent for him and Serena, who came by train accompanied by a cousin (*Come by Here*, 208–10). The one year of her original plan had turned into four. It is difficult, of course, to know the underlying reasons for this delay. It can be explained, in part, in financial terms; the wages of a young woman, regardless of race, would have been low, though better in retail and dressmaking than in domestic service. Living expenses in Chicago would have been relatively high, especially for someone repeatedly invited to move in higher social circles in the black community. Bringing her children to live with her would have added enormously to that burden. But I would also suggest that Inez might well have been reluctant to take on that responsibility. For the first time in her life, she had a sense of freedom. She had moved from a small-town world in which she was an object of some derision and rumor, despite the respectability of her family, to a marriage that was lonely and painful. In Chicago she was in a position to meet people, to move around as she pleased, to have a social life, and to enjoy herself at clubs and dances. She was not restricted by race to certain places and jobs; she was a woman shaping her own life. Though she loved her children, bringing them into her new world meant returning to a more limited life. It should not be surprising that she delayed that change until delay was no longer possible.

Once the children arrived, the three of them moved into the apartment of Sadie Crawford in a building on South Parkway (now Dr. Martin Luther King Jr. Drive) owned by former Congressman Oscar de Priest, who occupied a lower floor. Clarence Jr. remembers pleasant interactions with the retired politician. Crawford was a clubwoman who introduced Inez to important members of the city's African American community and took her to a number of major society events. These contacts enabled Inez to get additional work as a seamstress and also to meet a number of men, though her experience with Clarence Sr. made her reluctant to develop any serious relationship. Between de Priest and Crawford, we see the beginnings of the patterns of networks so important to the lives of both mother and son.

The children were initially placed in the Forestville School not far from their apartment. Inez was concerned about them being in a city school, fearing that they would be abused by bullies, so she would walk them to school each day. However, the two of them, especially Serena, found the presence of their mother awkward and even embarrassing. The problem seemed in part to be Inez's whiteness, which drew attention to her darker children. In effect, her color was as problematic for her own children as it had been for the black children of Lexington when she was growing up. Finally, Serena told her mother that it was no longer necessary to escort them, since she had beaten up the toughest girl at Forestville, thereby guaranteeing the safety of both herself and her older but smaller brother (*Come by Here*, 219).

Having brought her offspring into her new life, Inez now sought a home that would truly be theirs. She managed to find an apartment not far away. The building was owned by Elizabeth Williams, who also rented space to jazz musicians who performed across the street at a nightclub in the Ritz Hotel. Count Basie and Duke Ellington had been some of the previous tenants, and Lionel Hampton stored a vibraphone there for his performances. At the time Inez and the children were in the house, Johnny Otis was also renting an apartment, though he was seldom there ("Licking Stamps," 177).

FIGURE 8. The Majors' first house in Chicago

## CHILD ARTIST

The move meant that the children now attended Wendell Phillips School. During this period of the late 1940s, young Clarence began writing poetry and short stories and continued drawing and painting. His efforts won him a number of prizes, a pattern of reward that continued when he enrolled at Dunbar High School. He was not especially studious, however, later recalling that while some teachers praised his talent, others criticized his laziness and some students questioned the masculinity of his activities ("Licking Stamps," 177). At the same time, he began reading "adult" literature, first introduced to him, he recalls, by a girl sitting behind him in fifth grade, who loaned him a copy of Raymond Radiguet's *Devil in the Flesh*, translated by Kay Boyle (*Necessary Distance*, 16). While his teachers were having his classmates read O. Henry and Joyce Kilmer, he took up Hawthorne, Conrad, Melville, Dostoevsky, Salinger, Rimbaud, and eventually the twentieth-century modernists in both fiction and poetry. He continued this pattern of somewhat random reading, of one writer leading to another, until after he graduated.

Around the same time as receiving Radiguet's book, he made his own first attempt at a novel, a twenty-page narrative about "a wild, free-spirited horse leading a herd." He was so confident about it that he mailed it to William Self, who was then the producer of the television series *Schlitz Playhouse of Stars*. Major remembers receiving, with the returned manuscript, "a letter of encouragement" (*Necessary Distance*, 15). Dunbar High School was attended by a number of talented students, including future jazz great Herbie Hancock. Major recalls deciding to write a symphony that he conceived in visual terms. Without musical skill himself, he asked the teacher to play it. He refused but encouraged Hancock to attempt it. It was a twenty-five-page manuscript; Hancock got through about three pages before giving up on what Major called "a Dadaist symphony influenced by Bud Powell" ("Licking Stamps," 179).

His approach to painting was more focused. Around the age of eleven, he started taking private art lessons from Gus Nall, a South Side African American painter who studied at the School of the Art Institute of Chicago (SAIC). Nall's own work makes use of elongated figures and cubist elements. He later had some reputation in the 1960s for his representation of African Americans. More important to Major's development was his association with the art institute itself. It was here that he saw the work of the Impressionists and Postimpressionists, most significantly Vincent Van Gogh. A major event for him was the 1950 Van Gogh exhibition, cosponsored by the AIC and the Metropolitan Museum of Art in New York. The show broke attendance records for both museums and was extended in Chicago because of its popularity. Major reports having gone to the show several times and pushing through the crowds:

> I was not sophisticated enough to know how to articulate for myself what these things were doing to me, but I knew I was profoundly moved. So on some level, I no doubt did sense the power of the painterliness of those pictures of winding country paths, working peasants, flower gardens, rooftops, the stillness of a summer day. . . . Something in me went out to the energy of Vincent's "Sunflowers," for example. I saw him as one who broke the rules and transcended. Where I came from, no socially well-behaved person even

went out and gathered sunflowers for a vase in the home. No self-respecting grown man spent ten years painting pictures he couldn't sell. On the South Side of Chicago, everything of value had a price tag. (*Necessary Distance*, 20)

What is clear from this statement is the psychological as much as the artistic significance of this experience. Here was a bohemian alternative to both the hustler life of his father and the desire for respectability of his mother. Its value was that it brought recognition in the larger world through self-expression; it also provided a heroic model for a child unwilling to follow the usual paths open to African Americans at midcentury. As will be seen, it can be argued that artistically he remains under the influence of Van Gogh, even more than fifty years after his first exposure.

Clarence Jr. found himself obsessively sketching everyday scenes around his home in an attempt to capture the compositional and color patterns of Van Gogh. He further attempted to capture something like them in his writing, with poems that made strong use of images. Never one to conceal his talent, he collected the poems into a book that he paid an uncle ten dollars to print. Once he had the fifty copies of verse reflecting the influence of Rimbaud, Van Gogh and other impressionists and symbolistes, including "French words I didn't understand," he realized he had no one to sell them to. He gave away a few to teachers and his mother and stored the others until he realized how bad they were and destroyed the remaining copies (*Necessary Distance*, 21–22).

His painting technique was aided when he received a James Nelson Raymond Scholarship while in high school, which allowed him to attend drawing classes and lectures at Fullerton Hall of the SAIC with Addis Osborne and Cynthia Bollinger. He continued these sessions even after graduation. The SAIC also had around this time (1952) a show of the works of Paul Cézanne; what is important about Major's viewing of it is that he recalls *not* liking what he saw. It seemed to him "lifeless" and heavy. This sense led him to the realization that he could appreciate art for what the artist did technically, even if he did not care for the result (*Necessary Distance*, 22). This intellectual recognition appears to be the first moment he realized that he was more committed to technique than to content, a preference that holds in all of his work, regardless of medium.

On 17 June 1950, his mother married Halbert Ming, a mixed-race businessman. Ming had been born in Mississippi and seems to have been part of the Great Migration that brought tens of thousands of southern blacks

FIGURE 9. Major in Chicago, 1952

to Chicago. The marriage allowed the family to move to a larger apartment and for Inez to start her own dry-cleaning business. Clarence had occasional problems with his stepfather and sometimes lived with friends of his mother's to relieve the tension. Given his observations about what constituted an acceptable life and vocation for middle-class blacks at the time, such strains would not be surprising. After graduation from Dunbar High School, he spent a year in miscellaneous jobs and continuing with his writing and art classes. He was something of an oddity on the South Side, since he showed little interest in sports, money making, or the local social life; he was more at home with the artistic communities of other parts of the city.

In 1955, he decided to join the air force. He received basic training in San Antonio, Texas, and then worked in offices in Pensacola, Florida, Cheyenne, Wyoming, and Valdosta, Georgia. Despite the civil-rights activities of the time, the municipalities of both San Antonio and Valdosta, especially, maintained strong white supremacist views and imposed restrictions on the movements and activities of black airmen. He has stated that he probably would not have survived without the presence of a number of other northern black airmen ("Licking Stamps," 179). He used the time to take correspondence classes through the Armed Forces Institute and to do independent reading in philosophy, religion, anthropology, history, and biography, as well as literature. During this period he also began submitting material to small literary magazines and established his lifelong pattern of creating networks through correspondence.

# CHAPTER TWO

# Becoming an Artist

Upon completing his military service in 1957, Major returned to Chicago, where he lived for a time in his mother's home and worked at a factory that made loud speakers while continuing to paint and to write poetry. His first show was at Gayle's Gallery in 1957, where his work was exhibited alongside that of Archibald Motley, who had achieved a reputation during the 1920s and 1930s for his depictions of the nightlife of Chicago. By the fifties, Motley was emerging from an extended period of depression and his reputation was in decline, though he remained the best known of the city's African American artists. While the two of them had very different concerns as painters, they shared an interest in the technical aspects of their art as well as an ambivalent relationship with the black community of their city.[1] The joint show was in part a result of Major's skills at networking. Through a childhood friend, Jimmie Hunter, he met the owner of the gallery, who often displayed Motley's work. He also met through this connection Willard Motley, Archibald's nephew, who had gained a considerable reputation for his novel *Knock on Any Door* (1946). An additional relationship was established through another friend, Bob Ingram, who introduced him to Lil Armstrong, Louis Armstrong's former wife; she put him in touch with her cousin, the novelist Frank London Brown, the author of *Trumbull Park* (1959). A number of these figures later became subjects for essays Major wrote that helped to define the nature of fiction (and art more generally) for him. Given the association of Brown and Willard Motley with what became known as the Richard Wright school of black fiction, it was useful for Major to both place himself in a tradition and differentiate himself from it.

## BECOMING A POET

He had put out his first volume of poetry shortly before he went into the air force. It was a collection of seven pieces that were printed and bound by his uncle, who ran a business making stationery, calling cards, and other items. The poems in *The Fires That Burn in Heaven* (1954), while not very accomplished, do suggest some of the methods and concerns of his later work. "Simultaneously," the first poem in the collection, opens with images of domestic violence that may reflect a working-through of the relationship of his parents:

> A man rises his gun and shoot seven times in
>   The head of his wife!
> She feels funny and fall down.
> Somewhere else at the same time a brute is
>   beating his,
> And she, such a lovely girl. However he is
>   jealous of her ability to atract any man!
> Hence he gets his justice by whipping her! (*Fires*, 4)

The girl's attractiveness as the source of the brute's anger can easily be seen as a reference to Inez's light skin color, which Clarence Sr. might have taken as a threat to his control of his wife, a control that he attempted to establish through violence. In a community in which colorism would often determine beauty, a darker-skinned husband might see physical force as a crucial means of maintaining the "justice" of his claim to his wife.[2]

The status of bodies, and what is done with and to them, is a motif found throughout Major's work. His fiction is replete with acts of violence and sexuality; his poetry uses body parts and actions as ways of characterizing emotions and ideas; his paintings break apart bodies or play with representations of them. He notes in an early interview that his first published work of fiction, *All-Night Visitors* (1969), "was a novel I had to write in order to come to terms with my own body" (Bunge, *Conversations*, 12). It is apparent that such a concern existed at some level at least fifteen years before that work.

Another persistent aspect of his art, the arbitrariness of time, is also evident in "Simultaneously." He plays out the title by presenting a series of events connected only by their simultaneous occurrence. They are random in that they have no relationship of place or actors or quality (such as consequence or emotional weight). Some are rendered as vignettes, as in the violence of the "brute" and others as a single word: "Death." While in this first poem he uses markers ("Somewhere else at the same time") to signal changes in focus, he will in later work require the reader to construct links or the lack of them.

Finally, this initial effort reflects his interest in language and the creation of identity. He will later repeatedly argue that the literary work is not a reflection of external reality but rather an object in its own right generated by words. Thus, the poem or the novel is self-consciously constructed and often draws attention to itself as a construct. In "Simultaneously," the series of events are related only because the speaker in the poem has named them as connected. They exist only because the poet has called them into being. At the end, he looks at his "world" and declares his enjoyment through language play:

> Life comes!
> A pun!
> A laugh!
> I? (*Fires*, 4)

The wordplay is itself imposed by the creator of the work; nothing leading up to it would have required such an adolescent sexual joke. His telling us that it is a pun guarantees that we will not mistake the first exclamation for a romantic embrace of the universe. At the same time, it does suggest the erotic pleasure he derives from having crafted something new in the world.

This point is tied to the last line: "I?" The interrogative raises questions about identity that again the speaker insists on. Nothing in the poem before this implies uncertainty about a self. These two concluding typographical characters open up a new set of issues and questions when we least expect them. Major speaks in *Necessary Distance* and elsewhere of the oddity of being an artist in the community in which he grew up: "I had to be very quiet about my plans to become a writer. I couldn't talk with friends about what I read. I mean, why wasn't I out playing basketball?" (19). Furthermore, his professional goals had gendered implications: "A smart boy was a sissy and deserved to get his butt kicked" (19). "Smart boy" here is more associated with reading and artistic activities than with conventional academic achievement. He, in effect, violated both the idea of the good student and the idea of the athletic black boy in pursuit of his own interests.

Thus, the "I?" takes note of the fact that the creator of the poem, precisely by being able to make a poem, is a self that is open to question. Can this seventeen-year-old be both a man and a writer? In a community where the two terms are mutually exclusive, what will he be if he chooses the way of art? At the same time, by writing the poem, he makes possible the option of an identity that is not limited to the roles defined by South Side Chicago. This, even more than the pun, may be the source of the penultimate line ("A laugh!"): he surprises himself that he can achieve mastery in life through words. He has crafted something that never before existed in the world, and he did so out of his own being. Unlike the young men around him, whose lives will be circumscribed by the racial and gendered conditions of their environment, he can be and do whatever he wants through his art.

While in the air force and after in Chicago, he published work in various little magazines, including *Existeria*, *Olivant*, and *Blue River*. But even more significantly, he began creating the networks that were central to his career. He attended programs of the College of Complexes on the city's North Side; the college was a free-speech forum established in 1951 to provide a safe space for the expression of often radical ideas when the nation was entering a period of ideological repression.[3] What most interested Major, of course, were the conversations about art and literature. He also accumulated a significant library of little magazines. He recalls poet Marvin Bell, then a Master of Fine Arts student at the University of Chicago, commenting that Major's apartment on Drexel Avenue contained more little magazines than the university library ("Licking Stamps," 179). What is important here is not merely the collection, or the submission of work to the editors; rather, it is his correspondence with editors and authors. Bell, for example, was the editor of *Statements*, a magazine in which Major later published a poem. *Statements* was published from 1959 to 1964 and included both poetic and visual material, making it similar in some ways to the *Coercion Review*. Such connections made it possible not only to find outlets for his work but also to get advice and to expand contacts exponentially. James Boyer May, for example, was the editor of *Trace*, which began as a service publication for writers but soon incorporated stories and poems. May not only published some of Major's work but also encouraged his reading of a range of authors ("Licking Stamps," 180). By 1960, his work, including poetry, fiction, and essays, was appearing not only in a number of U.S. periodicals but also in journals in India, Canada, and Brazil.

A major early correspondent was Sheri Martinelli, who was well known for her ties to the avant-garde of the fifties. She was a protégée of Anaïs Nin and the inspiration for a character in William Gaddis's *The Recognitions* (1955). Her Greenwich Village apartment was a cultural salon, with regulars such as Charlie Parker and several of the Beat artists. Her artwork was collected by Marlon Brando, Rod Steiger, and E. E. Cummings. After moving to San Francisco, she began the *Anagogic and Paideumic Review*, a mimeographed periodical devoted primarily to little-known writers (S. Moore, "Sheri Martinelli"). As a result of their correspondence, Major published poems, reviews, and an essay in the magazine. In the letters between them, there was even discussion of his moving to the San Francisco area to manage the journal. This never came to fruition, in large part because of money. It was around the time he was becoming involved with Olympia Leak, and her pregnancy foreclosed the option.[4]

At the same time, he is the object of some harsh commentary in the correspondence between Martinelli and Charles Bukowski, from whom Major had solicited material for his little magazine the *Coercion Review*. As Bukowski tells this story, Major had accepted some of his poetry "then heard through the grapevine that I was a son of a bitch, so he returned it. Then later came a rather abject letter of apology, asking to see more of my work."[5] This material was never published because, according to Bukowski, the journal closed down as a result of Major's breakup with Joyce Sparrow. This incident may explain some of the criticism of Major found weeks later. It is clear that the correspondents are both deeply racist, as they are obsessed with Major's interest in white women, with the idea of a race war, and with generalizing from Major to all black people. Their letters reveal in addition a concern, not with Major's art, but with his artistic personality. Bukowski observes:

> Re Major: it disturbs me to think that M. believes modern poets prefer Ray Charles to Mozart, especially when he is discussing Bukowski. It also disturbs me that Major would think Bukowski is the type who would come right out and say: "sssssssssshit it's beautiful!" And if Major in his fantasy wants to screw white girls in the park, why hell, let him do it, of course. Only I would say it shows weakness of soul. Major is full of enthusiasms, young enthusiasms, about art and people and ideas, and when this wears thin, as it must, I wonder where he will stand?[6]

In her next letter, Martinelli agrees and requests permission to publish the comments in the next issue of the journal. A comment by Bukowski a few days later reveals their fundamental ignorance of Major's work: "And Major must not confuse an involved poetry with intellect. If Clarence would

ever bother to take a paint brush in his hand he will find that the most difficult thing in Art is to make something simple. All the great secrets of the
world are simple secrets, never spoken but felt."[7] Thus, two of the people
that Major admired in his early career are revealed as seeing him primarily
in racial terms and denigrating him behind his back, even though he had
given a positive review to Bukowski's *Flower, Fist and Bestial Wall* in *Anagogic and Paideumic Review* and had had several poems published there.

In the summer of 1958, he released the first issue of the *Coercion Review*;
the inside cover added the phrase, "of contemporary power in literature."
The idealistic and ambitious statement of purpose reveals the mindset of the
young artist: "The intention of this publication is to print the best poems,
stories, essays, and reproduce the best drawings and photos sent to the editor. The editor hopes to expand this mag into a large widely-circulating mag
eventually, without any changes in policy." While standards are of primary
importance, success is obviously also a goal. His inclusion on the cover of
"A Clarence Major Venture" reveals that he is the son of his entrepreneurial father. He also had bigger ideas for his journal than Sheri Martinelli;
unlike her, he sought out the work of established writers. The inaugural
issue has work by Paul Valery, Paul Eluard, Kenneth Patchen, and Lawrence
Ferlinghetti. The lesser-known artists include Carl Larsen, David Cornell
DeJong, Charles Shaw, E. W. Northnagel, D. V. Smith (who had published
Major's first short story), Harland Ristau, Trumbull Drachler, "Cerise Fa-
rallon" (Judson Crews), Mary Graham Lund, James Hunter, Bob Nystedt,
and himself. All of the work is poetry, except for Major's brief essays on
Bud Powell and French prose writers; he also offered eleven one-sentence
reviews, including books by Gregory Corso, Larsen, and Ferlinghetti. The
essay on bebop pianist Powell seems a clear expression of Major's own artistic credo. He insisted on the importance of inventing one's own rules, even
to the point of madness: "insanity has nothing to do with genius" (*Coercion Review*, 1:11). He saw in art curative powers for the troubled creator; he
compared Powell to Ezra Pound and Van Gogh in this regard.

In the second issue, which came out in the spring of 1959, he expanded
the number of pages from sixteen to twenty-eight, in part to incorporate
a long article by Henry Miller. He has also tried to give the journal more
visual appeal by replacing the simple gold cover of the first issue with a
beige cover printed with blue ink. The inside pages are green. He added
Miller's name in large print and lists other contributors and the price
(raised from fifty cents to $1.50). The most important element for this study

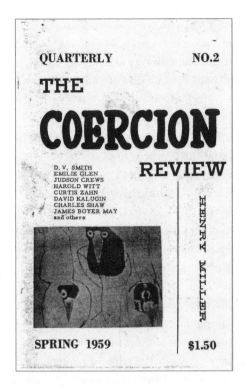

FIGURE 10. Cover of second issue of the *Coercion Review*

is the inclusion of an image of birds reproduced from one of Major's own paintings. This makes it the earliest of his visual works known to be in the public realm.

The issue appears designed to establish Major's avant-garde credentials. Over a fourth of it is devoted to Miller, with most of that a long diatribe against modern suburban life, especially as it affects children. Major later notes that when the essay was reprinted elsewhere, he was not given credit for first publishing it ("Licking Stamps," 179). This essay was supplemented with a brief bibliography of Miller's work. In addition, the issue contains two pieces by D. V. Smith, whose journal *Olivant* included Major's first published story. Smith's short essay attacks religion, especially as represented in the United States. His long poem "Heroine of the People" is an attack on the nation as the source of violence both domestically and internationally. The issue also contained the work of Emilie Glen, James Boyer May, Harold Witt, Judson Crews, David Kalugin, and Curtis Zahn. What is noteworthy about the writers in both issues of the magazine is that they were either already established as authors or soon would be. Several were also involved as editors of little magazines or, in the case of Emilie Glen, as the host of a literary salon. Thus, in his early twenties, Major was seeking to place himself within the network of contemporary art. His agenda is in part expressed in "Notes." He states that "THE COERCION REVIEW will consider no more traditional poetry" (14). He also asserts that "#1 in the COERCION POETS SERIES will be released late this year"(14). Not only did the book never appear, but the magazine itself was not published again for several years and then only as a combined issue.

The two early issues contain relatively little of Major's own artistic work. Number 2 prints a short piece by Cassandra Ming, his eight-year-old half sister. His own literary contribution is a five-line work titled "Moonlight." A "surrealistic photograph" is a collage that incorporates a face taken from one of his paintings, a Captain Kangaroo–style hat, and a refrigerator. The cover art is a section of a painting of birds that is similar to the work on the cover of his 1998 collection *Configurations*.

As mentioned above, his first short story was published in *Olivant* while its editor, D. V. Smith, was serving in the military in Japan. The issue came out in 1957 and included work by several of the authors Major used in *Coercion*. His name is misspelled "Majour" in both the table of contents and the heading of the story. The narrative is brief, around 1,200 words. Titled "Ulysses, Who Slept Across from Me," it portrays the life of Smithmunn, a recruit going through basic training with the narrator. He has joined the army in order to escape joblessness and domestic problems. Though only twenty, he has been married twice and is seeking his second divorce. The first marriage ended after the death of an infant, and the second after he found his wife with a lover. The only line of dialogue comes after he has been informed that Sara Alice will not grant him the divorce but expects him to support her now that she is pregnant. He then says to the narrator, "It's not my child" (56). This leads to a misogynist epiphany for the narrator: "And I instantly saw, in a split second, a vision, nothing more, what women were: a race of animals possessed by an inert nature, an unrealist temperiment a fast talking mob of worried, nervous, and cheep animals" (56). After a short time, he modifies the feeling to the final statement of the story: "When my mind was more sober, I thought of my mother, and I knew that both Smithmunn and myself, and all real men, could never live without these animals, greater in so many ways than ourselves" (56).

The tale is clearly apprentice work. There is no development of the protagonist's character; he is a cipher to whom things just seem to happen. We are told that he marries the second time because of "this love inside him," but we see no evidence of it in thought, feeling, or action. We also have no idea why Sara Alice has the affair or later becomes a prostitute. Likewise, the narrator is given no history or personality, so it is impossible to know how to judge his observations at the end. What the story does do is suggest some of the directions both the art and the life will go in. The emptiness of characters will evolve into the postmodern figures that populate his early novels, just as the jerkiness of the narrative will become nonsequential storytelling. Even the male-female relationships, which often depend on reflections on the nature of manhood and womanhood, can be seen in simplified form here. And finally, the play with mythological references, often to ironic purposes, will be seen in the fiction, poetry, and painting as his career develops.

## EARLY ADULTHOOD IN CHICAGO AND OMAHA

As for his own life, the story's unstable domestic world predicts Major's own experience over the next several years. On Valentine's Day 1958, he married Joyce Louise Sparrow, who was born in North Carolina but raised in Chicago. Her family lived in his neighborhood. The couple moved to an apartment on Oakwood Boulevard in the same building where Clarence had lived as a child. They had two sons, Aaron and Darrell, during the short time they were together. Aaron was born 29 April 1958, and Darrell on 13 June 1959. At this time, Major was working at the loudspeaker factory. When he lost this job, they were no longer able to keep the apartment, and Joyce moved with the children back to her mother's home. The relationship had deteriorated quickly, perhaps in part due to his commitment to his art, which he considered more important than establishing himself in a conventionally secure job or career. There is no evidence of any effort at reconciliation, and Major lived on South Drexel Avenue for a short period of time while producing the second issue of the *Coercion Review*.

After the separation, he moved to Omaha in late 1959 on the advice of a friend, Hugh Grayson, who wrote that there were good jobs there. He took on short-term work before finding employment as a steelworker. He taught himself welding and also crane operation. He also began a relationship with Olympia Leak, though he was still married to Joyce and would remain so until November 1964. He and Olympia, who was from his neighborhood in Chicago and whom he had known since fifth grade, produced two children before they were married (the first on 2 July 1960) and another two after that event. They were divorced in late 1966, and Olympia moved with the children—Serena, Inger, Clarence, and Angela—to Los Angeles. Thus, in a period of eight years, Major fathered six children, none of whom lived with him after the second divorce.

In place of a domestic life, he became part of the Omaha artistic community. He frequented Paul Allen's tavern, which was the site of the local jazz scene. There he met saxophonist Eddie "Cleanhead" Vinson. At this time, Vinson's career was on the decline, though he had earlier had his own big band and had performed with Bud Powell, Charles "Cootie" Williams, Miles Davis, and Julian "Cannonball" Adderley. In the mid-1960s, he found work as part of the blues-folk revival. One result of the interactions between Vinson and Major was a tribute article published in the first issue of the African American magazine *Bronze Mirror* in 1962. In addition to participating in the writers group to which Hugh Grayson belonged, Major also made friends with the black stage actor William Jay Marshall, who later left Omaha to become one of the principal players in the Negro Ensemble Company. Strikingly, Major claims not to know what happened to Marshall, though they were both in New York during the same period of several years ("Licking Stamps," 182).

The artistic output of this period was largely poetry. A vita created by Major shows no exhibitions or reproductions of his paintings between the 1959 issue of *Coercion* and a 1974 show. Similarly, only one short story was published between 1960 and 1968. The poetry appeared in a variety of little magazines: *Free Lance*, *White Dove Review*, Martinelli's *Anagogic and Paideumic Review*, *Galley Sail Review*, and *Kauri*.

The poems themselves include several examples of experimentation similar to what he sought for the *Coercion Review*. "Viewpoints," for example, is presented as free association:

> stimulate a viewpoint in viewpoint minds
> & such canny concerns are fumbled points
> media press souls for time & draw the outlines
> in love and money. (*Swallow the Lake*, 34)

The poem refuses to accommodate itself to the conventions of syntax or semantics and yet keeps teasing the reader with possibilities of sense, as in "chopped chives in cream cheese" which "should speak out of the context of politics."

"The Agony of Pain," published in the same issue of *Anagogic and Paideumic Review*, offers a clearer structure but is constructed as surrealism:

> around the hospital an interpreter of pain
> wanders in a mosquito net.
> His eyes are two fat Women. (*Swallow the Lake*, 52)

The "interpreter" is, in fact, a representative of a failing culture:

> His civilization
> is in his pocket and his precious
> English Language is Dead now that America "is free."
> But he uses it anyway.

The reference would appear to be to modernist poets such as Ezra Pound and T. S. Eliot, whose Anglophilia had been made archaic by the emergent culture of the Beats. At the same time, the speaker refuses the notion of an American art that is truly different. After all:

> The administration of the hospital is sound and
> from all appearances the interpreter of pain
> will have a job nightmare after nightmare,
> as long as howling men cannot explain their depth.
> Death is nothing. (52)

Since the poem was published in the magazine established by Martinelli, who was closely associated with Pound during his confinement at St. Elizabeths Hospital, Major can blend his social critique with the experiences of one of the key poets of an earlier generation. The fact that Pound had been released just a year before the poem appears would seem to reinforce the connection. At the same time, the reference to "howling men" links the poem to Allen Ginsberg, who also spent time in a mental institution. Like many of the Beats, the speaker of the work sees the society as insane, and the artists as the ones who must endlessly articulate that madness, even if their language cannot be understood by that society.

What distinguishes this piece is an image of Africa: "Around Africa— his body is shaped like the map of Africa— / he wears a large admiration belt to hold up the net." Since the "net" is the mosquito protection mentioned in the second line of the poem, the interpreter seeks to avoid those attacks conventionally associated with Africa. Because he himself is identified with that continent, one that the Western world defines as the opposite of civilization, the "admiration belt" is necessary to prevent assaults on his being. Significantly, these lines are an intrusion into the middle of the poem that would seem to belie the reading of the interpreter as the representative of Western art. The deeper connection may be found in the earlier comment on Bud Powell as joining genius to madness. If Africa is marked as the space of the irrational, the savage, then the "madmen" Pound and Ginsberg are "African."

"Something Is Eating Me Up Inside," published in *Artesian* in 1960, is one of the early statements of Major's persistent theme of the fragmentation of identity. The speaker is a young man trying to find a place and a meaning for himself. Though he has a space and a neighborhood, he cannot stay still:

> I go in & out a thousand times a day
> & the round fat women with black velvet skin
> expressions sit out on the
> front steps, watching — "where does he go
> so much" as if the knowledge could give meaning to
> a hood from the 20s I look like in
> my pocket black shirt button-down collar & black ivy
> league. . . . (*Swallow the Lake*, 19)

The endless movement of the speaker suggests some form of neurosis that afflicts him. At the same time, he adopts the persona of the "hood" to give the women something to talk about. He undermines the value of community by asserting that they lack knowledge of him and, further, that the presence of such knowledge would make sense of his being. He offers an explanation, which only reinforces despair:

> . . . In & out to break the
> agony in the pit of skull of fire for a drink a
> cigarette bumming it anything the floor is
> too depressing. I turn around inside the closet to search
> the floor for a dime / a nickel (19)

The inside is claustrophobic, a space that he finds intolerable because it leaves him alone with himself.

The source of this anxiety is in part an experience of emptiness that is paradoxically a presence:

... but seriously something is
eating me up inside I don't
believe in anything anymore, science, magic—
in tape worms inside philosophy inside (19)

His nonbelief is a kind of parasite that feeds on the nothingness that has become his being. He refuses to name the "something," even metaphorically, as evidenced by his rejection of the tapeworm. To name it is to somehow diminish it and perhaps to rid himself of it. In other words, the poem is a performance of existential angst. The ending is not despair:

—this is what I move full of,
slow young strong & sure of nothing myself a gangster
of the sunshine the sun is blood in my guts:
moving me from gin highs to lakesides to sit down
beside reasons for being in

the first place
in the second place looking
outward to definitions for definitions like
a formal ending would be unlawful unfair (*Swallow the Lake*, 20)

The emptiness, the nothingness, turns out to be a possibility, not a failure. To be "sure of nothing" is to have a faith, but one that is outside social expectations. Instead of being the "hood" as seen by the black women (and presumably by the society generally), he can be a "gangster of the sunshine" and thus not so different from Emily Dickinson's inebriate of air. He may not believe in philosophy, but he can "sit" with the reasons for being. He can look outside himself for definitions precisely because he has already declared those definitions invalid. In effect, the poem revels in fragmentation, in an unstable identity. Ironically, then, just as the poem comes to a formal ending by denying such an ending, so the speaker denies the self in order to gain it.

One culmination of this early period is *Human Juices*, published as *Coercion #5* in the summer of 1965. Though it is very short (nine leaves), Major manages to incorporate three rather distinct themes that will affect his work for the next several years: the erotic, black pride, and art and the artist. Sexuality will find its fullest expression in his fiction, especially in the 1969 novel *All-Night Visitors*, but it is already apparent in his poetry. The emphasis is sometimes on the senses, as in "Sales Il'Erotisme":

> your forbidden exotic flesh . . .
> 　　Clothed in silk, green silk
> Drenched in red confession perfume . . .
> 　　Studded with the sounds of churchbells
> And jewishhorns; blowing . . .
> 　　Fascinate the exclusive (twisted, lost person)
> Itch of the run of the catalog. . . . (*Human Juices*, n.p.)

Here sight, sound, smell, and touch reinforce the exotic aura. The "you" of the poem is praised for violating the rules of the Victorians and the "Good Sisters."

In contrast, "Throw Them, Somehow" is straightforward in its depiction of Freudian family romance:

> Strikeback at his own mother:
> Fallatio performed on him forever;
> He did instinct intact see the difference
> Between themselves; They were very walked,
> Had a direct connection with similar states
> Of mind; relationships at the earliest
> Failure in the face of her anger: he was scaed
> Faces soared; it runnind down his security.
> Fallatio, he loved; it meant he had to give nothing. (*Human Juices*, n.p.)

Sexual activity almost always carries special psychological weight in Major's work. Oral sex becomes a means of revenge on his mother. The willingness of women to pleasure him becomes a means of neutralizing maternal power. The fact that the mother is the only woman mentioned implies that the behavior itself both conceals and reveals incestuous desire. It has the virtue of requiring nothing of him, in contrast to the demands of the mother.

In this collection, we also see some of Major's early efforts at explicitly racial poetry, an approach he will engage for relatively short periods in his various art forms. Some of this work takes on the personal quality most often associated with women writers such as Mari Evans and Nikki Giovanni. The piece in this category is "My Daughter":

> Is no reflection in plaited curls of black girls
> Hair? My daughter is Beautiful / Black Beautiful. I am
> A mirror—a father to her. A shadow. An edge to her love.

My daughter has a fleecy personality . . .
She undulates everything she says / She is brimming
    With the love I gave her. (*Human Juices*, n.p.)

Even though the poem is about the daughter, it tells us at least as much about the father. He is in fact the source of virtually everything that is valuable about her. She appears to have little in common with other black girls. Instead, he is her mirror and her shadow. Her best quality, her love, comes from him. An effort at racial pride resolves itself into masculine narcissism. If we take the subject to be one of Major's own three daughters, then he is asserting the primacy of fatherhood shortly before his relationship with their mother breaks down.

At other times, his work engages in social criticism that is only indirectly racial. "A Poem Americans Are Going to Have to Memorize Soon" carries in its title the urgency often associated with Black Arts writing. The work itself, however, is a critique of the notion of American exceptionalism:

Americans have a fatal
touch of shallowness;
    or they are great (sizewise) people.
Great in that they did not
    Exist ever like this anywhere.
Americans are a unique lot.
For instance / an American doctor
Would never have dismissed a fee
    for restoring the sight to a child
Like a doctor did somewhere in Italy.
They are fatal. (*Human Juices*, n.p.)

The specialness of Americans is not in their democratic principles or their economic success but rather in their selfishness. Major carefully uses the language of Americanism in order to subvert it. The word "fatal" in the last line carries double weight: Americans are deadly, since presumably doctors (and others) who are not paid will not deal with suffering, and they seem to be fated to be a nation of the selfish and shallow. In this view, Major brings together the attitudes of the Beats and the Black Power advocates.

His work can also be explicitly racial, as in "News Story." The poem situates itself in the present moment:

Heard over radio
  A white woman from Can. / with
  Sticks of dina
  mite trans ported from Can.
  (her home
  &
some serious Afro-Americans
(called NEGROES
                    were uncovered
    but not in bed.
by the curious group
titled FBI
        In a plot to BLOW      UP
                    BLOWUP
                    BOM
                    BLAM
Items listed
Lady Lib
Lib Bell
Wash Monu. etc
            Teach our country a thing or 2 ???
If the serious saboteurs
Had succeeded / who could say
    We would have a deeper sense of reality
& self (*Human Juices*, n.p.)

Major uses many of the devices of nationalist writing here: abbreviations, short lines, onomatopoeia, and typographical innovation designed to produce what Stephen Henderson referred to as the "mascon" effect of black art. The work also plays with other kinds of American fears in a poem about violence. "Uncovered / but not in bed" suggests the miscegenation that obsessed J. Edgar Hoover as well as many other whites. The word *curious*, applied to Hoover's organization, carries the double meaning of an interested party in the events and an oddity in its obsessions and its police techniques. The speaker also implies some sympathy with the activists by twice labeling them "serious." For him they carry some moral authority, especially given the previous poem. Their actions might have forced the nation to consider why a group of serious people would attempt to destroy the symbols of national identity. The targets are specifically those linked to freedom; it can even be argued that the abbreviations of the names of the monuments signal that aborted nature of American democracy. In this particular piece, Major demonstrates his ability to manipulate the discourse of black nationalism, though his connection to it is short-lived.

The most significant theme to emerge from this early period is the nature and function of art and the role of the artist in society. It becomes the issue by which Major tries to distinguish himself during his career, especially among African American writers. The first and last poems of *Human Juices* explore this issue. "Cast Reality" offers a somewhat tentative response to the question of the relationship between art and the world:

> What lurks in this pose?
> Is it a pose?
> Am I sure that this person
> Is a proxy for the real one?
> He walks straight toward the center
> Of his nerve pith. He tells us
> A series of established myths;
> And th[r]ough his actions we see
> For awhile at least our lives,
> Projected for good or bad,
> In that effort put there to bleed.
> Then there comes the reality again,
> Dull & pitiful.
> But we thank the art for it's escapism.
> Tho not escapism. (*Human Juices*, n.p.)

He begins with a series of questions that engage the issue of mimesis immediately. The figure presented is fictive, offering to us a pose not a person; but the speaker quickly backs away from this assertion by asking whether it is in fact a pose. *If* we assume that the artwork is a movie, then we need to know if the character we see is a version of the actor or perhaps a representation of a living or dead person. We can also read this opening to suggest that the character, even if totally fictive, does exist, not as the image of someone else, but as a created object in the world. After all, "He walks straight toward the center / Of his nerve pith." He speaks in myths, which both marks him as a work of art and gives him the language to address our lives, since presumably our identities are shaped by those cultural narratives. At the end, we are returned to the mundane world.

The poem ends in paradox: "But we thank the art for it's escapism, / Tho not escapism." This conclusion can be read in two different ways. Consistent with the questions that open the work, the final statement can be understood as the art reflecting back to us, either in mimetic or mythic terms, a transformed version of reality. Through its imaginative processes, it can enable us to see what is so hard to see when we are caught up in the everydayness of the world. In taking us away from reality, it brings us back to it. The other interpretation, as suggested above, is the one that Major eventually claims for his work generally. In line with experimental and postmodernist thinking, he comes to see the art object as a new thing in the world, as a reality of its own that has no necessary relationship with what already exists. "Escapism" implies that a work of the imagination takes the observer-reader out of the world; in contrast, Major will come to say that his work brings something new into the world. The world is no longer the reference point; rather, the artwork becomes its own self-contained being.

The final poem in the collection moves more clearly toward this position. "Young Actor" tells the story of a man who becomes real to his friends through his performances, not through his life. His lived experience is dull and even depressing:

> He was a young man
> Who did not feel beautiful
> Nor calm,
> Nor real,
> Nor happy. (*Human Juices*, n.p.)

What transformed him was the ability to perform:

> We were his audience;
> When we were there—
> He would stand on a table
> jump through the room, redo ing his part from some silly USA musical

This audience, because they are his friends, know the harsh truth about his past:

> We all knew he came from a very cruel
> ly treated crib

& thru many bleak yrs on playgrounds &
in alleys with broken whiskey bottles.

They could easily have taken this as his reality and drawn a variety of con-
clusions about him. They could read him as victim, as ghetto child, as failure; they could have constructed that information as his identity. Instead,
something else happens:

but now:
he was real: before us: a living reality,
On the table singing, jaws swelling.

The reinvention of the self as a work of art takes precedence over whatever the "real world" says about him. The truth of his being is the object he
has created. Moreover, the poem constructs this biography; a man is presented to us who has reality for us as readers, with a life history that may
or may not be linked to any actual person. It would be possible to read him
as a version of William Jay Marshall, Major's friend from his Omaha days,
but it would be meaningless to do so, since what is important for the author
is his ability to make us believe in the character through the words on the
page, not through any external knowledge.

Major came to see this period in his career as one of frustration, despite
his success at getting the attention of a small group of avant-garde writers and editors. Omaha simply did not provide the cultural resources and
intellectual and artistic community he felt necessary to his work. It was also
the period of urban disturbances. Major recalls looking out of his second-
story window one day and almost being shot by a white policeman ("Licking Stamps," 183). Given the circumstances, he decided it was time to move
again, this time to New York in December 1966.

# CHAPTER THREE

# Making It in New York

Major had visited New York briefly after his release from the air force in 1957. Like other African American artists of his generation, including LeRoi Jones and Ishmael Reed, he believed the place to be was Greenwich Village, not Harlem. This was the area associated with the Beats and with the avant-garde in the arts. Given his correspondence with Sheri Martinelli and his publication of work by Lawrence Ferlinghetti and Henry Miller in the *Coercion Review*, it is not surprising that he would take up residence in a bohemian rather than ethnic area of the city. He moved into the apartment of a friend from Omaha who lived on Twelfth Street on the Lower East Side. He quickly established a connection to Walter Lowenfels, with whom he had been corresponding and who had helped to place some of his poems. His relationship with the Omaha friend soon became strained, and he found work that enabled him to get his own apartment nearby.

He taught creative writing at the New Lincoln School in Harlem, a job secured for him by his friend Art Berger, a poet and member of Umbra, a group of black artists living in or frequenting the Lower East Side. In 1967, Major had printed an anthology of the work of his students from the school. But more important for his career, he began working as a research analyst for Simulmatics, an information consulting firm based in New York City. Major traveled to Milwaukee and Detroit as part of a project to examine media representations of and citizen responses to the civil disturbances of the period. He chose to interview residents of the ghetto areas, in barbershops, diners, and other venues where members of the black community gathered. He was in Detroit at the time of the Algiers Motel incident, in which young black men were killed by the police, apparently for being in a room with white women. This event, which came near the end of the civil disturbance that took forty-three lives, placed Major in the center of the action. Strangely enough, he never used this material in any of his works other than "Licking Stamps." The report of the corporation, funded by the federal government, was largely ignored, though it has come to be a part of the historical record of the time.

## THE MAKING OF *ALL-NIGHT VISITORS*

During this period, he continued to write on his own, but he succeeded only in placing individual short pieces, though there were many of these; between 1966 and 1968, he published nearly forty poems, in addition to several short stories, essays, and reviews. Correspondence with his agent Howard Moorepark demonstrates the problems he had with his longer fiction. Several manuscripts were sent to major publishers, but none were accepted. It was this frustrating experience with mainstream houses that probably led to the decision to approach Maurice Girodias at the New York office of Olympia Press, a French publisher. Major's breakthrough came in 1969, with the publication of *All-Night Visitors*, by Olympia. Within four years of its release, he came out with four books of poetry, an anthology of black verse, a dictionary, and another novel. His reputation as an avant-garde artist, one who refused to follow any traditional set of ideological or racial principles in his writing, was established by these works.

The story of *All-Night Visitors* is a complex one. Major's reputation as an experimental novelist was initially based on the fragmented narrative method of this first long work of fiction. He has told the story several times of how Girodias, who supported the work of avant-garde writers by printing and selling a line of pornographic novels, insisted on editing the manuscript to emphasize the erotic material (e.g., "Licking Stamps," 185). There is no independent documentation of this claim; letters between Major and the publisher indicate a need for some specific cuts, but nothing as wholesale as he has stated. His explanation is that all of this interaction was verbal, since both he and the press were located in New York at the time.[1] Having failed to attract a U.S. publisher, the novelist reluctantly agreed to the changes.

In addition, he attempted to combine parts of three separate manuscripts—one each on New York, Chicago, and Vietnam; a fourth set of chapters, situated in an orphanage, appears to be part of the Chicago material. Though these manuscripts are not held in the Clarence Major Archives at the University of Minnesota, a corrected typescript in the archives suggests that Major's initial effort was to juxtapose them rather than create a sequential, coherent narrative. In this draft version, chapters linked by time and place are grouped together and given a location and date as part of the chapter title. The narrative starts in New York in 1967, then moves to Chicago in 1966, Vietnam in 1963, the orphanage in 1957, Chicago again in late 1966, New York in August and September of 1967, then several deleted chapters (some of which reappear in the published version) called "Anita" set in Chicago in late 1966; it concludes in New York in late 1967.[2]

Major and a new girlfriend, Sheila Silverstone, a recent graduate of Queens College, who had also worked at Simulmatics, left New York for Puerto Vallarta, Mexico, to live while he made the revisions over several months in 1968. His journal of this period focuses primarily on their everyday living experiences and the difficulties of their relationship rather than on the activity of writing. He has described one source of those problems as Sheila's sense that he was compromising his artistic integrity by cutting his manuscript so drastically to please a publisher ("Licking Stamps," 185). There was regular correspondence among Major, Girodias, and some of the Olympia staff during this time. Frequently, it would involve requests from the author for funds to help support them in Mexico. These requests were sometimes granted, though Girodias often accompanied his agreement with comments on the financial difficulties of the publishing company.[3]

There was also a period before and after the time in Mexico during which Major considered writing for Olympia's pornography line. He requested several of the books and tried out pseudonyms, including the name he used for the heroine of *Reflex and Bone Structure*. The idea advanced far enough that Girodias provided a five-hundred-dollar advance.[4] The sample that Major submitted was deemed "too literary" for the market, but Major was allowed to keep the advance—an act of generosity not generally associated with Girodias, who was better known for his contentious dealings with authors over money.[5] This latter point is supported by Major's later thought of taking legal action against Olympia; documents in the Clarence Major Archive include lists of possible violations of the contract. There is no evidence that he followed through legally, though he was in correspondence with those who handled the bankruptcy case.[6]

When the book was finally released in 1969, it received good reviews, though it never sold significant numbers. Many of the comments came, not surprisingly, from the writers with whom he was associated. Both Ishmael Reed and Walter Lowenfels gave it positive evaluations. Christopher Lehmann-Haupt in the *New York Times* called Major "a sincere and passionate writer" on his way to saying that "the trouble with his novel is that the arrangement of the material doesn't build or sustain anything but boredom."[7] What is truly important about this commentary, however, is that it appeared in a review titled "On Erotica" and was accompanied by comments on two other Olympia Press works. The net effect was that Major was introduced to the reading public as part of the avant-garde of literature, a position he had been trying to gain for himself during his apprentice years.

An interpretation of the novel should begin with a brief summary of the text, since both the author and the work have, unfortunately, received limited attention even in African American literary and critical circles. *All-Night Visitors* is the first-person narrative of Eli Bolton, who spends his childhood in an orphanage and later attends Roosevelt University in Chicago. During this time he has a series of sexual experiences that are reported in detail. He then goes to Vietnam as a draftee, where he witnesses the sexual and other violence of white soldiers against the local population. Suffering both mental collapse and physical injury, he is released from the army. After traveling around the country, he returns to Chicago and works at the soda fountain of a neighborhood drugstore, while deciding whether to return to school. He falls in love with a white girl, whose race is relevant in that it is the source of much of the sparse commentary on racial matters in the text, from both black women and white strangers. Eli and Cathy decide to go to New York, where they live on the Lower East Side, until she decides to leave for California. Despondent, he moves to a residential hotel, where he works as a desk clerk and encounters prostitutes and transients. He takes up for a time with Eunice, though he knows she is leaving to go to Harvard. In the last scene, he offers refuge to a Puerto Rican mother and her children, who are escaping the violence of her husband.

This is the sequence of events as narrated in a "restored" 1998 version, discussed later; each section usually included lengthy, explicit sexual passages. These make up much of the 1969 version. In fact, Major has suggested that the narrative disruption thought by critics to make the original text experimental was the result of Girodias's demands for a more sexual and less literary text. Since such revisions would destroy the storyline in any case, Major decided to randomize the chapters (Bunge, *Conversations*, 90). The effect is a series of narrative fragments or freestanding stories unified only by the voice and sensibility of Eli Bolton. Thus, Cathy leaves him before she is introduced as a character, and some New York hotel experiences are related before the stories of childhood and Vietnam. Readers, in a very postmodern way, are forced to attempt the construction of a coherent narrative from a work filled with gaps and erasures; it is a novelistic puzzle with about half the pieces missing. And because the 1969 text focuses so much on Eli's sexual needs, desires, and practices, Major encourages readers to believe that the novel is either a radical rendering of the black male as sexual predator or somehow a deconstruction of that stereotype.

Plot, motive, and character development have little relevance to the story that is told; Eli's experiences in the orphanage tell us nothing about his reactions in Vietnam or his relationships with women in Chicago or New York. This suggests a compositional strategy consistent with Major's other work. This will be seen in his frequent emphasis on the line as distinct unit in poetry. We also know that his 1975 novel *Reflex and Bone Structure* was written as blocks of prose; he has compared this to some of his paintings being done as blocks of color. Thus, we could say that *All-Night Visitors* follows this same principle, though he seems not to have been conscious of it at the time of writing. In an essay in *Nickel Review*, he calls the book an "epic collage poem," which draws together his interest in working across artistic genres.[8]

The most salient characteristic of this work is, of course, the sexuality. Every chapter contains extended sexual descriptions, often running for several pages. Eli presents individual experiences in great detail, in effect pleasuring the reader with erotic language that also delays gratification. His narration controls the reader's response, just as his physical control delays the gratification of his partner. The few chapters that do not contain such material offer the indefensible killing of a dog at the orphanage, an old man in New York, and civilians in Vietnam. Between the thanatos and eros offered here, there is a sense of the emptiness of Eli's existence; he takes menial jobs and appears to have no purpose in his life except for intense sexual experience. Stylistically, however, the narrative is generally rendered in a realistic manner, with precise details and sequencing of events within chapters.[9]

BECOMING A NEW YORK WRITER

Once the manuscript was completed, Major immediately began planning his return to New York with Sheila. However, they had lived together at 533 East Twelfth Street only for a few months before they ended the relationship. He worked as the director of the creative writing program at New Lincoln School during the 1967–68 academic year and was for a short time a writer-in-residence at the Center for Urban Education. From 1967 to 1971, he taught as part of the Teachers and Writers Collaborative of Columbia University Teachers College. This experimental program brought professional writers—among them Grace Paley, Muriel Rukeyser, Kenneth Koch, Sonia Sanchez, June Jordan, and Nat Hentoff—into the public schools, especially those in "ghetto" areas. The program enhanced the network Major had been developing since arriving in the city. Perhaps most significant for his career was his acquaintance with Jonathan Baumbach, who aided him in getting work at Brooklyn College and later worked with him in the Fiction Collective.

Also during this time, he worked to establish his credentials in Black Arts circles. He became part of Umbra, which held workshops, conducted readings, and published *Umbra*, a literary magazine. Through it, Major met Ishmael Reed, Tom Dent, David Henderson, and Calvin Hernton, among others. While the group played a key role in creating the Black Arts Movement, its membership tended to divide between those whose interests were primarily social activism and those whose concerns were primarily literary.[10]

At the same time, Major began publishing in the *Journal of Black Poetry*, which had been established in San Francisco by Joe Goncalves. One of the leading publications for the voices of the Black Arts Movement, it lasted for nineteen issues from the mid-1960s to the early 1970s. Major came to be listed on the masthead as a contributing editor. He also initially published in the journal his essay "Black Criteria," which spelled out exactly how far he was then willing to go with activist art. He opens with a rather straightforward assertion: "The black poet confronted with Western culture and civilization must isolate and define himself in as bold a relief as he is capable of. He must chop away at the white criterion and destroy its hold on his black mind because seeing the world through white eyes from a black soul causes death" (*Dark and Feeling*, 147). In speaking of the "black mind" and "white criterion," he is clearly echoing the claims of Amiri Baraka, Larry Neal, and others. But his references to "white eyes" and a "black soul"

FIGURE 11. Major and Sheila
Silverstone in New York, 1968

also allude to W. E. B. Du Bois's notion of double consciousness, which is a
more complex articulation of the relationships of blacks and whites, since
for Du Bois there is no escaping a deep connection to Western and specifically U.S. society.

Major's ambivalence is further expressed when, in the midst of a discussion of the poet's social responsibility, he says this: "A work of art, a
poem, can be a complete 'thing'; it can be alone, not preaching, not trying to change men, and though it might change them, if the men are ready
for it, the poem is not reduced in its artistic status. I mean we black poets
can write poems of pure creative black energy right here in the white west
and make them works of art without falling into the cheap market place
of bullshit and propaganda" (147–48). Here he is in direct conflict with
much of the thinking of the Black Aesthetic, which demands an art that is
primarily useful for social and political action.[11] It is not surprising, given
his views, that he had a contentious relationship with the *Journal of Black
Poetry* and representatives of the movement and eventually resigned from
the editorial board. The break came when an issue that Major guest-edited

was changed by Goncalves to include both work Major had rejected and an attack on Ishmael Reed written by Goncalves.[12]

## SEEKING OPTIONS

The kind of network he sought is indicated by a party he attended in 1973 at the Park Lane Hotel. It brought together a group of young black male writers with the visiting expatriate novelist Chester Himes and his white wife Lesley. Included among the visitors were Ishmael Reed, Steve Cannon, Joe Johnson, and Quincy Troupe. Himes had a long-standing antagonistic relationship with U.S. publishers and with politicized black writers such as Richard Wright. He moved to Paris and later to Spain in the mid-1950s; in Europe he achieved literary success through his generally realistic representations of working class and criminal life. By the time of the party, his detective fiction and the films made from them (including *Cotton Comes to Harlem*) had gained him celebrity and wealth. Thus, for the group of young visitors associated with the Lower East Side, Umbra, and a nonnationalist impulse in their writing, Himes was a father figure. Even though they were all primarily known as poets at this time and were often engaged in experimental work, his critical attitude toward U.S. culture, his expatriate life, his sexual conquests, and his persistent individualism provided a model of how to be a black male artist who put his literary ahead of his racial identity.

The younger men were themselves largely independent-minded artists. They made up much of the aesthetically rather than politically oriented element in Umbra; they all had close associations with the Lower East Side and had or developed multicultural perspectives intended to transcend a racially specific view of literature. They also tended to work across genres. Three of them later formed Reed Cannon and Johnson Communications as an alternative to mainstream publishing companies. While all of them made use of African American cultural materials in their work, they did so more in the manner of Ralph Ellison in *Invisible Man* than in the manner of cultural nationalists. Thus, this moment in Major's early career shows him seeking out like-minded individuals rather than a broader ideological grouping.

Major's most significant editorial contribution at this time came in the form of the 1969 anthology, *The New Black Poetry*. In the introduction, he indicates his desire to put into print the work of a wide range of writers, especially those under thirty. As in "Black Criteria," he insists on the value

FIGURE 12. Left to right, back row: Major, Ishmael Reed, Joe Johnson, Steve Cannon; front row: Lesley and Chester Himes

of black consciousness: "Black poets are practically and magically involved in collective efforts to trigger real social change, correction throughout the zones of this republic. We are mirrors here, and we know that anybody who has ultimate faith in the system is our enemy" (12). Given this ideological view, it is striking that the only person he quotes at length in his introduction is Walter Lowenfels, the white Marxist anthologist and critic who was important in the development of Major's career. Moreover, the criteria for selection of material were only secondarily political: "In collecting these poems, my primary concern has been, first, with the artistic quality of the work, and second, with the quantity of the poets' social black conscious-ness, i.e., the degree to which IT is intrinsic to the human quality of the poem" (20). The last statement suggests Major's deep ambivalence about any ideological position. He seems to be attempting to sell his collection as nationalist without demanding any particular stance from the writers included. It is not surprising that one reviewer described the introduction as "incredibly sloppy."[13]

The selections suggest an aesthetic that had little to do with nationalism. It included several writers who built their reputations on Black Arts principles, including Larry Neal, Ed Bullins, Nikki Giovanni, Baraka, and Don Lee (Haki Madhubuti); but next to them were Russell Atkins, Calvin Hernton, Bob Kaufman, Audre Lorde, and Darwin Turner. His choices indicate that this is an anthology of poets who happen to be black, rather than a work defining a particular aesthetic or ideological position. He said as much in an interview done the same year: "What I've come to realize is that the question of a black aesthetic is something that really comes down to an individual question. It seems to me that if there is a premise in an artist's work, be he black or white, that it comes out of his work, and therefore out of himself. Or herself. I think that it's also true with form. It has to be just that subjective. I don't see any objective way of dealing with the work as an artist does, solely along racial lines" (*Dark and Feeling*, 115).

The publication of *The New Black Poetry* aroused controversy, not so much because of who it included or excluded, but because its publisher, International, was created to publish primarily Marxist works. Ed Spriggs, a poet who had not contributed to the anthology although he had been invited, organized a boycott of the book because Major had not published with a black-owned company. Spriggs made the attack in the *Journal of Black Poetry* even before the book was released (*Dark and Feeling*, 150). Around this same time, William F. Buckley, in the journal *Combat*, took issue with the Metropolitan Museum of Art bookstore selling *The New Black Poetry* during the Harlem on My Mind exhibit. Buckley's accusation was that the work of a "communist" publisher should not be openly available. The museum director first removed the volume and then, after counterprotests, sold it from behind the counter (*Dark and Feeling*, 150–51).

## A CORNUCOPIA OF POETRY

Major's own poetry began to appear, not only in little magazines but also in a flurry of books. Between 1970 and 1972, four volumes appeared under four different imprints. Because these came out in such rapid succession and they include work that was produced over the same time period, the works can be discussed as a unit. The histories of the volumes themselves, however, are distinct.

*Swallow the Lake* (1970) was the result of Major's social connection with William Meredith, a faculty member at Wesleyan University, and also the efforts of Walter Lowenfels on Major's behalf. As early as 1966, Lowenfels had suggested the title for the volume, and a year later, Major was in touch with Meredith about using his influence with the press.[14] Their combined efforts led to the acceptance of the collection by Wesleyan University Press, which was establishing itself as a significant force in poetry. One problem with the material was that the author sent in a wide range of pieces without indicating how they should be arranged. In addition, Major kept writing to the press director, José Rollins de la Torre Bueno, with new work and with questions about the book's production details.[15] Finally, according to Major, Meredith had to drive to Middletown, Connecticut, to make the final selection and arrangement himself ("Licking Stamps," 187). The collection won a National Council on the Arts prize in 1970.

The other projects were more straightforward, with Major sending letters of inquiry, followed by a collection of material. In doing this, he thought in terms of the logical outlets for a writer both black and avant-garde. Paul Breman, the London publisher, had since 1962 put out a Heritage Series, focusing on poets of African descent, including Robert Hayden, Audre Lorde, and Ishmael Reed. On September 14, 1970, Major sent Breman an inquiry about the work that became *Private Line* (1971). This success allowed him to claim his place as a "racial" artist while aligning him with those not directly linked to the Black Arts Movement. He maintained contact with Breman for several years, even staying at his London apartment on a trip to England.

*Symptoms and Madness* (1971) was published by Corinth Press, which was operated by Ted Wilentz, who had established his reputation through first the Eighth Street Bookshop (where LeRoi Jones worked) and then Corinth, where he focused on the work of Beat artists, including Jack Kerouac, Allen Ginsberg, and Gary Snyder. His location on the Lower East Side was not far from Major's various apartments at this time. Corinth was also putting out volumes by experimental African American writers, such as Jones and Jay Wright. In effect, Major was able, through this connection, to move in the literary world he had desired when he was putting out the *Coercion Review* back in Chicago.

His fourth volume, *The Cotton Club* (1972), came out of Broadside Press, which Dudley Randall created to give expression to the emerging voices of the new black renaissance. Randall himself had appeared in Major's *New Black Poetry*, as had several of the poets published in the Broadside Series, including Jones, Nikki Giovanni, and Don L. Lee. Publication here established Major's credentials as a "black" writer, since his other three volumes, as well as earlier books, had been done by white publishers. Significantly, the two shortest of the four poetry books were with presses—Paul Breman and Broadside—that had a focus on African American writing.

The poems from this set, which date from the mid-1950s to the beginning of the 1970s, tend to be personal rather than racial in nature, despite the fact that publishers were marketing them as black literature. The social commentary which appeared followed the pattern of Beat literature generally; that is, a broad critique of materialism, narrow-mindedness, and cultural superficiality. According to "A Poem Americans Are Going to Have to Memorize Soon," citizens are "these huge teachable slangy people / touched with giddy shallowness" (*Swallow the Lake*, 32). In "Don't send me no more inter-viewers," the media are said to be "simple, opaque" (*Private Line*, 20). The nation as a superpower is rendered as

> the comic moneypowerdream
> of this octopus
>   of the globe
> sunstruck with the
>   silent dangers
> of goofy operations and
>   unholy jive with
>   sham visions
>   of honor drugged with
>   the weight of propaganda. (*Symptoms and Madness*, 37)

Even when the work is clearly designed for an African American audience, as in the case of *The Cotton Club*, Major carefully distances himself from the work of the Black Arts Movement. The cover photography, which shows him with Sharyn Skeeter, who would later become his third wife, was taken in Barcelona and depicts them as typical American tourists. In addition, few of the poems offer a social or racial critique; the number is even smaller than in *Swallow the Lake* or *Symptoms and Madness*. The pieces that are racially specific focus on black expressive forms and black artists. Several are apparently based on images in the Schomburg Library in Harlem. For example, "1915 Interior" describes a woman the speaker addresses as "sister," though clearly she is an image. What is important is neither the identity of the woman nor the details of the picture. Rather, it is the response of the viewer-speaker, who believes that she is capable of revealing some secret that will help him understand himself. "Ladies Day: 1902" engages race, though through a double distance. We again have an image (this time clearly a painting, since it refers to the colors used by the artist) and one from an earlier era. The subject is a group of whites going boating on the Harlem River. The persona notes that they are dressed up and that the boats are colorful but observes that "they don't have / any fun" (*Cotton Club*, 9). This last observation reflects attitudes about whites common in the Black Arts Movement, but the displacement of time and medium blunts any critical edge.

Another variation of the art theme is the underappreciation of black performers. The title poem of *The Cotton Club* describes the work and person of Duke Ellington. The poet pairs the public image of the all-night performer with the often-tired human being. He notes the endless demand for pictures but makes the point that the real Duke is invisible to his audience. Similarly, "Ventriloquist 1900–1968" describes the photograph of the performer that is sometimes on display at the Schomburg. But though "people downtown begin / to go uptown" to see black art, almost nobody pays attention to the man or his photograph (7).

In these pieces, we see Major's concern with his own reputation as an artist. He is caught in a double bind. His race creates certain expectations about what he should produce and how he should be marketed. If he follows the Black Arts formula (or even seems to follow it), then white critics read him as a propagandist and black ones question his ideological purity. If he goes the way of a more subjective, experimental art, which could include forms of social commentary, then he limits his audience, regardless of race. Thus, we see him in these four volumes trying out different styles and devices, hoping that something will work.

What is generally consistent through these books is a reluctance to follow principles of syntax and image-building. A poem, such as "The Bust," from *The Cotton Club*, is made up of fragments that do not quite cohere:

> you black, soft, your voice
> remember me speak call me
> from a dream not sure really
> whether it happens
>
> if it really is not to laugh.
> at. like the white boys
> telling corn planting jokes
> busting up
>
> over the hoghead and peas
> bit, and your mama, your
> woman, white out gigging
> to pay. for love, cause

she hates her father. yet
she grew up on the nicodemus
from detroit thing the
hants and snake jokes

about your people. but knows
she was tricked by her daddy
who hated all women like
account figures (*Cotton Club*, 11)

The referent of "you" of the opening line is not clear; it could be "the bust," which is not otherwise referred to. But given what is said later, it would make sense for the bust to be male. However, the soft voice would normally (certainly in the environment of 1960s activism) imply a female referent. The mention of a dream in the opening stanza suggests a surreal quality that only partially explains the poem. Periods fall at points that do not appear to call for stops, whether for reading or speaking purposes. The poem offers various folk references, but they do not tell us anything about "your people," who presumably are connected to the "you" of the first line. Moreover, it is whites throughout who have this folk knowledge. Finally, it is the white characters whose stories we know, at least in a minimal way. The poem works only if we consider it as an experiment of the same sort, though in miniature, of *All-Night Visitors*, in that it operates as only marginally related pieces, connected principally by the fact that an artist has put them together.

The title poem of the first volume, "Swallow the Lake," is more successful because it organizes the fragments around the image of Lake Michigan and the subjective responses of the speaker. It also uses periods and line breaks in a communicative manner rather than at random:

Gave me things I
could not use. Then. Now.
Rain night bursting upon & into. I
shine updown into Lake Michigan

like the glow from the cold lights of the Loop.
Walks. Deaths. Births.
Streets. Things I could not give back. Nor
use. (*Swallow the Lake*, 14)

As in much of the verse from this period, Major provides limited connections; readers have no idea, for example, who or what "gave me things." As with much of the beat writing that served as an early influence on him, the source of his malaise appears to be American culture generally rather than a specific set of conditions. He has "feelings I could not / put into words" that are connected to "Blank monkeys of the hierarchy," which presumably are the leaders of society who enjoy "stupidity & death turning them on" (14).

While the sources of the distress are not clear, the effects on the speaker are:

my middle
passage blues my corroding hate my release
while I come to become neon iron eyes stainless lungs
blood zincgripped steel I
come up abstract (14)

The "middle passage" links him not only to the experience of slavery and its denial of basic humanity but also to the Great Migration that brought early twentieth-century African Americans to work in the foundries and steel mills of Chicago and other northern cities. Major himself left Chicago to work at a steel mill in Omaha. His corroding hatred destroys the metallic structures that might enable him to survive such a world. Instead, he is

not able to take their bricks. Tar. Nor their flesh.
I ran: stung. Loop fumes hung
                    in my smoky lungs

. . . . . . . . . . . . . . . .

Illusion, illusion, and you
would swear before screaming somehow
choked voices in me.
The crawling thing in the blood. . . . (14–15)

He cannot resist being infused with the threats of the society. The bricks, tar, and flesh suggest the experience of lynching, though only indirectly. He is choked when he tries to articulate the voices within and is infected with the "crawling thing." But what comes out is a kind of immunity, though at a price:

One becomes immune
to the bricks the feelings. One becomes
death. (15)

The very ability to survive comes at the price of his humanity. But this threat produces what is for Major the Great Refusal:

> I could not whistle and walk in storms
> along Lake Michigan's shore. Concrete walks.
> I could not swallow the lake (15)

He has talked in a number of interviews, letters, and remembrances, as well more indirectly in poetry and fiction, of Chicago as a place he found uninhabitable for a young man seeking to be an artist. Even as it gave him some of the cultural tools and influences in painting and literature that were essential for his career, it robbed him of the sense of opportunity to achieve status and recognition as an artist. This was especially true in the black community of the city, which, he felt, valued much more highly the accumulation of material goods. To continue to live in Chicago meant that he would have to "swallow" all that and to deny his deepest aesthetic instincts in order to be successful. Both the structure and the content of the poem serve as an assertion of an artistic identity that resists racial, ideological, cultural, and aesthetic boundaries.

He has also linked this poem to *All-Night Visitors*:

> They came out of the same experience in Chicago. I was young then and
> very angry, poor and unhappy most of the time. All the young men are
> angry, it's true. Some more than others. We are all promised more than the
> world can deliver. My anger had a cultural, social, and economic basis. But
> I had enormous confidence in myself. It just at times seemed that the world
> was too indifferent to what I believed I had to offer. And I saw all around
> me young men like myself giving up at an early age because they too felt
> the same way about the world. But I was still very optimistic. At times fool-
> ishly so. In any case, I knew I had to change my life. "Swallow the Lake" and
> *All-Night Visitors* represent that period in my life. (Bunge, *Conversations*,
> 168–69)

The source of that confidence is his ability to give artistic expression to those emotions, in a manner similar to Richard Wright and James Baldwin, who also worked through their dysfunctional environments by turning experience into story and image. Unlike them, he had from an early age received positive attention for his skill, even if it was dangerous to publicly display it. The result was a willingness to try various approaches, as evident in the range of genres, approaches, and themes already being employed.

Ironically, the reviews of these books of poetry, which were few in number, consistently read them in social and racial terms and praised or attacked them from that perspective. Bill Katz in *Library Journal*, in the only significant review of *Private Line*, commented that "these are direct black poems filled with explosive expressions of events and feelings. The voice and passion are real enough, but the poetry is minimal." In contrast, Jerome Cushman, also in *Library Journal*, said of *Swallow the Lake*: "Major ... writes about his people with a passionate but controlled lyricism. While his language is sometimes harsh and street oriented, the prevailing tonality of the poetry is quiet, almost philosophical. He knows about the desperate young men and women of his generation and he delineates with tender honesty their struggle to keep things together. More literary than polemical, his work shows exciting promise." The primary virtue of the work appears to be its lack of anger and ideology; virtually nothing is said about its poetics.

In February 1970, Major met Sharyn Jeanne Skeeter at a restaurant party on Fourteenth Street. She was poetry editor for *Essence* and also had worked for *Mademoiselle* magazine and had reviewed *Private Line* positively in 1970 for *Black Creation*. Her family lived in Brooklyn, and she was also a distant relative of Langston Hughes. The family, by Major's report, did not care for him. Married at the time, she left her husband for Major, and they lived first in his apartment on St. Mark's Place and then moved to 11 Waverly Place. She managed to get his work published in the magazines, though he had difficulty getting paid for it.

The early seventies was a time of extensive social interaction; in "Licking Stamps," he refers to 1971–73 as the "period of literary parties." The name-dropping in the memoir becomes as important as the artistic history. He met W. H. Auden, Josephine Baker, Robert Hooks, Chester Himes, Ralph Ellison, Kurt Vonnegut, James Jones, and Adrienne Rich. In his correspondence, he asks Reed how he can become a member of PEN, and he later attends a number of their social events.

## ON THE ROAD WITH SHARYN

He and Sharyn traveled to Europe in the summer of 1971, both as tourists and to establish connections with professional acquaintances, who were consistently helpful to Major. They went first to London, where they stayed in an apartment at 4 Eton College Road, arranged for them by Paul Bremen, the publisher of *Private Line*. They saw a number of the sites but were

FIGURE 13. Outside one of Major's New York apartments, 11 Waverly Place

anxious to move on to Paris. There they initially stayed at an apartment arranged by the poet Norman Loftis, who was living in the city with his new bride. They seriously considered moving to Paris, going so far as to look at apartments to rent long-term, but decided that it was too costly. It was also apparently here that Major told the anthologist Robert Lee that he was "tired of theme and ethnic anthologies, including my own, primarily because of the journalistic and propagandistic work they inspire."[16] Thus, within two years of its publication, he was repudiating *The New Black Poetry*, even though, as we have seen, it was not as ideological as reviewers claimed.

They traveled from Paris to Milan by train and then to Venice to see many of the tourist sites. In early August, they moved on to Florence, which was of special interest to Major for its art. Sharyn's facility in Italian was helpful during this segment of the trip in enabling them to find cheap accommodations. They stayed at a hotel near the river. In his journal of the visit, Major portrays the city in aesthetic terms, emphasizing its color and detail. They then moved on to Rome, where again they focused on tourist locations, including Saint Peter's, the Sistine Chapel, the Forum, and the Coliseum. In a bookstore, he found an Italian translation of *All-Night Visitors*, about which he had a negative response: "A sex goddess is on its cover! What does a sex goddess have to do with growing up black and poor in Chicago?"[17] His reaction was curious, since the novel is intensely sexual, and he had elsewhere downplayed the role of race in his work. It was as though he had to constantly remind himself, and whomever he considered the audience for a particular text, that race is relevant to his art.

From Rome, they went to Barcelona, where the cover photograph for *The Cotton Club* was taken. Here they stayed at the Hotel Cristal, near the center of the city. While in Barcelona, they went to their first bullfight, which Major found fascinating despite his repulsion at the violence.[18] From there, they went to Madrid, where they again took in the bullfighting and visited the zoo, as they had done in Milan. They stayed at the Gran Hotel Colón. Like the Barcelona lodging, this was also a four-star hotel near the cultural center of the city. At the Prado, Major took special interest in the work of Goya, which he had learned to appreciate during his apprenticeship at the Art Institute of Chicago.

From Madrid, they returned to the United States; they had spent six weeks on their version of the grand tour. Major went back to teaching writing at various universities while maintaining a faculty position at Brooklyn College, which he held irregularly from 1968 to 1975. He continued to publish both poetry and short fiction, though increasingly the work appeared in mainstream periodicals and anthologies. For example, in 1973, eight poems appeared in *American Poetry Review*, for which he later became a columnist, as well as *Essence*. In the summer of 1972, they visited Montreal and Quebec, again primarily as tourists. That fall, he began teaching at Sarah Lawrence College, where he worked until 1975 as adjunct faculty. He and Sharyn moved to Darien, Connecticut, near the end of this period in order to be closer to the college. There they were married in the backyard of a justice of the peace on 9 July 1975. They moved to Maryland when he was offered a two-year position at Howard University. This position was arranged by Charles Nilon, who was serving as temporary chair of the English Department. Major comments in "Licking Stamps" that his relationship with Sharyn had begun to disintegrate around the time of the move to Maryland, which suggests that the marriage itself was perhaps an attempt to resolve conflicts.

BECOMING AN EXPERIMENTAL NOVELIST

As suggested earlier, Major's initial reputation as a postmodern fictionist was in part an accident, in that the structure of *All-Night Visitors* was
the result of pressure from the publisher and aggressive response from the
author more than a deliberate aesthetic decision. In 1973, with the publication of *NO*, Major demonstrated his commitment to the experimental
mode. The novel was actually completed in 1969, but he again had difficulty
finding an outlet for it. The creation of the novel was perhaps the easiest
of his career. At the time, he was coteaching with Victor Hernandez Cruz
a summer teachers seminar, "Black Excellence in American Literature," at
Cazenovia College in Upstate New York. While the goal of the program
was to prepare teachers to introduce African American materials in schools
for the first time, Major and Cruz chose to challenge preconceived notions
about racial identities and the literatures that emerged from such identities.
Among the required readings was *All-Night Visitors*, which had recently
been published.

 While engaged in this subversive work, Major produced a draft of a novel
about a metaphorical penal system that imposes identities on its characters. He says in "Self-Interview" that he did the first draft on a roll of tele-
type paper spun off a spool into his typewriter. He finished the first draft
in "about two months of very casual work" (*Dark and Feeling*, 129). The
second and final draft was completed in the fall of 1969 on regular typing paper. The principal work of revision involved developing charts of the
characters and their personalities as well as the wealth of cultural allusions
running through the text (*Dark and Feeling*, 143). While the method and
speed of writing suggest the model of Jack Kerouac's *On the Road*, Major
never refers to that work when discussing his novel, though his sense of
discovering what the story was doing after finishing the initial draft suggests something like "automatic" writing.

 It took three years for *NO* to find a publisher and, as with *All-Night Visitors*, the arrangement was unusual. It was brought out by Emerson Hall, a
new African American house focused primarily on social and behavioral
science studies about black life. Established in 1969 by Alfred E. Prettyman, a former executive at Harper and Row, the press did not issue its first
volume until 1971, two years after Major completed his novel. Significant
authors on its list included sociologist Kenneth Clark and psychiatrist Alvin

Poussaint. Emerson Hall's goal was to provide an outlet for high-quality black work.[19] The booklist did include a collection of poetry by June Jordan.

The reasons that Major went to a nonliterary and inexperienced publisher and that Prettyman was willing to take on an experimental novel remain points of speculation. George Davis raises these issues in one of the few reviews of the novel: "It makes one wonder where [Major] will find readers for this brave but often confusing work. It is also surprising that a new black publisher struggling for survival would choose to publish so esoteric a book." The answer may well be found in the oddity of the pairing. A publisher not devoted to literature might give a writer much more freedom to tell the story his own way. Moreover, Major had been moving in the circles associated with black nationalism and was engaged in the current experiments in public-school programs in New York. He had also edited a slang dictionary. All of this would make him attractive to a publisher of African American material of any genre.

In addition, the statement Major submitted to Prettyman about the book would have made it consistent with the press's larger mission:

In *NO* I am interested in probing deeply and evenly and fully the combination of conscious and unconscious experience. I mean for the work to create its own terms. It is not meant to be satire. It is realistic work of what we call fiction. Its realism is as real as that middle land between sleep and wakefulness. And in terms of theme, mainly, I am exploiting a range of taboos, fears, cultural limitations, and social traits, springing from attitudes concerning a wide range of human experiences, sexual, racial, historical, national and personal. In *NO* the "spirit" of the narrator's "head" is meant to function both as a "scheme" (plot) and as central force, conveyer of the "story" and a screening device for the development of the work as an entity. The main concept involves demonstrating the plight of Moses Westby's tragic imprisoned birth and growth and ultimately how he transcends this penal system. The "prison" is spiritual; it is also "physical" and it refers to an area of human activity (in this case largely concerning black Americans) that is as precisely personal as it is political. The logic that the action and ideas depend on is meant to be as implicit as the plot in that it is a "secret plan"—as one finds in but cannot quite define in a good poem. This manner of mind and these activities will be both familiar and at the same time, distant, strange; which is, in all of our minds, exactly what the fusion of unconscious and conscious reality amounts to. I am not writing more about the penal system than the people trapped in it. (*Dark and Feeling*, 16–17)

This long passage reveals Major's strategy for selling the project to Emerson Hall. This was a press that made money from *The Mind Game*, a study of psychotherapy by E. Fuller Torrey, and Poussaint's *Why Blacks Kill Blacks*. A summary of a novel that talks about the unconscious and prisons and about its realism but says almost nothing about the plot would entice further attention. In fact, the language Major chooses is as unlike a description of a novel as it could be. Terms such as "plot" and "story" are buried in commentary about social traits, penal systems, and logic. Major's parenthetical that *NO* is also about "black Americans" closes the deal. He projects it as a psychologically rich *Native Son*.

The fact of the matter is that *NO* would in any case not be easily recognizable as a novel to those unfamiliar with the fictional experiments of the time. It has greater coherence than *All-Night Visitors*, which is a pastiche of different subjects. *NO* more deliberately fragments its unitary subject, much like a cubist painting. Instead of chapter divisions it has three titled parts, and the segments within the parts vary in length from two to more than twenty pages. Generally speaking, the segments fall into chronological order, but with no necessary transitions between them. There is a consistent narrative voice, an adult man mostly telling of his childhood experiences. Individual sections violate time and space order internally, such as the one that tells in reverse chronology of a trip to a stock-car race. There is also a fluidity of discourse that allows references to popular culture and folklore from different times to be contiguous. Nonetheless, the novel is similar to the antiheroic stories published by John Updike, Saul Bellow, and Philip Roth during the post–World War II period. The narrator has some of the same personal inadequacies and social failings. He displays the same inability to develop a strong sense of self. Major does construct more graphic scenes of violence, sexuality, and family conflict, and he makes more use of dream sequences and challenges credibility when, for example, we learn that the narrator's father kills all the members of the family, including himself and the narrator. The story nonetheless continues to be told by the same narrator.

Major told John O'Brien in an interview that the novel was not autobiographical, though "its roots are very deep in my emotional life" (Bunge,

*Conversations*, 19). In fact, almost all the characters and a number of events are drawn from life. The narrator has the same name as his father, who is a hustler; the mother is a light-skinned woman who suffers abuse from her husband and eventually leaves him. The narrator and his sister live with their maternal grandparents; the "white" grandfather was an architect and builder who has suffered a series of strokes, while the grandmother traces part of her ancestry to Native Americans. In the last section, the trip to a "Latin country" is clearly modeled on Major's trip to Mexico with Sheila. Even the references to Moses's sexual inadequacies have a source in the author's Mexican journal, where he talks about premature ejaculation.[20] The bullfight that concludes the novel corresponds to the first one he saw in San Miguel de Allende in 1968.

This accumulation of personal history is transformed into a narrative that pushes the tensions of childhood and early adulthood to extremes. Major's experiences as an undersized child in a dysfunctional family become a series of humiliations in which young Moses repeatedly experiences abjection and social ridicule, especially in matters of sexuality. Violence is commonplace, as animals are sexually molested or killed, children are beaten, and women are assaulted. A cousin is apparently castrated by his own father, though his action appears to have no physical, psychological, or legal repercussions. The father is driven to kill his family and then himself, though his motive is unclear. The world of restriction that includes adult authority, racial discrimination, and male domination is captured in the motif of the prison system. The narrator labels various characters as guards, trustees, wardens, and "free folk." The story is racialized in that whites are the only ones who can be free. Even the powerful father figure knows how to behave deferentially in the presence of whites.

If the novel can be read as an experimental bildungsroman, then it is the story of a quest for identity in which the author questions the very notion of a unitary self. Major has said that one of the flaws of story is its overreliance on a Freudian way of thinking (Bunge, *Conversations*, 14). Clearly there is an obsession with dangerous fathers, seductive mothers, and a castrated male self. He tries to mitigate these elements by breaking the narrative into pieces, but in fact all of the pieces lead in the same direction and reinforce the point of the fragility of the modern (black) male self. In the end, we even have a notion of emerging wholeness. At the bullfight, Moses (the narrator) jumps into the ring and runs toward the bull. He seeks, not to kill it, but only to touch it. He senses that his freedom somehow is linked to the risk. He succeeds, then leaves the girlfriend who has been demeaning him, and returns to the United States and a future outside of the penal system that has been his life. Ultimately then, despite its questioning of both cultural values and the literary structures that embody them, *NO* affirms individualism and the process of self-creation.

One of the few remaining paintings from this period reflects the themes of this work. Titled *The Long Road* (1968), it appears to be a variation of Edvard Munch's *The Scream* (plate 1). In some ways it is more stark than that existential iconic work. While both paintings focus on an elongated figure in the foreground who looks out at the viewer, Munch's image is recognizable as human. Major's, in contrast, has virtually no features. Two holes that might be eyes are encased in a brown imperfect circle linked to a thin neck and a triangle that suggests shoulders. No other features are represented. In addition, while Munch offers swirls of contrasting color and the presence of other figures in the background, Major's work is fundamentally monochromatic and geometric. The beige road of the title disappears into the beige sky in the background. Perspective is gained through the use of dark, elongated triangles bordering the road.

Thus, the figure Major creates lacks even the capacity to scream. It is alone in an empty landscape, a man without qualities. Like Eli Bolton, it is merely a body, without even Eli's ability to tell his story or function with other human beings. Like the younger Moses Westby, it has no one on whom it can rely. If the road is to be read symbolically, it is not clear that it leads from or to anything. Given the dark brown color of the figure, it is possible to understand it to be African American and thus to encode the message from Invisible Man: "keep this nigger boy running."

But it is dangerous to suggest too much about a work by Major, who always insists on the technical aspects of what he does. Thus, what dominates much of the canvas is the creation of the vanishing point, as blocks of color are used to form geometric figures that move to the same point. Even the neck and shoulders of the body contribute to this effect. Thus, just as the blocks of prose or verse in his writing are used to break any straightforward interpretation, so the technical concerns in this painting challenge the reader/viewer to impose a conventional meaning on Major's work.

# CHAPTER FOUR

# Beginning a Professional Career, 1975–1980

The mid-1970s marked the period when Major, in his late thirties, emerged from his itinerant, bohemian life into what can be considered a career as artist and teacher. This did not mean that his life became entirely settled or stable, only that it became more so. He had now established himself as a poet and was gaining a reputation as a novelist among the avant-garde with whom he identified. It also meant that he was less engaged in the ideological struggles that had shaped the late sixties and early seventies.

## PAINTING

During this time, Major took up painting again as a regular activity. He had largely given it up since leaving Chicago, with a few exceptions, such as *The Long Road*. While he has always insisted on the influence of the Impressionists and Postimpressionists on him, the work produced during this period suggests different sources at work. Another complication with the art is that Major has a habit of reworking paintings over several years, thereby obscuring his original design. Thus, for example, *Family Five* is dated 1976–83. It appears to be a parody of late nineteenth-/early twentieth-century family portraits. It includes parents on either side with three children in the middle. But the artist is not interested in naturalistic representation; simple lines indicate features, and the only color occurs in the middle of the frame. The maternal figure appears to be late Victorian, with very formal hair, dress, and posture. The paternal figure is far less distinctive, represented by a few lines to indicate basic facial features and limbs. What draws the eye is the child in the center. The head is dark brown, with white holes for eyes and mouth. The rest of the body (except for rectangular shapes for hands) is pastel pink. He stands with one arm akimbo and the legs forming an arch. Though the small figure next to him is also in color (blue and turquoise), it is the central image that appears ready to burst out of the frame. He is being held back by the hand of the father. By reducing the figures to lines, by suggesting then breaking the formality of the portrait, and by focusing attention on the rebel in the portrait, Major continues his tendency to undercut respectability while acknowledging its presence.

*Yellow Chair*, which he began (and apparently completed) around the same time, shows the influence of Van Gogh (plate 2). It is simply a table and chair, with nothing else in the frame. The most direct reference is "Vincent's Bedroom in Arles," radically simplified and reorganized. While done with watercolor instead of oil, it makes the same effort to blend color and simultaneously obscure and emphasize lines. The lines delineate shapes but are wavering and muddied. Yellow dominates, but it merges into red and even into the white background. There is no effort at realistic portrayal; unlike Van Gogh's room, there is no clear depiction of either object. In addition, both appear to extend beyond the canvas. As in much of his other work, Major works primarily with geometric patterns: triangles, rectangles, semicircles. He plays with light in a way that makes it difficult to determine the source of the light; color is washed out in different locations on the canvas, giving the effect of various intensities of light. He would seem to be attempting to examine a series of problems of composition and perspective by reworking an iconic painting. The eye is at the edge of the table, yet the table appears to be tilting down toward the viewer. The chair, in contrast, is tilting away from the table at a different angle and out of the frame. The overall effect is instability.

Another painting from the same time, *Grief* (1976), also shows Major signifying on Edvard Munch (plate 3). The specific reference is *The Death Chamber* (ca. 1892). While Major's work is in an expressionist style, it contains some elements very similar to those in Munch: three of the figures are in virtually identical positions, both in terms of their postures and in terms of their relative locations on the canvas. The chair in the background, though much more detailed in *The Death Chamber*, is the same shape. While *Grief*, like Major's work discussed above, reveals little detail, the lines around the heads of the female figures suggest similar hairstyles; their dresses also follow the same pattern.

It is the differences, however, that are striking. First, there is the realism of Munch's painting, down to the inclusion of a bedpan at the right center, the collection of medicine bottles on the nightstand, and the design of the wicker chair. *Grief*, in contrast, is blocks of color given shape by wide lines in contrasting colors. Only one of the characters has facial features, and those are very broad. More important is the change in palette. Consistent with his subject, Munch chooses subdued tones of blue and gray, with a hint of purple. The contrast is provided by a spectrum of browns, moving toward, in some places, orange, yellow, and pink. The background is a muted green. Major chooses strong versions of the secondary colors to create garish effects. The floor and chair are different shades of purple, two of the dresses and the top of the frame are green, and the third dress and the dead body are bright pink, with the latter outlined in purple. The artist sets off these colors with white space in both the foreground and the background.

What is most significant, and clearly affects the meaning of the work, are the changes in the placement of certain figures within the frame. Major has eliminated all but one of the males, suggesting that mourning is a female experience. And whereas Munch conceals the dead (or dying), Major places the body in the foreground, naked. Interestingly, he seems to have rotated the seated figure in *The Death Chamber* so that it is now in a fetal position on a white surface. Munch's painting incorporates in the background a framed image of Christ with a crown of thorns. Major moves that image to the right foreground and enlarges it. It is also the only figure with facial features, though they are done in broad lines. He takes the bloodshot eyes of Munch's dominant female figure, changes them to the same pink as the body and gives them to Christ, in addition to a pink beard. The face is outlined in purple, and the face and shoulders of the body are ecru. This image may also be the artist himself, just as Munch placed himself in *The Death Chamber*. The difference is that Munch is turned away from the viewer, while Major/Christ stares directly out.

The effect of this revision, in which Major enlarges and exaggerates what Munch conceals or underplays, is to desacralize death and the emotions associated with it. The body is laid out like a piece of meat. Since the mourners have no faces, we as viewers have no sense of their sorrow or pain. Whereas Munch wants to depict simultaneously the privacy and communal nature of grief, Major suggests the raw, public fact of death. He brings Christ off the wall as a dominating image of comfort and presents him instead as a voyeur, invading private space, just as the artist in the original invites us to see sorrow as a spectacle. While Munch turns his own head away, Major positions the Christ/artist in the space between viewer and mourner, welcoming us to exploit the emotions of others. As in his fiction and poetry, he breaks the boundaries between public and private, between self and other so that his audience is left in the uncomfortable position of seeing what they might prefer not to see and perhaps cannot resist gazing upon.

A very different work from the same time refers to a much earlier period, the one in which Major lived with Sheila Silverstone in Mexico. *Dream of Escape* (1976) is a small work done in gouache on artist board (plate 4). The clearest influence is Marc Chagall. The scene is a street in a Mexican village, with an indoor-outdoor cantina bar on the lower left, at which are seated small dark-brown figures. Above them is a lighter figure extending out of a second-floor window. The lower center depicts a golden donkey with a very full udder; it is noticeably larger than the human figures. Above the donkey floats a nude silver-white woman, with light yellow hair, proportionally the largest figure on the canvas. The woman's posture suggests her intention to land in a sitting position on the back of the donkey. The background color, from top to bottom of the frame, is bloodred. None of the figures, including the donkey, have any individualizing features. The disproportion in size and the colors of the woman, the donkey, and the background make this literally a gynocentric work. The males are small and marginal. The woman's leap is a kind of dance, and the blood that is both sky and earth is presented as natural, in the sense that it is contained neatly within the frame, as though it were simply street and sky.

The work is clearly based on Major's time with Sheila in Puerto Vallarta and elsewhere in Mexico while he was revising *All-Night Visitors*. In effect, he has reconstituted that experience, which he had previously described as difficult and painful. Here, in the context of the writing of *Emergency Exit* in the mid-1970s, which critiques society's repression of women, he reinvents the past as a celebration of the feminine. The woman becomes the central figure in this visual narrative, precisely because of her liminality; she rides the air, forever free of thresholds and bathed in the vital fluid of her own being. The male figure, the version of Major, can only look on. The title, however, calls us back to reality, or at least to personal history. *Dream of Escape* implies incarceration of some sort. Why is this woman leaping into the street? Why has she left the male figure behind? Is his gesture toward her an attempt to catch her, a sign of farewell, or a dismissal? Is this a leap of faith or a suicide? In other words, the text that the artist creates for the painting raises challenges for any unitary interpretation of the work.

## SYNCOPATED CAKEWALK

Major again brought his New York network into play with his next book of poetry, *The Syncopated Cakewalk* (1974). After failed attempts to find a publisher, he turned again to Walter Lowenfels, who had recently come out with a volume of poems from Barlenmir House.[1] Major wrote to Barry Mirenburg, who ran the company out of his home. The press was a small house that Richard Kostelantez, in an essay on small presses, said produced "collections by otherwise unfavored poets."[2] Such poets included William Packard, Adrian Vance, Robert Burdette Sweet, Philip Wofford, William Childress, and Major's friend Quincy Troupe, whose *Embryo* was published the same year as Lowenfels's *Found Poems* (1972). Though they never met in person, Major and Mirenburg collaborated closely on what was in effect an art book, and the volume came out in 1974.[3] The boards were hand-painted by Steffan, an abstract artist who worked for the company. Of the fifty-one poems, slightly fewer than half had been published previously, though in a wide variety of places. The oldest had appeared in the 1965 issue of *Coercion Review*, while others turned up in anthologies by Lowenfels and Woodie King (*Black Spirits*). Two of the pieces came out in Ishmael Reed's *Yardbird Reader*, two in *Essence* while Sharyn was poetry editor there, and three in *American Poetry Review* while Major was a columnist and two years before he became a contributing editor. He obviously used his connections carefully as a means of overcoming the difficulties of poetry publication.

Given that *The Syncopated Cakewalk* was published just two years after the last of his earlier poetry volumes and that several of the poems come from the same time period as the earlier collections, similarities among the collections are not unexpected. We find very little political or racial commentary, though some pieces take on racial subjects. Emphasis is given to patterns of love, to personal experiences, to history, but primarily to the workings of language.

The love poems concern themselves with frustration or possibility rather than realization. The situation can be humorous, as in "Flowers for My Date," in which the girl is hip and the boy is square. She

Fucked in hallways.
Played the dozens
with her mama. (*Syncopated*, 34)

He, in contrast, shows up with yellow roses, to which she responds:

Roses are straight
out of the Stone Age
Plus they ain't Soul.

Voiced by the young man, the poem expresses the gap that emerged in the late 1960s between conservative "Negro" identity and black pride. An irony at work is that the yellow rose in the popular song "Yellow Rose of Texas" refers to an African American woman and thus the young man's gift is racially relevant.

One of the few poems that offer a positive experience of love is "The Way the Roundness Feels," and it offers more verbal play than emotional substance. Typical of several pieces in the collection, it is structured on individual lines. Only three lines (of twenty-three) do not have an end stop. The speaker develops variations on the idea of roundness:

your strong fingers cruise the rotunda
As our secret world turns in on us

. . . . . . . . . . .

Your neck and breasts are round.
So are the peanuts we eat.
And the teacups we drink from. (*Syncopated*, 6)

Together the two people form a whole; they effectively complete each other. But even in the erotic moment, we are returned to language:

Your mouth, I know your lips.
Your hands, I know your fingers.
I feel you moving all through my speech.
Inside this poem, you are speaking.
Your tongue in my ear. Rotating me.
Giving shape to my thoughts. (*Syncopated*, 6)

It is words, not human relationships, that take center stage in the poem. As in the fiction, so here we have not the emotion, or the verbal representation of that emotion, but an artistic creation that is an artifice of emotion that calls attention to its verbal structure.

The personal poems are not necessarily specific to Major's own life. Some are his imaginings of the experiences of others and thus are fictive inventions. An example of invention is "The Jefferson Company," which originally appeared in *American Poetry Review*. In it, the speaker addresses someone from the black neighborhoods of St. Louis and, through an act of prestidigitation, describes that person's childhood environment:

> I need not spy on your place.
> It shows on your face.
> Your two hands. (*Syncopated*, 13)

He then identifies the specific streets and communities, as well as experiences of that life:

> Remember he [the best friend] beat you across
> The MacArthur Bridge.
> Remember Highway 70.
> And the lady
> With the shopping bag
> Dripping hog guts?
> Smell them and ragweed now.

Major has said repeatedly that his art generates reality rather than reflects or represents something outside that art. Here fragments of a life story are created. The speaker of the poem gives the addressee a history. While it supposedly originates within the hearer ("I see the names / in your eyes, touch them / on your lips"), that person only exists for us through the narrator.

The poet also crosses gender with this approach. "Her Emotional Feeling" constructs part of the life of a young woman from Philadelphia. Pregnant, she has a relationship with a man who "was not into his own style." The tension leads her to sexual encounters with members of a jazz band in Boston, "but it was his style she loved holding." Just as he is self-alienated, so

> Her profile was not her own, and her ability
> To sleep went out somewhere on its own.
> She grew to fear silence and white men in blue shirts. (*Syncopated*, 20)

She seeks emotional substance from him, but all she finds are "his gold cuff links / and diamond studded watch." Realizing the limits of the relationship, "she got an abortion and went to sleep."

In this case, Major creates a psychological landscape rather than a geographical one. His character's need for both physical and emotional intimacy is linked not only to the pregnancy but also to her sense of herself. In depicting her quest for sexual gratification, Major plays with folk traditions in referring to "hambone," which is tied to African American dance as well as being a sexual reference. He also speaks of "left handed sperm," suggesting intercourse outside the marriage. But the physical is not sufficient, and the emotional support that would sustain both the time of pregnancy and her fragile self are not available from either husband or lovers. So she gives up the child, so at least she can deal only with herself. It is a brief study in acceptance of the limits of one's life. The depiction of a different and specifically female perspective is something Major will return to later in both paintings and the novel *Such Was the Season*.

Other poems deal more directly (presumably) with the author's own experience, since they present locations and people from his life. "Sexual Conduct" portrays the speaker as a six-year-old being given a bath by his adult cousin, who is traumatized when he develops an erection:

In alarm, when I turned man on her, she called
The Cliffhouse, breaking her own rhythm.
My very pretty cousin, she was high class,
Even went to college, but wouldn't let the soap move
Between my legs,
Wouldn't trust the spirit of her own father.
She scrubbed my back but refused to listen
To the Indians, the Eskimos,
The Gulf of the Saint Lawrence in my voice;
She screamed when I resembled her dreams. (*Syncopated*, 29)

Major has indicated that "the Cliffhouse" is a reference to the clitoris, thus suggesting her erotic response to the situation; while there is no evidence of that connection in sexual slang, as he suggests, it does work as a pun.[4] The sexual element is reinforced by reference to the gulf, a symbolic orifice. But in order to maintain her status as "high class," she must deny the body even as it experiences pleasure. Her repression includes not merely femaleness and maleness, even in the form of a small child, but also any sense of racialized identity. We understand this as repression precisely because he "resembled her dreams." The voice that can be Indian, Eskimo, or anything else American opens up, like the sexuality, an abundance of possibilities for identity. But she sees those possibilities as threats.

The speaker himself reads this as a moment of loss: "What delight / lost between us at the pivot of that tub" (*Syncopated*, 29). For him, all that was involved was an experience of pleasure; in this sense he is another of Major's characters who embrace the physical. He turns this into an object lesson of sorts:

> Understand now she's opposed to alcholic beverages
> and her husband, a prominent clerk somewhere
> in the canyon of Cottage Grove, beats her ass.
> I hear their offspring grew up and headed for the Cliff. (*Syncopated*, 29)

She is apparently punished for her rejection of an identity that is connected to pleasure. The association of abstinence and domestic violence implies that she pays a price for her repression. And her self-denial has not produced results; her children engage in the same sensual acts she once refused. As the wife of a clerk, she has not achieved "high-class" status but is only an insignificant housewife on the South Side of Chicago.

The reference to the "canyon of Cottage Grove," in association with the allusions to cliffs, establishes a connection to Henry Blake Fuller's 1893 novel, *The Cliff Dwellers*. In this realist work, Fuller critiques the bourgeois life of businessmen who live and work in the new skyscrapers of the city. But Fuller's title also leads to another level of meaning. For the novelist, the title suggests how far the modern world has come from the ancient cultures of the American Southwest. The Anazazis and Pueblos, in this view, constructed their worlds within the realm of the natural and physical reality they were part of. In a similar way, the speaker's voice in the poem, in its connection to Native Americans, takes the body and the physical world as the basis for his identity. His cousin, given the same option, chooses instead the artificial, claustrophobic canyon of Cottage Grove. Her children, like him, are seeking a way out.

"Funeral" originally appeared in *American Poetry Review* and then in the first edition of *Pushcart Prize*. It tells of Major's stepfather's death and burial. The speaker is met by his sister Mae (Serena's middle name) at the Chicago airport. The body is presented as artificial:

And they have his face
Propped up in the casket. Powdered,
he is tucked neatly in a suit.
There is this quiet hysterical laughter we all share. (*Syncopated*, 12)

An undertone of absurdity is evident in this image and may explain the laughter. The face is portrayed as separate from the body and apparently unsupported by it. The placement of "Powdered" initially links it to the face, which would be realistic, but it in fact modifies "he" and thus implies an excess of powdering, as in theatrical makeup. The passive voice of "is tucked" invites the reader to visualize the work of the undertaker. While the poem does not go as far as the painting *Grief*, done several months after the poem was published, it has the similar effect of subverting the solemnity of the event. Specifically, it undermines the cliché of the lifelike corpse. Under the circumstances, the surprise of the laughter is not in its hysteria but in its quietness.

Nonetheless, an emotional ambiguity shapes the poem. At the beginning and end, the speaker expresses his affection for Mae. In the middle are realistic details of the wake, which express nothing about the deceased but speak of the liquor drunk and the food prepared. Significantly, it is the mother who provides the "fried chicken and mashed potatoes"; since she is the chief mourner, we would expect the visitors to follow the tradition of bringing food rather than assuming that she would provide for them. Snatches of conversation are provided, coming from a variety of strangers. At the end of one such story—

And a dude is talking about Wichita Falls
last summer, some fifty year old white chick
who fell in love with him (12)

—the words *"Daddy daddy"* are spoken by an unknown voice. Their intrusion suggests the cry of a stricken child, thus returning us to grieving. If we take the poem as autobiographical, the voice would be that of Cassandra, Major's half sister and the only child of Halbert and Inez Ming. Halbert died on 28 November 1971, making Cassandra around twenty at the time.

The poem jumps in time to the burial, which takes place in Alabama. The crucial line feeds the ambivalence: "Mother's face / does not know what expression it should hold" (12). It returns us to the propped-up face of the corpse by disconnecting the mother's visage from her body, mind, and emotion. The line implies that she is trying to perform grief but cannot quite step into the role; it leaves unanswered the question of what she is feeling at this moment. We know that the Mings had separated long before Halbert's death.[5] Sympathy for her uncertainty is not evident in the speaker: "As we drove back I hold the airline tickets and Mae" (12). The speaker's devotion to his sister is the only absolute in the poem.

A psychological reading of "Funeral" begins by returning to Major's problems with Ming during his childhood; those difficulties were serious enough that, as indicated in chapter 1, young Clarence periodically would go to live with his mother's friends. It was also the case that Ming would naturally be considered an interloper in a tight-knit family unit in which Clarence received significant attention. The boy, who was entering adolescence at the time of his mother's second marriage, would be struggling to construct a masculine identity in a female environment, an environment in which he was the physically smallest member of the family, though not the youngest. He was trying to create a self that did not follow the expectations of the local community, which, according to Major's depiction, emphasized money making and social status, both of which Ming represented as a successful businessman. Moreover, Clarence had experienced abandonment by his mother when she left him in Georgia to start her new life in Chicago. For her to marry a stranger again sets him aside in his mind. Finally, there is some question about the timing of this new marriage. If Major is correct on the date of birth of his half sister, Cassandra, then his mother was pregnant at the time of the wedding.[6] Such a situation would only reinforce the sense of Ming as an intruder, as well as tarnish the image of the mother. It would help explain the coldness of the speaker toward both the deceased and the widow.

By this reading, the stepfather's propped-up face and tucked-in body in "Funeral" signify both the artificiality and restriction of the life he chose to live. The lack of mention of him during the wake reveals the lack of meaning and substance of that life. While many people have come to the event, from many places, their concerns are not with remembering the deceased or with comforting the widow, who, after all, is preparing the food. In addition, Major displaces the burial from Ming's origins in Mississippi to Alabama, thus displaying an indifference to his stepfather's personal history. The mother's uncertainty at the ceremony about which face to wear reveals her to be something other than a straight-forward mourner at the grave of the man to whom she was married for over twenty years. The speaker in the poem effectively robs her of her grief. It suggests a coldness in her response.

The only emotional expressions associated with characters in the piece are the cry of the half sister, who is not named, and the intimacy between the brother and sister, the two who have had to survive the mother's vagaries and, as in childhood, had only each other to cling to. "Funeral" thus can be read as a subtle act of revenge on the adults in their lives.

Another kind of revenge comes in "Gothic Westchester," a poem about Major's time as an adjunct faculty member at Sarah Lawrence College in the early 1970s. Typical of portrayals of university life, he focuses on the social rather than intellectual realm. He imagines a home at which faculty parties take place as the residence of Dracula. He lives in the "mossy basement"; meanwhile

On the dark stairway,
pink silk ladies are waiting
to be seduced. (*Syncopated*, 25)

These are, the reader assumes, faculty wives anticipating a sexual experience unlike anything their husbands can provide. One reason would be that the men are zombies: "In the living room, / the other guests have no eyes." In this surreal depiction, where

The Woman of the House, Miss Lust,
Jumps from the attic window,
She floats over an empty pool out back,

a key question is the identity of Dracula. Thematically, vampire narratives involve sexuality linked to fear of the other. Sexual inadequacies, fantasies, and pursuits are standard themes of academic fiction and drama. The best candidate for Dracula would be Major himself. In a world like that of Sarah Lawrence, with its emphasis on the training of the daughters of the elite, but also a desire, especially during and after the 1960s, for a sense of relevance, the presence of an African American male, particularly one involved in creative writing, would draw considerable attention. In this context, he is both forbidden and irresistible, an embodiment of racial and sexual fantasies and fears. Dracula is presented as a mystery, sleeping in black smoke and wearing a black suit; he also "lives in the past." And, of course, even in this supposedly liberated environment, embracing the black man is to risk contamination of one's "white" blood. Thus, Major has updated the campus and vampire stories by bringing them together in a critique of the contemporary elite.

Expanding upon the personal, Major also includes in *The Syncopated Cakewalk* poems that engage U.S. history, especially its multicultural aspects. It is not surprising that he would incorporate African American elements, but he also includes Native American and American West elements that have not previously appeared. A key example is "Queen Pamunkey." The title character was the chief of the Pamunkey tribe of Virginia during the early colonial period. Major's interest in her probably has to do with her link to mythic American history. An earlier leader of her group had captured John Smith and brought him to Powhatan and thus to Pocahontas. As a later leader "Queen Anne," as she is referred to by the English, helps to maintain peace between the two groups. Her service results in King Charles providing to her a crown engraved "Queen of Pamunkey."[7] But for the author, there are other issues:

> Grief
> She lost Totopotomoi
> And the warriors and never forgot
> Nor forgave: English ends (*Syncopated*, 18)

In exchange for promises of better treatment from the English, with whom they had allied from early settlement, Queen Anne had committed warriors to the struggles against other tribes. The crown was given, but the treatment never improved, despite her repeated requests. Thus, the story becomes a parable of the failure of Western civilization in its dealings with nonwhite people. Thus, it both continues the cultural critique that has been apparent from the beginning of Major's career and is an early version of his interest in Native Americans, which will emerge fully in his Zuni writings.

The portrait "Young Woman" constructs a narrative of the child of an Indian mother and black father. She is "sensitive dark lovely angry hot cold." Her parentage has left her with no respectable place in society:

> old people are spending their last days
> deep in your life
> You help them yet they do not trust you.
> You empty their clear piss;
> And joy drains from your warm cruelty. (*Syncopated*, 47)

Ironically, the second-person narration robs her of her voice even as the speaker seeks to express the meaning of her life. He is the one who asks: "What kind of lady can you become?" To suggest that lady is a status to which she ought to aspire imposes on her an expectation we cannot know she desires. What we know instead are the circumstances under which she lives:

> Whores in the Valley knew your Indian mother,
> the gambling drunks in town
> were cheated by your black father.
> Who are you? Where can you live? (47)

The problem of identity becomes central, but not merely as a result of racial mixing or racial difference. It is the specific behavior of the parents that create the young woman's situation. Significantly, the poem uses stereotypes of the promiscuous "squaw" and the amoral black man to make the point. Moreover, the girl herself is untrustworthy:

> The young mothers on the hill whisper your name.
> The word is out: you're a threat.
> *Husbands are wild and helpless!*

The daughter combines the vices of the parents and becomes a kind of succubus, a woman the men cannot resist. Major appears here to be playing with literary notions of the dark woman, one who has little consciousness but exists primarily in terms of her sexuality. The very questions of identity the speaker raises appear largely irrelevant, since she is viewed from the outside. Yet despite her questionable being (or perhaps because of it), the speaker wants a relationship:

> Still, I love you
> And want to take you with me
> to Denver.

Since it is not clear that this is a "whore with a heart of gold," as many of the sentimental novels would have it, and thus not a woman who can or would be subject to moral reform so that she could become a "Lady," the speaker's motives must be interrogated. We cannot know her actual behavior or her character since she has no voice, but we can surmise that, like the "pink silk ladies" of "Gothic Westchester," the speaker is playing out a sexual fantasy in which he alone possesses the "young woman." She can be his construction of "woman" rather than an actual person.

As in some of the earlier collections, Major portrays figures from African American cultural history. Here as well, his concern is for the problem of identity. "Coon Showman" presents the various names and guises of Bert Williams, the pre–Harlem Renaissance vaudevillian. All of the stage designations for him—Jonah Man, Mister Nobody, King of Bandana Land—are applied to him. Pieces of his material and fragments of his life are mentioned. But what might be behind the performances is left unclear.

> :   A light skinned colored man in black paint.
> Glossy black face under lights!
> Nobody sees what's beneath the whipped grin,
> beneath the years of memory and vaudeville fame. (*Syncopated*, 48)

Williams's most successful stage characterization was as a man who suffered life rather than enjoyed or dominated it. Thus, any notion that the man himself was a victim of a racist society is, within the poem, speculation: "And late hours and poker game skits, so painful / I see people moving back from his dreams." His most famous song was "Nobody," and Major plays off it throughout the poem:

> Your paint hides nobody. Nobody is beneath the grease,
> The laughter; nobody rubbing elbows with you
> In Matheny's Café 125th & Seventh; while you are
> singing and dancing one part of the self to pieces.

In effect, Major utilizes the various literary motifs of negated black identity to provide a sense of Williams. Implicitly present here are Paul Laurence Dunbar's mask, W. E. B. Du Bois's double consciousness, and Ralph Ellison's invisibility as ways of understanding someone locked into a stereotyped image. Yet ironically, Williams himself spoke of the source of his success as his naturalness in his role. He gained fame precisely because audiences took his blackface stage performances as reality. The poet imagines that confusion (or willful ignorance) and the performer's awareness of it as the essence of the self. But this essence can only be hinted at and in fact is inverted. Rather than locate the expression of racial identity, Major calls for its concealment:

> Yellow nigger! Yellow nigger!
> Where you gonna hide your blackness?
>
> .  .  .  .  .  .  .  .  .  .  .  .  .
>
> where you gonna hide your yellow? (48)

The logical question is why either needs to be hidden. Certainly Williams himself did not desire to be nonblack: "People sometimes ask me if I would not give anything to be white. I answer . . . most emphatically, 'No.' How do I know what I might be if I were a white man? . . . There is many a white man less fortunate and less well-equipped than I am. In fact, I have never been able to discover that there was anything disgraceful in being a colored man. But I have often found it inconvenient . . . in America."[8] The answer can be found in the word "inconvenient"; Williams was so skilled at being white Americans' idea of a black man that there was no place where he could simply be himself. In the poem, this confinement within the performance kills him at age forty-seven: "Singing and dancing / each part of your passion to pieces!" (*Syncopated*, 48).

The piece enacts its perspective through the use of exclamation points, italics, and repetition of the names of stage characters. But in addition, it also, in its rendering of Williams, creates the image of the suffering artist, and specifically the racially identified artist whose work is judged according to expectations about that identity. In this sense Williams is a figure for Major himself. The stage performer cannot step out of his stereotyped role to do serious theater or music. Likewise, as seen already, the writer is evaluated by his contribution to black letters and not to literature in general. And just as Major is criticized by both blacks and whites for not consistently matching his efforts to those of the Black Arts Movement or the Richard Wright school of social criticism, so Williams was taken to task for feeding negative racial images or for not doing so. In both instances, as Major suggests through constant references to aliases and disguises, it is race as constructed by audiences and not as understood and accepted by the individual that determines one's artistic career.

The final category of poems, on language, brings Major's poetry into line with his technical concerns in fiction and painting. *The Syncopated Cakewalk*, more than any other collection published to this point, explores the possibilities and limits of wordplay in shaping or deforming meaning. Questions of identity, love, and personal experience are reframed as problems of language. It also takes the form of humor, as in "Doodle," in which the poem misbehaves. The events are set in a creative writing class, where a student appears to be acting out: "he giggles and falls on his face" (21). But the next line opens up to the absurd: "I say sternly, *Stand up! and read, The Papaya!*" The placement of the comma suggests that "The Papaya" is the name of the student, not the poem. Further confusion occurs in the next lines:

> Then he goes into the poem from its rear,
> struggling through its warm blood, clawing his way.
> Charlie Chaplin strutter, this boy is a doodle-squat
> who walks to the wall
> and with it—holds a great conversation. (*Syncopated*, 21)

The difficulty in determining whether the initial line refers to anal sex is intensified by the appositive "doodle-squat," an unusual variation in slang of diddly-squat or doodly-squat. The choice actually enhances the sexual reading, since one meaning of *doodle* is *penis*. Thus, the author suggests that the interpretation of a poem is an assault upon it.

The boy continues to disrupt the class, running around, jumping on the furniture, acting literally like a monkey. Finally in exasperation the teacher cries out: "*Listen, is this any way for a poem to act?*" (21). Thus, the transformation is completed from the impish student to the recalcitrant poem. The writer seeks to bring his creation under control, as Major makes literal the trope of the work of literature taking on its own life. But he is not yet finished with his verbal play, for the boy-poem has his own poem:

> "I am a frog with bat wings.
> I want to eat cars on the freeway.
> I want to stroke my mother's butter." (*Syncopated*, 21)

Poetry here takes the form of the id, seeking pleasure in sounds, images, and vulgar impressions designed to satisfy itself. The poet must play the role of superego:

> *Look, go stand in the corner—*
> *and write a hundred times:*
> "I will understand what it means to be a poem."

According to the instructor, the freedom of imagination must be brought under the control of the artist's literary intelligence if it is to communicate with an audience.

But it is not clear that this is Major's final word on the subject. The work is a version of ars poetica and may be read as an act of signifying on Archibald MacLeish's dictum that "A poem should not mean / But be."[9] While Major has expressed repeatedly his agreement with the view that a work of art is not the representation of something else but a thing in itself, he differs from his modernist predecessor in emphasizing the play (in both senses) of language. MacLeish's poem is decorous and instructive; it repeats the phrase "a poem should" throughout. Major, in contrast, shows, rather than tells; what he shows is a barely controlled, disreputable, erotic struggle to give shape to words. His poem is garish, with references to "green teeth," "yellow moustache," and "pink tinted eyeglasses." It is disrespectful of authority, as the misbehavior of the student and ineffectuality of the teacher demonstrate. At the same time, it is no less a poetic construction than "Ars Poetica." It follows a clear narrative line, with clearly defined roles for the various characters. It leads to closure, albeit a ridiculous one. It is in the tradition of commentaries on the nature of poetry that go back to Horace. The difference is that Major is not interested in what "should be" but in what happens when the imagination and the words that express it freely work in the poet's mind.

A different kind of consideration of the working of language is found in "Words into Words Won't Go." Here there is no narrative, only a series of images. What links them is the "problem" of figurative language. The claim of the poem is that the devices of simile and metaphor are unreliable since the objects they refer to exist only as themselves. In a rhetorical twist, the poet consistently uses simile to question it:

> There are no things the rain is like.
> The trees are like brick walls.
> But there are no things the walls themselves are like. (*Syncopated*, 3)

The comparisons are simply asserted or rejected; they are not explained. Some are absurd on the most obvious level:

> The contents of a book
> is like margarine. The hard green surface of my car
> is like a forest fire.

Others invite more comment: "I am like you," but "The handyman who sweeps the leaves in the yard / is not like himself" (*Syncopated*, 3).

Clearly the validity of the comparisons does not inhere in the words or in the things to which we assume they refer. The figures claim our attention simply because the poet insists upon them. His use of language implicates us in a search for meaning that may not exist except in the artifice of the poem; the sequence of words adheres because the artist has put them together in a manner that readers would expect to yield insight into the world. But it is not clear that the figures, the claims of what is or is not like something else or is or is not like itself is other than arbitrary. The concern for Major then in "Words into Words Won't Go" is to test the limits of figurative language as a device of the art form.

The title poem of *The Syncopated Cakewalk* works with language in a different manner, this time by defamiliarizing constructions of history and the self. Major does so by incorporating as many references to jazz and slang as possible. Just as the cakewalk was itself an African American performance that signified on white formal dance, in part by shifting the musical structure through syncopation, so the poem breaks down notions of identity and history through fragmentation and anachronism.[10] The self is first offered as a media production:

> My present life is a Sunday morning cartoon.
> In it, I see Miss Hand and her Five Daughters
> Rubbing my back and the backs of my legs. (*Syncopated*, 53)

A Sunday morning cartoon, of course, would generally be more elaborate, larger, and more colorful that the daily version; but the line also suggests a life that is episodic and an artistic projection rather than something connected to the actual world. It is a passing entertainment rather than a substantial part of reality. But the second and third lines break with this notion, since the cartoon involves "Miss Hand and her Five Daughters," which is a slang expression for male masturbation. But here that notion is not carried through, since the speaker apparently prefers massage to sexual release.

The poem then becomes a travel narrative in which the speaker finds himself on a Mississippi riverboat, like a character from Mark Twain; however, his version emphasizes the role of black entertainers. In fact, it becomes a catalog of such figures, their songs, and their language: the Original Dixieland Jazz Band, Nat King Cole, Louis "Satchmo" Armstrong, Charlie "Bird" Parker, Ella Fitzgerald, Mister B (Billy Eckstein), Zoot Sims, Sarah "Sassy" Vaughn, Stan Getz, Lester "Prez" Young, "Cootie" Williams, Leadbelly, "Big Butter and Egg Man," "Texas Shuffle," "Cow Cow Boogie," "Illinois Central Blues," "Rock Island Blues," Snake Hips and Lindy (dances), Freak Lips (musician who specializes in high notes), chase chorus, and "Jump Back," from Paul Laurence Dunbar's "Negro Love Song." He shifts some of the terms so that, for example, Texas Shuffle and Snake Hips become characters, Jump Back and Freak Lips become places, and Bird becomes money. All are embedded in a version of a tall tale. The narrator's personal history is the story of twentieth-century African American music:

> My past life is a Saturday morning cartoon.
> In it, I'm jumping Rock Island freight cars, skipping
>     Peoria with Leadbelly; running from the man,
> Trying to prove my innocence. Accused of being
> too complex to handle.
> Meanwhile, Zoot, Sassy, Getz, Prez, Cootie, everybody
>     gives me a hand.
> Finally, Mister B comes in. Asks about my future.
> All I can say is, I can do the Cow Cow Boogie
>     On the ocean and hold my own in a chase chorus
> Among the best! (*Syncopated*, 53)

Identity here depends on improvisation within structure. The cartoon must be new each week, though recognizable to its viewers. The cakewalkers must create their own style, while moving gracefully to the music. The chase chorus performers must respond to the challenge of the other musician within the framework of the measures. The blues singer needs to incorporate his signature into the form of the lyric. The speaker keeps shifting shape: cartoon, masturbator, traveler, employment seeker, fugitive, musician. But all of them are expressed within the language of the African American vernacular. Many of the terms are included in Major's *Dictionary of Afro-American Slang* (1970) and thus are self-referential. The poem can be seen as a language game in which he seeks to embed as many allusions from that culture as he can in a relatively short (forty-line) narrative poem. It can also be seen as a modern syncopated cakewalk in that, like the original, in which slaves both imitated and parodied the formal dance of whites, the poet imitates and parodies the allusion-rich work of modernist writers. Like Pound and Eliot, Major constructs a work that requires a range of often esoteric knowledge in order to understand it. But he creates his out of the putatively low-cultural forms of black life. In doing so, he subverts the claims of high modernism.

EDUCATION

Major began his post–high school education with courses from the U.S. Armed Forces Institute while he was serving in the air force. These were a combination of correspondence and self-paced classes, both of which required final examinations in order to receive credit. There is no record of his having received such credit. Later, while teaching in New York, he took courses at the New School for Social Research and Norwalk College. He made arrangements to consolidate the credits through a program of the University of the State of New York, which is the governing body of education for New York State (and not to be confused with SUNY, the State University of New York). To do so, he added courses in the sciences while teaching at Howard University in Washington, D.C. In 1976, he received a Bachelor of Science degree from the State of New York, based on that course work, his experience teaching at Brooklyn College, Sarah Lawrence, and Howard, and his publications.[11]

By that time, he had realized that he needed substantial academic credentials if there were to be any end to his itinerant life in college teaching. The fact that he was able to work at important universities even without a bachelor's degree indicates his ability to market his skills as a writer and teacher. However, the uncertainty and need to move frequently disrupted his efforts as an artist. For this reason, he began a search for a program that would provide him with a legitimate advanced degree without the necessity of becoming a graduate student. The solution was the Union Graduate School (UGS), a part of the Union of Experimenting Colleges and Universities (UECU), which was established in the mid-1960s as a means of providing higher education through nontraditional programs.[12] It began as a consortium of liberal arts colleges, including Antioch College and Sarah Lawrence. The graduate school was designed to counteract a belief that advanced professional training was too narrowly specialized. The UECU was based at Antioch and authorized by the State of Ohio to grant bachelor's and doctoral degrees. The primary work that Major did for this degree was the composition of *Emergency Exit*, which was published by the Fiction Collective in 1979. One problem he addressed to the UGS was the length of time needed to get the degree; the difficulty was that he lacked a master's degree, so he had to enroll for several semesters while working on his manuscript.

He put together a doctoral committee consisting of Raymond Patterson, who had been a member of Umbra; Jerome Klinkowitz, a critic who was an early advocate for Major's fiction; Jonathan Baumbach, who had been a colleague at Brooklyn College and one of the founders of the Fiction Collective; Patricia Greenwald, a fellow student in the program; and Jonathan Daube, the director of graduate programs for UGS and the core faculty member required for all defenses. Greenwald participated because it was standard practice at UGS for a student who had not yet gone through the defense to be involved. Since some members of the committee had to travel and received a stipend, there was discussion of expenses; in the case of Baumbach, this was an issue that did not get resolved for a while. The defense itself took place on 25 August 1978, in the loft apartment of Barbara Ann Ryan, located at 137 Greene Street in Soho. Ryan had been Major's student at Sarah Lawrence and had visited him in Boulder, Colorado.[13] The defense went smoothly, and the degree was conferred the following day. Later correspondence concerned the bankruptcy of UECU, with Major named as a creditor for fees paid but not used.[14]

## BECOMING AN ACADEMIC

Now fortified with a legitimate, if unconventional, doctorate, Major sought more permanent employment. In 1976, he applied for a position at the University of Washington. He was highly recommended by Charles Nilon, whom he had known at Howard, and was offered an assistant professorship in creative writing. He moved to Seattle with Sharyn in the fall of 1976. He became friends with African American writers Charles Johnson and Colleen McElroy. He wrote of his experience there: "I liked Seattle very much. The drizzle was well suited to my temperament. (When I went back there later to give a lecture, I still felt close to it. It was one of my cherished homes)" ("Licking Stamps," 192). He became involved in university life, serving on various committees and as contributing editor for the campus literary magazine, *Dark Waters*. However, the situation for Sharyn was different; he says in a letter to Russell Banks that she did not care for the West Coast.[15]

She did go with him when he made the move to Boulder, Colorado, a year later. He went in the summer of 1977 as a consultant for the University of Colorado writers conference and then made a permanent move in the fall. While Washington was attractive, Colorado was becoming a center for postmodern writing. Nilon was able to smooth the transition, but it was the presence of Steve Katz and especially Ronald Sukenick that was crucial to the change. The creative writing program at the University of Colorado had been established in 1975 as an experimental effort with Peter Michelson, Marilyn Krysl, Reg Saner, and Sidney Goldfarb as the first director. Ed Dorn was brought in the same year as Major. Nearby, the Naropa Institute was the home for Allen Ginsberg, William Burroughs, and others. Thus, he found himself at the center of the innovative writing universe. In addition, he came in as an associate professor. As will be seen in the next chapter, this situation provided a wide variety of opportunities, as well as criticism of his teaching and editorial work.

## TRAVEL

Major's earlier trips out of the United States, to Western Europe, Canada, and the Caribbean, were mainly taken as a tourist. With his new status as a scholar and established author, he began to be invited to international writers conferences. The first of these was the Struga Poetry Evenings festival in 1975 in Struga, Yugoslavia (now in Macedonia). The trip, as so many things in Major's life, came about because of a social and professional network. Galway Kinnell, who also taught at Sarah Lawrence, had suggested Major's name to the Macedonian writer Meto Jovanovski, who in turn proposed him as the official U.S. representative to the festival. An invitation was extended for 1974 but had to be turned down. In early 1975, Major was invited to Columbia University to work with a group of students through the visiting writers program. William Jay Smith, poet and translator, was director of the program and had participated in the 1974 festival. Around the same time, a renewed invitation arrived. A key difficulty was the cost: the festival would cover local expenses but not international travel. Smith used his influence (he had been poetry consultant to the Library of Congress) to have Major's trip arranged through a cultural grant provided by the U.S. State Department. Major speculates that the government was responding to the fact that Leopold Senghor, president of Senegal and a founder of Négritude, was to receive the Struga Poetry Evenings' most prestigious award, the Golden Wreath of Poetry. It would serve U.S. foreign policy to have an African American as the country's official representative (*Necessary Distance*, 35).

Whatever the motive, he and Sharyn were able to travel first to London and then to Belgrade and Struga. The festival itself had been established in 1962 as a specifically Macedonian celebration of its cultural history and artistic achievements. In the following year, invitations went out to poets throughout Yugoslavia. In 1966 it became international and is now recognized as one of the leading arts events in the world; it counts UNESCO among its sponsors. It has attracted a number of Nobel Prize winners, including Joseph Brodsky, Eugenio Montale, Pablo Neruda, and Seamus

Heaney, and has recognized W. H. Auden, Ted Hughes, and Allen Ginsberg, among others.[16]

While Major did meet and talk briefly with Senghor, the more important
aspect of the experience was that it involved him with a significant group
of international poets, including Fathi Sa'id of Egypt, Melo Castro of Por-
tugal, Eddy van Vliet and Frank de Crits of Belgium, Kjell Erik Vindtorn of
Norway, Ayyappa Paniker of India, Sergio Macias of Chile, Lassi Nummi
of Finland, Waldo Portal of Cuba, and Hans van de Waarsenburg of the
Netherlands. In "From Chicago to Yugoslavia," he recalls that a hotel was
built specifically for the occasion and that many of the speeches, by political
leaders and academics, were long and boring. What was much more important to him was the social interaction with other writers. There were evenings of drinking, dancing, storytelling, and complaining about the organization of the festival (*Necessary Distance*, 38).

He also discovered that some of the principles of his own art were clearly
understood by others and were even part of cultural traditions:

> Later, Paniker gave me a copy of the Indian magazine *Chitram*, in which he
> had published an article. In it he says, "I know what reality is. It is what I
> imagine to be real. And art at its most sublime is the creation of that reality."
> Repeat: *the creation of that reality*. My own ideas coming back at me. A non-
> representational art. It was the position, years ago, that Senghor had also
> taken when defending the flexibility of African languages as a medium for
> poetry. It is the position the innovative fiction writers in America take: art is
> an extension of reality, not a mirror image of it. (*Necessary Distance*, 40)

What he finds is validation of the work he has devoted himself to in his
career, often at the cost of being attacked for his lack of ideological commitment or, conversely, for the racial character of his work. Here he found
a community of those with the same values he had been proclaiming from
the beginning. He also found an audience for his work and ideas. As the
official U.S. representative, he received considerable press attention. He was
interviewed by a young Yugoslav poet for Television Skopje and a journalist for a Macedonian newspaper. He then had the opportunity to discuss his
distaste for functionalist definitions of art with a reporter for Radio Skopje.

Throughout his remembrances of the event runs an undertone of criticism of Senghor. He noted the formality and self-importance of the older
man's participation in the activities. At one point he noted about a social
occasion, "after Senghor left the picnic area, the fun started again" (*Neces-*

*sary Distance*, 41). Later, when Senghor received the Golden Wreath award and read an "old" poem, Major struggled not to laugh when someone on the stage whispered a comment about Senghor's decades of artistic sterility. In contrast, Major's reading was given an extensive ovation and Senghor himself praised it (*Necessary Distance*, 42–43). Thus, the festival marked the passing of literature to a new generation, of which he felt himself a key member.

The acquaintances he made in Struga enabled him, two years later, in June 1977, to participate in the International Poetry Festival in Rotterdam, the Netherlands. Eddy van Vliet recommended him. One distinct event was his involvement in a workshop on translation. The organizer was Talât Halman, whom Major refers to only as "an American professor" ("Licking Stamps," 192). In fact, Halman is much more important to the world of poetry. He has taught at Princeton, Columbia, the University of Pennsylvania, and NYU. In 1971, he was Turkey's first minister of culture and that same year he was awarded the Knight Grand Cross (GBE) by Queen Elizabeth II. More directly important to Major, he served on the executive board of PEN and has been a member of the Poetry Society of America. While Major enjoyed the workshop, he seemed not to have used the opportunity to promote his career. It may well be that Halman, though only five years older, was in fact too much of a mainstream poet and critic to be of use to an artist building his avant-garde credentials.

On the second night of the festival, Major did his reading in conjunction with poets from Belgium, Poland, Indonesia, the Netherlands, Britain, and Brazil; also included was the Turkish writer, Fazil Hüsnü Dağglarca, whose work had been the subject of the workshop. Other writers attending were Seamus Heaney, Stanley Kunitz, and John Ashbery. He also met Renate Rasp, a poet and novelist associated with the German movement Schwarzer Realismus (black realism), which in her case incorporates sadism and masochism into fiction.[17] The connection was significant enough that she dedicated two poems in *Junges Deutschland* to him, and he used a line from her novel *A Family Failure* in *Emergency Exit*. While he sees both gatherings as having limited value in terms of the official purposes, he obviously gained significant social and professional connections. His audience is now global, and if he is often not understood by readers in the United States, he can now believe himself part of something much larger. In this sense he has achieved a cosmopolitan status that he had desired since reading Radiguet in the fifth grade.

# CHAPTER FIVE

# The Machinery of Postmodernism

Having established his credentials as a "certified" academic and as an internationally recognized poet, Major set about the work of entering fully what might be called the Avant-Garde Establishment. He brought together his nonfiction into *The Dark and Feeling*. He took up his position at Colorado, primarily in the creative writing program and became part of the staff there of *American Book Review*, a journal established by Ronald Sukenick to discuss literary works outside the commercial mainstream. He had two novels published by the Fiction Collective and became an active member of that group. He also spent more time with painting, including works that are incorporated into *Emergency Exit* (1979). He largely turned away from poetry during this period, preferring perhaps to belong more to the fiction community in which he found himself artistically.

## THE DARK AND FEELING

For the publication of his first collection of nonfiction prose, Major turned once again to a little-known house. The Third Press was established by Joseph Okpaku, a Nigerian-born businessman who earned advanced degrees in structural engineering and dramatic literature from Stanford University. He started the press in 1970 in New York initially as a means of bringing African writing to the United States. To this end, he published work by Wole Soyinka, Chinua Achebe, and Léopold Sédar Senghor. His list also included Angela Davis, Sonia Sanchez, and Ruby Dee. Interestingly, he solicited and published the official biography of Gerald Ford and published his own study of the Chicago Eight trial in 1970. Thus, Third Press, while clearly racial in its mission, was not particularly narrow in its focus. It was also the case that Okpaku was clearly entrepreneurial in his approach; he was the CEO of Telecom Africa International Corporation and a consultant to the United Nations. He made Third Press into one of the most successful black publishers in the United States during the mid-1970s, and it continued until 1986.[1] It may well have been Okpaku's business sense that attracted the man who had subtitled his little magazine "A Clarence Major Venture."

*The Dark and Feeling: Reflections on Black American Writers and Their Works* (1974) includes interviews, book reviews, and commentaries on individual writers as well as more general observations about black writing. Of the nineteen pieces, seven originally appeared in *Essence*, where Sharyn was poetry editor. The first part focuses on the nature of black writing, in both fiction and poetry. Major continues his effort to define a position that both recognizes the "racial" character of literature and claims the validity of an individual aesthetic. In the first piece, "The Tribal Terrain and the Technological Beast," he uses his experience at Cazenovia College in 1969 as an example of the bind black writers find themselves in. The title of the seminar was Black Excellence in American Literature; he asked the participants how that differed from Excellence in Black American Literature. The problem, as he describes it, is that no one understood the difference. His argument here, and elsewhere in the book, is that art and ethnicity have been made inseparable for readers, teachers, critics, and the artists themselves. The "technological beast" of the title is the process by which language is turned into marketable product. He condemns what he calls the Black Literary–Political Establishment, which serves as judge of what counts as black literature. He notes, for example, the tendency of black critics to read Ralph Ellison out of the race because of his refusal to serve a social-realist ideology (*Dark and Feeling*, 19). It is important to understand that Major is not, at this point, making the claim for "art for art's sake." He is perfectly willing to accept fiction that engages social problems and moral dilemmas, as seen in his review of George Cain's *Blueschild Baby*. The issue is the commitment of the writer to an artistic rendering of material: "I wanted to suggest to the Cazenovia participants that black writers were whole people who, when they were lucky, produced whole books, works with a rounded sense of humanity" (15). Thus, one can speak out of what he calls the "inner tribal terrain," the space where social constructions such as race are personally experienced, and can speak to whatever audience is willing to take seriously one's artistic expression of that landscape.

The following two essays from part 1 of *The Dark and Feeling* develop in detail the ideas of the initial statement. It is worth noting that these pieces are footnoted, suggesting that Major was beginning to measure his work by the standards of conventional scholarship. Nonetheless, as in "Tribal Terrain," the work is dominated by the author's personal experiences and preferences. In "Formula or Freedom," he is even explicit about any ideological test for art: "My own feeling is simple: the most functional and valid method of examining a work of art is by first discovering the terms on which it exists and then judging it on its own terms alone. The racial identity of a group of writers is not grounds for a critical formula to which all may be subjected for analysis" (28). He offers in the essay his sense of the problems for the black novelist who is evaluated by publishers and critics on the basis of the formula rather than his "valid" method. He cites a number of works that he considers successful, primarily from the postwar era. These include Richard Wright's *The Outsider* rather than *Native Son* and several experimental works, from Jean Toomer's *Cane* (1923) to Charles Wright's *The Wig* (1966). Most of the authors and works he values were little known (such as Toni Morrison and John Wideman) or devalued (such as Ellison, Himes, and Baldwin) in the early seventies; some have remained obscure, including Robert Boles and Henry Van Dyke. The reason for this obscurity is clear to him. He concludes a paragraph comparing Jewish American writing to black writing, noting that Jewish writers were always evaluated in general literary terms. However, "the word 'literary' is never applied to black writing and many black writers themselves considered the idea of a 'literary work' obscene, irrelevant or strange" (23). In effect, Major is defining a true "black aesthetic" and tradition precisely in the language that he has most often applied to his own work and that therefore would explain the relative neglect of his career.

The primary cause of this negligence can be found in criticism. He divides this section of the essay into black and white critics. Among blacks, he finds a link between recent cultural nationalists, such as Harold Cruse and Joe Goncalves, and an older generation, including Nick Aaron Ford and John Henrick Clarke, in that both insist on a political model of writing. He finds little to like, except in Larry Neal's apparent reversal on Ralph Ellison and Sherley Anne Williams's attention to "the work" (29). Among white critics, there are the cowardly, such as Richard Gilman, who quit trying to discuss black writing, and the harassers, as in Irving Howe's attack on Ishmael Reed, long after his more famous confrontation with Ellison. "Howe performs police work for a dying culture" (29). Major cites reviews of his own *The New Black Poetry* to demonstrate that white critics denigrate black writing in ways that have nothing to do with the artistry.

The final essay in this section offers a brief summary of recent black poetry, clearly designed for the *Essence* readership rather than a more scholarly audience. It describes the themes, both universal and racially specific, as well as the modes of circulation, which were often oral rather than written. He then provides lists of poets and critics that he recommends to readers. Significantly, he mentions Sharyn among both the critics and the younger poets. The essay was originally published in June 1972, a year after the two of them traveled together to Europe. Her inclusion, like the inclusion of his younger sister in the *Coercion Review* years earlier, suggests a willingness to blend his personal and professional lives. The readers of *Essence* would be familiar with her name, since she wrote reviews as well as edited the literature sections.

The remainder of the book can be said to provide a range of opportunities for Major to articulate his aesthetic ideas. For example, his review of Addison Gayle's *The Black Aesthetic*, another *Essence* piece, devotes little space to commentary on the book; instead, it focuses on what he sees as the problematic relationship between criticism and art: "The cultural fermentation current in the United States is radical, and that alone is the healthiest aspect of this new phase for Afro-American writers. The best black critics recognize this fact. This is not to say that the scene is not crowded with would-be dictators making frenzied efforts to squeeze every black person in the act of creating into the limitations of the network of one theory or another; some call it 'The Black Aesthetic'" (49). The virtue Major sees in Gayle's collection is its variety; he does not comment at all on the editor's own position as one of those arbiters of black art. His evaluations of work by June Jordan, Ishmael Reed, and Ernest Gaines reinforce his rejection of any black nationalist prescription for literature. In every case, he is willing to acknowledge the validity of cultural critique, but he explicitly repudiates any relevance of ideology to art: "Whether or not one chooses to believe that a novelist should try to solve social problems through his work, there simply is no evidence that social propaganda has ever helped anybody toward a larger or deeper vision and sense of life" (58). Instead, he emphasizes originality, language, and artistic control.

The third section of *The Dark and Feeling* offers a model of how black writers might be read outside the framework of race. He discusses five of his predecessors in fiction, paying attention to their careers rather than analysis of their work. Richard Wright, James Baldwin, John A. Williams, Willard Motley, and Frank London Brown all offer something to Major's sense of himself as a writer, even if he gains little from their literary practice. One element is the reality of struggle in the quest for art. He pays attention, for example, to the difficulties of being taken seriously as someone who creates art, in terms of both family and publishers. He also notes the importance of hard work and persistence as crucial to artistic success; Motley chooses to share the poverty of his immigrant subjects in order to give authenticity to *Knock on Any Door*, while Baldwin has to start over repeatedly before he gets *Go Tell It on the Mountain* right. Importantly for an emerging novelist like Major, the devotion to art paid off; each of the writers he profiles eventually achieves recognition. He notes book sales and other forms of reward that come even to a minor figure like Brown, who died in his early thirties. An additional element in this narrative is the importance of writing from one's experience rather than from political commitment. Wright is admired for his willingness to move away from the naturalistic, political work that earned him celebrity when his sense of the world changed. Even in the case of Brown, whose *Trumbull Park* took up the cause of integration, Major points to his ability to produce a skillful novel out of the personal experience of facing racial hostility. Finally, in each instance, attention is drawn to the turning away from fiction that is fundamentally racial and ideological. Major quotes Williams, with whom he was well acquainted, approving of Wright's expansion of concern to the general human condition. Williams, in fact, epitomizes the serious artist. He struggled for years to find outlets for his work, he writes in a variety of genres, he has a cosmopolitan sensibility, he demonstrates integrity in the face of literary infighting, and he achieves his success on his own terms. It is also noteworthy, of course, that he befriended and aided the struggling young writer Clarence Major. Through these short articles, then, that young author established a tradition for his own literary principles.

He reinforces these ideas with his comments in "Self Interview: On Craft." He offers a variation of Wordsworth's linkage of feeling and poetry:

> Subject matter is usually directly from my own experience. I try to wait
> until the experience is completely internalized before trying to handle it
> in terms of art. If I try to write about something that happened recently it
> usually turns out badly. I have to be emotionally removed to a degree. But,
> at the same time, if I am too far removed, emotionally, it won't work that
> way either. It becomes a question of balance—how I handle the interplay
> between what has gone into my unconscious and what remains controlled at
> a conscious level. (126)

Since it is the experience of the individual subject that is the source of artistic material, no political agenda or ideology can provide the basis for a work of literature. Moreover, the transformation of that material into art also has a psychological basis: "I try to rely on a sort of unconscious screening device or selector. I try to let the feeling (somewhere behind the mind that guides the front part of the mind) determine everything" (127).

This romantic element, however, does not lead to mere subjective effusions; he always also has in mind aesthetic control:

> But the artistic quality, itself, for me, is the first consideration. It comes before shit like "message" and such jive. A lot of black writers tend to get hungup in militant rhetoric, thinking they can save their people. The deliberate effort, propaganda, has never helped anyone toward a larger sense of self. It has always been the novel or poem that begins from and spreads all across the entire human experience that ends liberating minds. These militant fictionists, hungup in their slogans and dialect-writing, are simply competing with newspapers and the six o'clock news and house organs and cheap politicians. Apparently they never once stop to think about the artistic quality of their work, mainly, I guess, because white folks never told them it applied to them. (128)

The claim here is double edged. On the one hand, writing based in black nationalist or any other political principles is not as effective as artistically serious writing in that ideological work narrows rather than expands human understanding. It does this because ideology abstracts from rather than expresses human experience. Major's description of his process reveals that, for him, experience, and the emotion connected to it, is not only the raw material of art but also a constant reference point as that art takes shape. Because it emerges from both the conscious and the unconscious mind, it can connect to readers at a level that ideas cannot. The formal elements give the audience the sense of structure and therefore meaning for a work that through these transformations is neither political assertion nor purely private expression.

The second point is perhaps much more contentious from a nationalist perspective. Baraka, Larry Neal, and others claimed to be seeking an art that arose from the lives of ordinary black people, that used the language of black people, and that was to be judged by its value to black people. Any writers who failed to apply such standards, or who considered the opinions of whites to be relevant to this literature, were written out of the new black canon. Thus, Phillis Wheatley, Ralph Ellison, and James Baldwin were not sufficiently "black" to be taken seriously by other blacks. Major has, in effect, reversed this argument. In his view, the reason for the indifference of Black Arts Movement writers to aesthetic concerns was an inferiority complex growing out of the long-standing view of white critics that African Americans could not and should not attempt to be artistically serious. The argument, going back to Thomas Jefferson's attack on Wheatley and up through Irving Howe's debate with Ellison, insisted, first, that blacks lacked the capacity for aesthetic mastery, and, second, that racial issues required work that emphasized protest and social critique. Thus, there was no talent or time for developing the artistically successful novel or poem. Major brings these two points together by showing that demanding a propagandistic art was a way of accepting one's own inferiority. It is his revenge on Ed Spriggs for denouncing having *The New Black Poetry* done by a white publisher and on Joe Goncalves for subverting his work on *Journal of Black Poetry*.

The few reviews of *The Dark and Feeling* follow the pattern of connections apparent in Major's career. John O'Brien, having published his conversation with Major in *Interviews with Black Writers*, praises Major's book for "some long overdue insights" in a review published in the *Chicago Sunday Sun-Times*.[2] Nancy Clare, in *Essence* (which had published several of the essays in the book), uses such words as *sensitively, vigorously, humane, masterful,* and *finesse* to express her views on the work. Jerome Klinkowitz, who had served on Major's doctoral committee, wrote about the book in *Chicago Review* shortly after it came out. He emphasizes the author's commitment to artistic freedom and the imagination, a concern that had led Klinkowitz to early support of Major's career as a fictionist. His own position was (and remains) a defense and promotion of experimental writing, and in this critical work by one of its practitioners, he finds validation for his own efforts as well as Major's fictions.

## LIFE IN BOULDER

At the University of Colorado, Major was for the first time working with those he considered his peers. Although part of the English Department, the Creative Writing program had its own faculty, which was primarily interested in literary experimentation. He was now working full-time with creative writing students at both the undergraduate and graduate levels. Moreover, Ronald Sukenick, who had helped to recruit him into the program, was a significant force in avant-garde fiction. He had been one of the founders of the Fiction Collective, established the *American Book Review* as an alternative outlet for the evaluation of new writing, and was considered a serious spokesman for the importance of that writing. He was joined on the faculty by Steve Katz, another of the key figures of the Fiction Collective with a national reputation for experimental writing. He had also been, for a short time, one of Major's colleagues at Brooklyn College. Boulder was, moreover, a community that was comfortable with the bohemian world-view that so appealed to Major.

Despite all this, Major's life continued to be unsettled. Less than a year after they arrived in Boulder, he and Sharyn formally separated. In April 1978, he wrote to Ron Sukenick that Barbara Ann Ryan (who hosted his doctoral defense) and Sharon Mayes were separately coming to visit him for two weeks each.[3] He and Sharyn were divorced on 22 September 1978, though she remained in Boulder for several months. She later moved to Seattle and then to Massachusetts, where she remarried. Later in 1978, Major wrote to Russell Banks that he had bought a house and was "living with Diane." The following September, he met Pamela Jane Ritter, and by January of 1980, he wrote to Banks that they were planning to marry.[4]

At the same time, he became involved with the *American Book Review*, a magazine established by Sukenick to focus on writing that did not generally receive national press attention. The intent was to have writers serve as editors and often as reviewers; thus, the first issue (December 1977) included reviews by Ishmael Reed, William Demby, Joyce Carol Oates, and Frederick Busch. Six numbers would be published each year. Sukenick received a Guggenheim Fellowship in 1977 that he used to live in France for much of 1978. Major was given significant responsibilities in his absence but apparently was in over his head. Correspondence to and from Sukenick while he was in Paris reveals a series of problems, both financial and editorial. Material in the Ron Sukenick Archive shows a pattern of complaints about

FIGURE 14. Major's home in Boulder, 1751 Norwood Avenue

Major during the spring of 1978, concerning both his editorial work and his teaching in the creative writing program at the University of Colorado. In May 1978, he resigned from the journal.

This pattern of instability would seem to suggest an unwillingness to settle into either personal relationships or positions of significant responsibility. Despite the sponsorship of Charles Nilon, the English Department chair, and the presence of colleagues whose work he respected and who respected his, despite a wife who was ambitious (she taught at the nearby Naropa Institute with Allen Ginsberg and others), talented, and beautiful, and despite the opportunity to settle into an environment that would be conducive to both writing and painting, he managed to explode the situation within a year of arriving in Boulder. It would seem that disruption was essential to his being and his work. The everydayness of marriage and an academic career were perhaps threatening to those creative juices he used to make his art. At the same time, he wanted to be both bohemian and successful and famous. His position was somewhat marginal. After all, his credentials were suspect for an academic position and all of his books had come out of little-known publishers. Unlike most of his colleagues, he came from a working-class background, and many of the complaints about him implicitly claimed that he was not really competent for the work at hand.

Proving himself worthy was difficult under the circumstances. For some-one who had spent his first forty years hustling jobs and chances to get his work in print, stability may have been a frightening future. What saved him, as always, was his art.

## THE FICTION COLLECTIVE

The networks that Major had been building over the years came together in the mid-1970s to create new options for his writing. During this period he published around twenty poems in little magazines, including several that appeared in Dutch in *Poetry International* of Rotterdam, through the inter-national connections he had made. He also produced eleven essays, most of which appeared in *American Poetry Review*, and fifteen short stories, some of which were later integrated into longer fictions. Most important are two novels, *Reflex and Bone Structure* (1975) and *Emergency Exit* (1979), both published by the Fiction Collective.

The collective was established in 1973 by Jonathan Baumbach, Peter Spielberg, Mark Mirsky, Steve Katz, B. H. Freidman, and Ron Sukenick out of frustration with New York commercial publishers, which showed little interest in new and especially experimental fiction and little ability to mar-ket it. The alternative the founders developed was not designed as another small press. As Baumbach has noted: "We wanted no less than to publish the best new fiction around and have it acknowledged as such in the media and carried in bookstores everywhere. We hoped to create something com-parable to the wide-reaching writers' cooperatives in Sweden and England, although there had been no tradition for it in the U.S."[5] The decision was made to base the Fiction Collective at Brooklyn College, where Major was teaching at the time and, in fact, shared an office with Baumbach and Spiel-berg. The college agreed to provide office space and mailing privileges. After extended efforts, distribution arrangements were made with George Braziller, a small company primarily handling European novels.

Once this infrastructure was established, the guidelines for participation were set up. Writers became members by having their work accepted for publication. The manuscript had to be approved by a majority of the mem-bership, though this quickly evolved into a decision by three readers. At that point, the author was obligated to provide a production-ready type-script and to pay production expenses, normally around three thousand dollars, minus whatever funding came through grants from the New York

State Council on the Arts and the National Endowment for the Arts. The money from the author was considered a loan, so as to avoid the appearance of vanity publication. It would be repaid out of earnings from book sales. As a member of the collective, the author then was required to serve as editor for another writer, to read manuscripts, and to work in the group's office when possible. No royalties were paid, and books were permanently kept in print for the life of the press.[6] Finances were aided over the years by a variety of grants, university subsidies, and donations.

The plan was to bring out six books each year, three in the spring and three in the fall. The first group—Baumbach's *Reruns*, Freidman's *Museum*, and Spielberg's *Tweedledum Twaddledum*—came out in the fall of 1974. Their publication was accompanied by an article by Sukenick that immediately became the manifesto of the group: "For American novelists, the publisher has played the role of unacknowledged father, boss and sugar-daddy, whose recognition legitimizes one's identity as a writer. The Fiction Collective offers recognition by one's peers. This clear insistence on the standards of those who, finally, know what the art is all about, opens a path toward the maturity of the American novel, as well as a way for American novelists to assume their full prerogatives and responsibilities."[7] Correspondence in the Fiction Collective archive shows a constant concern on the part of Baumbach over management of the enterprise, which seems to have largely fallen to him, despite the presence of members in the city and in his department. He complains about finances, about arrangements with Braziller, about other members not handling office or editorial work. An additional worry was the reputation of the project, since some of the public commentary suggested that the collective was too much like a closed society.

Responses to the work of the Fiction Collective were mixed: nearly fifty publications noted or reviewed the first series, with long positive commentaries in such major venues as the *New Republic*, *Newsweek*, *Village Voice*, *Los Angeles Times*, *Chicago Tribune*, and *American Poetry Review*.[8] An early negative statement came from novelist Michael Mewshaw in the *New York Times Book Review*, in which he attacked the quality of the publications, both the writing and the printing of the works. The collectivists responded en masse. As Baumbach notes in a letter to Sukenick, "reaction to letter exchange in *Times* seems to be that Mewshaw comes off stupid and malicious. Our letters seem to have flushed him out."[9] A more substantial attack came in 1978 from Gene Lyons in *TriQuarterly*, who pointed out that, despite the Fiction Collective's claim of independence, it depended on government and academic support, its claim that commercial publishers refused to accept truly new work was dubious, and it was not necessarily putting out the best fiction. He saw most of its output as mediocre at best. It was, in his view, simply another version of a vanity press, since the writers approved one another's work. Lyons's underlying problem was that the group included primarily academics working in creative writing programs who needed publication for tenure and promotion. He admitted to having difficulty reading the work of J. M. Alonso but indicated that his struggle was part of the issue of having good writers produce second-rate fiction. Baumbach wrote in the same issue a defense of the organization, pointing out that the only negative reviews appeared in the *New York Times*. He noted that, despite the generally good reception of their work, they had so far failed to change the attitude of commercial publishing.

Members of the collective and critics committed to the value of experimental fiction offered defenses in several venues. Sukenick wrote a piece for the *Co-op Publishing Handbook* (1978) explaining the necessity of such an approach given the economic realities of U.S. publishing. He noted the number of stories about it in the press and the number of awards given to its writers. Larry McCaffrey wrote articles in *Contemporary Literature* and *Chicago Review* tracking the history of the group and the nature of some of the work. Jerome Klinkowitz served an insider-outsider role, hoping to shape the fiction but also commenting on it. He also appears to be the person who introduced Major to Sukenick. He was involved in a controversy with Joe Bellamy of *Fiction International*, who rejected work by Raymond Federman, Major, and others. Klinkowitz's first wife, Elaine, offered to type Sukenick's *98.6* manuscript.[10] Most important, he consistently wrote books, articles, and reviews advocating for the specific authors and for the principles of their fiction; he was an especially strong supporter of Major, who attended Klinkowitz's wedding to Julie Huffman.

This history is important to a discussion of Major, not only because his next three novels came out through the collective, but also because it suggests the kind of environment in which he could successfully do his work. He was not an original member of the group, though he was in New York at the time and on the faculty at Brooklyn College during early discussions and the period of formulation; as already noted he shared an office with Baumbach and Spielberg. In fact, his first letter to Sukenick came just a week before Baumbach also wrote Sukenick about plans for a cooperative that had reached the staffing stage. Major may well have had some involvement in preliminary conversations, as he suggested to me, but his name

FIGURE 15. From left: Russell Banks, Clarence Major, and Jonathan Baumbach, circa 1978 (photo by Sharyn Skeeter)

doesn't appear in the correspondence or historical accounts of the group until his submission of the *Reflex and Bone Structure* manuscript.[11] Given the reputation of the group as a closed circle, it might have been desirable for the members to take public advantage of the presence of the diversity (both racial and geographic) that Major represented. Of course, the very opposite may also have been true. Despite his residence in the city and his publication of two experimental novels by this point, he could still have been deemed an outsider. The others had doctoral degrees from major institutions, held tenured positions, had substantial academic publications, and had published fiction with respected and usually major houses before undertaking this new approach to the publishing business. Thus, it may well have been that the others saw Major as a secondary player in the project. For example, while Sukenick was still writing *98.6*, Baumbach approached him about having the collective publish the novel; such work presumably would add prestige to the enterprise.[12] No one from the collective made such overtures to Major about his work, however, though they didn't turn him down when he approached them.

What is clear from reading the correspondence of this period is how important the group was to Major as a community. He would include comments about his relationships and his teaching; he requested information about and recommendations for grants and fellowships; he complimented others on their recent publications and let them know that he was using their materials in his classes. He arranged readings for them at his institution and received invitations in return. Sukenick, Baumbach, Raymond Federman, and Russell Banks were the closest thing he had at the time to a circle of friends. This circle seems to have lasted for about five years, ending around 1981.

# CHAPTER SIX

# The Art of Postmodernism

Over the next eleven years (1975–86), Major responded to this new community by publishing three highly experimental novels with them and by actively involving himself in the other editorial work and business of the collective. He reacted positively to recommendations for revisions, and he assisted in involving others, such as novelist Charles Johnson, in the operations of the group. He also helped to secure funding for the costs of books by himself and Sukenick. But his most significant contribution was, of course, the fiction itself.

## REFLEX AND BONE STRUCTURE

The first documented link between Major and the Fiction Collective appears in a letter to Sukenick in September 1974, though the contents suggest a longer connection. In it, Major notes his support for the publishing effort and his struggle to find the money to pay for *Reflex and Bone Structure* if it is accepted. He also reveals that he has had Klinkowitz read the manuscript.[1] His consequent experience with the text reveals the workings of the collective. Within two months of this letter, Baumbach wrote Sukenick that the ad hoc board of the collective (himself and his colleagues at Brooklyn College) had decided that the four readers for the novel would be the two of them, Steve Katz, and Peter Spielberg, all of whom at some time had been colleagues of the author.[2] Approximately a week later, he asked for Sukenick's vote, since there were three yes votes already. Five weeks later, he announced that the work had been approved, "with revisions."[3] Two months after this, Major wrote to Sukenick that he was completing the revisions, which were assigned to Federman to edit two weeks later. Meanwhile, Major had read and approved Mimi Albert's *The Second Story Man* and had agreed to edit Jerry Bumpus's *Things in Place*.[4] These three constituted the third series of publications, which came out in the fall of 1975. Significantly, this group breaks the impression Baumbach had feared of a closed group of author-members. It includes the first woman and a non-Jewish minority.

As Major wrote to Sukenick, he had "cleaned up REFLEX, cut the philosophy bullshit, really cleaned it up. It's going to be a good Fiction Collective book!"[5] The narrative is pared down to little more than dialogue and exposition; at the same time the author is represented as interacting with his characters, making them appear to be part of the "real" world. But this is not a text representative of realism. While Major has stated that he created "recognizable events and believable characters," he set out to challenge any mimetic qualities (Bunge, *Conversations*, 26). First, there is the issue of narrative voice: "I consciously played with the whole concept of author-narrator identity, though in fact there were several personae there: the narrator, the protagonist, and the implied author" (76). Second, the compositional method worked against coherent narrative: "[It] was a mock detective novel or a kind of murder mystery and that's all I had in my mind, that I was going to do this very, very strange murder mystery. But I never knew from day to day where it was going. I would just sit there and say, 'OK, typewriter, here I am' and that's the way I took it from day to day" (36). Third, he incorporated dreams into the texts: "I find it *really*, really remarkably easy to construct a fictional dream that makes sense as a dream and, in fact, that's what I tried to do with *Reflex and Bone Structure*. A lot of those episodes are based on what I like to think of as dream logic . . ." (112, original emphasis).

For such a text to work, it was important for Major to select a traditional form, such as the detective novel, which has a fixed and recognizable structure—one can even find online "10 Rules of Mystery Writing." The form exists as a puzzle or game with the goal of encouraging the reader to solve the puzzle before the author has revealed it. The solution comes through the application of logic and rational deduction. Secrets must be uncovered, pasts revealed, and information plumbed to reveal underlying truths. Though the successful protagonist must understand some of the more troubling aspects of human nature, he or she applies reason to that knowledge and emerges with an entirely credible answer to the problem. Major plays with such reader expectations in part to demonstrate the essential artifice of fiction. His goal is not enlightenment but rather deeper mystery, the unknown of human relationships and of the creative process.

The conventional mystery presents a crime near the beginning and then proceeds to solve it through a series of linked episodes that gradually make the evidence clear. The detective is usually a skilled reader of the information and slowly, through discarding what is irrelevant and analyzing and synthesizing what is pertinent, comes to the right conclusion. In contrast, Major suggests the crime on the first two pages of the novel but his narrator-detective offers mostly useless information, such as descriptions of items the police did *not* use at the crime scene. Variations of this episode are repeated throughout the novel, but little is offered as actual evidence derived from the procedure. We are told that Cora Hull, the center of the story, and her lover Dale (readers never learn his last name) are murdered. The narrator and his sometimes-friend Canada are both suspects, but they are also permitted to help at the crime scene. Periodically, the narrator attempts to figure out who is responsible, but he never sustains the inquiry for very long, and he does not use any evidence gathered by the police to help him. At the end, we know no more about the deaths than we did at the beginning, not because of incompetence, but because the detective/narrator refuses to detect, by which is meant that he rejects the logical processes by which the solution might be found. In effect, the novel is an antidetective story.

Major further complicates the tradition by conflating narrator, protagonist, and author, so that at any given time the reader is uncertain about what perspective is taken and what interests are at stake. This blending of points of views is added to fragmentation of the narrative itself. Part 1, "A Bad Connection," contains approximately 140 separate scenes, while part 2, "Body Heat," contains about 150. The scenes can be as short as one sentence or as long as three pages. Occasionally two or three episodes will be in chronological order and clearly related, but usually there is no pattern. Moreover, this fragmentation is not like that of *All-Night Visitors*, in which reconfiguring of the parts leads to more or less coherent story lines. In *Reflex and Bone Structure*, the pieces do not fit together to form a whole narrative, in large part because the narrator is unreliable. While virtually all of them involve Cora, there are gaps, contradictions, and admitted falsehoods in the narrator's telling of Cora's story. In addition, some of the scenes take the form of fantasies or dreams. Thus, the narrator makes it impossible for the reader to construct a coherent image of Cora or any other character, including himself. In fact, he often comments on the difficulty of getting her right as a creation.

He is even more explicit about Dale: "I mean I *should* be interested in him since he is one of my creations. He *should* have a character, a personality. And it is strange that I'm jealous of him since he's formless. I lie when I say he won't let me explain him. He doesn't give a fuck about me: whether or not I give him presence or talk about him" (*Reflex*, 12). Here we see the blending of narrator/protagonist/author that Major manipulates throughout the novel. It makes no sense for an author to be jealous of his or her characters, just as the literary creation of figures in the present text does not fall within the purview of traditional protagonists. It is not insignificant that the narrator makes Cora a successful actress and Dale and Canada minor actors. He constantly reminds us that what we are reading is a pattern of language that he has constructed, that the characters are not any version of actual people. In this sense, it is all a performance: can he keep us going through 145 pages of a plotless narrative, especially when he reminds us periodically that he is struggling to continue his invention?

So the mystery ultimately has to do with the making of fiction. Major claims a kind of absolute freedom for his creation: "I want this book to be anything it wants to be. A penal camp. A bad check. A criminal organization. A swindle. A prison. A devil's island. I want the mystery of this book to be an absolute mystery. Let it forge itself into the art of deep sea diving. Let it walk. I want it to run and dance" (61). While there is some ebullience to his claims, it sets forth the problematic nature of fictional creation. What are the process and problems faced by the writer sitting in front of the keyboard each day? How does he or she make a story, especially if one is committed to rejecting conventions of plot and character? Just as the mystery novel is the result of the detective giving shape to a set of apparently random pieces of information so as to produce a narrative of crime and guilt, so the experimental writer must negotiate the space between his or her private vision and the demands of the reader for something believable and enticing. In this case, it is the anxieties of the process itself, including the recalcitrance of language to do the work that needs done. Major has said repeatedly that he wants to leave the reader with a sense of a secret withheld, something just beyond the reader's ken. This novel can be said to be the revelation, not of the solution to the mystery, but of the fact of creative mystery. What is also significant in the statement is the association of novel writing with criminality; for Major, fiction must be transgressive. It must disrupt the reader's sense of order and propriety; to be truly new, it must violate our expectations, not just in terms of theme, but also in terms of the act of reading itself.

While these metafictional concerns dominate *Reflex and Bone Structure*, it is worth noting that the conscious blending of protagonist, narrator, and implied author is one definition of autobiography. A simple instance of this is that Cora's surname, Hull, is similar to Major's maternal family name, Huff (Hull is also the pseudonym Major uses for the family in his 2002 biography/memoir of his mother). Another example is that the novel contains references to his other novels, including a manuscript with the working title "Inlet," eventually published as *Emergency Exit*. In a more complex sense, the narrative tells of the artist's efforts to devise something truly new. In this sense, a mystery for him is the nature and desires of women, just as in his earlier works of fiction. Without suggesting that Cora corresponds to any actual person, we can see the author's difficulty in finding words that will adequately communicate her being to the reader. He makes her promiscuous, going as far as having sex with her himself in an act of metafictional incest. Yet she is also the character who displays compassion and family loyalty. The author divides himself into three male figures, all of whom have a relationship with her, one as lover (Dale), one as dominating husband figure (Canada), and the third (the first-person narrator) primarily as observer and commentator. But not even these three perspectives yield the full story of Cora. When Major was considering writing pornography for Maurice Girodias, the name "Cora" was one of the pseudonyms he tried out; thus, the idea of her existed for him beyond this novel. The frustration of the implied author is that his language is always inadequate for her. She seems to represent Major's difficulties with black women at this time in his life; he had already been through two divorces and was close to a third one. In the novel, he offers a solution not possible in real life: he can end his frustration by killing her off. Moreover, in many ways, Cora shares personality traits with Sharyn. In fact, Klinkowitz specifically argues that the novel is Major's imagining losing her.[6] Both Cora and Sharyn are confident and successful, much more accomplished than either the narrator or

Major himself, who, despite having published several books by this time, had still not achieved recognition for his work. Further, like his character, he remains a minor figure despite his creative power.

Finally, *Reflex and Bone Structure* reflects its author's interest in other arts. He had a clear sense of how the book pages themselves would look: "I knew that there would be a lot of space around each paragraph. And that's the way I wanted it to look on the page. That's all I knew about the shape of it: I wanted each paragraph to have a kind of presence, like a poem on the page—the space around it as important as the text itself" (Bunge, *Conversations*, 112). In fact, white space is placed between episodes, which may consist of several paragraphs. In some instances, these paragraphs use the concentrated language of poetry, generating an image or wordplay, without advancing the narrative:

> Cora is so exciting, yet, you can't do anything with her. She's like a tree.
> You can look at her. You can make her do nothing that does not comply with herself.
>     A tree. With green leaves you can chew.
>     Cora. She has sap.
>     A tree. You can rub your saliva into its gray wood. Watch it turn purple. Then blue. And possibly even pink. Wood is often as pink as pussy. Still it remains essentially untouched. It is only when you begin to approach it technologically, as an object, a thing of utilitarian possibilities, that it falls to pieces.
>     I haven't changed one degree in any direction.
>     And Cora waits for instructions. (*Reflex*, 16)

While this passage may contain some of the philosophical "bullshit" that Major said he had generally deleted, it does demonstrate as well the poetic impulse of the writing. The double figuration, of Cora as tree and of tree as woman, exists independently of the story and primarily as a form of verbal play. The change to second person also implicates the reader in the network of language and physicality, as we are invited to chew, touch, and watch. But we also then experience the stubbornness of language and reality, as the object (tree or Cora?) remains "untouched."

This section also presents the central paradox of the writer's effort in this novel and elsewhere. While both Cora and the tree are verbal creations, the narrator nevertheless acknowledges their essences: "You can make her do nothing that does not comply with herself." What is that self if "Cora" is simply a word, which is then linked to a string of other words? What does it mean to make such a character "believable"? She must gain that status in comparison to women in the "real" world. This is true even if we take the postmodern view that both gender and personal identity are constructs. Major's claim that he extends reality rather than reflects it depends on assigning to his inventions qualities that connect them to the world, even as he must subvert any straightforward mimetic assumptions (*Reflex*, 49).

A secondary element here is evident in the "philosophy": "It is only when you begin to approach it technologically, as an object, a thing of utilitarian possibilities, that it falls to pieces" (16). In some ways, he returns here to some of his earlier social critiques and those of Henry Miller (in the essay published in the *Coercion Review* years earlier) and in some of the comments Sheri Martinelli makes about U.S. society in correspondence with Major. The refrain is also evident in much of the late 1960s critiques made by Herbert Marcuse and Norman O. Brown about the suppression of the pleasure principle (to use Freud's term) in pursuit of material benefits. This view is consistent with the emphasis on the body and on sexuality in the early poetry, fiction, and painting. But it is also the case that Major's approach is "technological." He is concerned with formal problems; the ways to get from what sounds almost like automatic writing in the first draft of *Reflex and Bone Structure* to the finished novel published by Fiction Collective are technical. And his manipulation of language to keep up the guise of a detective novel is utilitarian; as always, he was very much interested in the design, marketing, and sales of his book. He cannot treat his novel as a book of poems, whatever his impulse. Cora must seem to be a person whose life and death matter; and the narrator's struggles to tell that story must matter to the audience, at least the primary audience of Fiction Collective members, whose respect he wants to gain through this work.

If the text sometimes takes on the qualities of poetry, it also displays painterly moments: "Naked, Cora stood before the window looking down at a sharp angle upon the heads of people moving across the pavement. The tops of cold painted cars" (105). The narrator likes this image so well that he uses it two more times, with different characters. It is as though he is trying out different versions of the composition, much as he has done with painting throughout his career. Another section brings color into play: "His right hand held a wine glass half filled with red dry wine. His elbow was against the red oak bar. . . . The black leather of the stool, through my thin brown pants, was cool. A small hacksaw was lying on the bar" (114). The picture is similar to those of Archibald Motley, with whom Major had an exhibition during his Chicago years, or like some of his own later works. He also notes that "Fiction is a stained glass window" (*Reflex*, 112). The most striking instance is offered as an image on a postcard: "I receive another card. The picture on it shows Cora wearing a delicate taffeta iris colored dress, and smiling. The background is yellow" (32). The figure corresponds almost exactly to a painting produced several years later of a young African American woman in a lustrous, light violet dress with a yellow background (plate 5). It even has dark bands framing the sides of the background, as though it were a card. Thus, in some sense, "Cora" has a long-term presence in Major's artistic life; she is an idealized figure to whom he must return again and again. In the painting, she has one hip thrust out in a dance move, with the folds of the dress both catching the light and embracing her body. In the novel, he kills her off in pursuit of literary necessity (a mystery has to have a murder), but that very act is a means of refusing to let her die. It frees him to invent a wide range of memories and scenes in which she as a character is deepened and enriched. So much invention is noteworthy in a work that generally follows the metafictional practice of flattening and simplifying characters. Even the difference in the two "postcard" versions of her is revealing. In *Samona* she is not smiling, implying perhaps that her creator has put her through much trouble in her imaginary life. The story and the painting suggest, then, how hard Major works to keep her alive.

The novel received generally positive reviews, though it did not sell particularly well. By the end of 1978, more than three years after publication, it had sold fewer than two thousand copies in cloth and paper. It was translated into French by Maurice Couturier and published as *Reflexe et ossature* in 1980. *Ebony* felt compelled to note it, though the editors did not even attempt a summary. Instead they simply listed some occurrences in the book. "J.S.W.," the reviewer of *Kliatt Paperback Book Guide*, seems equally befuddled, though he or she at least makes an effort to understand it as a mystery novel: "She is murdered during and probably because of an illicit affair she is having with a character named Dale." But the critic's attitude is made clear in the final statement: "The reader must be careful not to get lost during his journey into this unknown territory." Thomas Lask, writing in the *New York Times Book Review*, understands that Cora is the center of the narrative; he reads her as an earth mother, about whom literary analysis would be largely irrelevant, since the writing is impressionistic and poetic. Two other reviews examined the novel as part of the Fiction Collective set for that season. Bruce Allen, in *Library Journal*, sees it as the best of the three, "a wry, funky recording of the interconnections between writers and what they create." He sees this not only as the best of the set but also one of the two best (along with Sukenick's *98.6*) recently published by the collective. The most detailed review came in the *Baltimore Sun*, where Michael Scott Cain offers a brief history of the Fiction Collective, before evaluating the three texts. He gives half the review space to *Reflex and Bone Structure*. He sees Major as an author taking real chances but succeeding: "For the first 30 pages or so, you'll wonder why you are reading it, but then you'll be caught up in it and know. Major is daring, bold, but never self-indulgent and that's why his book succeeds: because he never forgets that art lies in discipline."

## EMERGENCY EXIT

Major's fourth novel was the writing project for his doctoral degree. It was a work that developed very slowly, taking, by his accounting, seven or eight years to complete (Bunge, *Conversations*, 36). Sixteen portions of it were published separately, beginning with an excerpt in *Essence* in 1972. He wrote to Baumbach on 19 January 1975 that he was working on a new novel, titled "The Inlet Picture Gallery—A Metaphor."[7] In the letter to Sukenick a month later about cutting "the philosophy bullshit" from *Reflex*, he noted that he was working on "Inlet." He reported that the editor Seymour Lawrence, who had an independent imprint associated with Doubleday, had become interested in his work (through an essay by Klinkowitz) and had requested a sample. He sent seventy-five pages, which were returned later with a note that, while the imagination and writing were very good, the book would have a very limited audience (as shall be seen, this was prophetic). He used the occasion to comment on the publishing business: "How is that for the future of fiction? If Seymour Lawrence feels that way novelists had better start fiction collectives in every town and hamlet. But come to think of it he never published Vonnegut or Brautigan til they were already famous. He's never been an innovative publisher so how come so many think of him as such."[8]

While Major was expressing his disappointment with his latest effort to reach a commercial audience, he was also not coming to terms with the implications of his literary choices. Certainly there was nothing in the fiction he had published thus far that would have made it readily accessible to a mainstream readership, and it was unlikely that any set of pages from the new work would have produced a different opinion. Even the shot at Lawrence about publishing Brautigan and Vonnegut after they were famous ignored the fact that, despite their innovations, both were in many ways traditional storytellers. Despite his views, he submitted the complete manuscript in 1978 to Dell, which, ironically, then included the Seymour Lawrence imprint. It was promptly rejected. At that point, he agreed to Fiction Collective publication in the same season as Baumbach's *Chez Charlotte and Emily* and Sukenick's *Long Talking Bad Conditions Blues.*

As early as June 1977, Baumbach had written to Major about getting the book into print, though at that point it had not received the approval of Major's doctoral committee or the collective members. Baumbach suggested that Klinkowitz might serve as editor, though he was not a member of the collective.[9] A year later, it was sent to members Peter Spielberg, Carol Sturm Smith, and Raymond Federman for votes.[10] One issue was the cost of publication, since Major intended to include artwork: prints of his paintings, a photograph, and charts and graphs. One solution was available because Sukenick and Major worked at the University of Colorado. The university, through the Committee on University Scholarly Publications (CUSP), provided funding for faculty publications. In a letter in support of the requests for funding, Robert Minkoff, assistant to the directors of the collective, wrote to Sue Dillingham of CUSP about the history and practice of Fiction Collective regarding publication.[11] He estimated at that time that *Emergency Exit* would cost approximately $4,500 to produce. Six months later, Major observed that the actual cost was closer to $6,000, despite a grant from the National Endowment for the Arts of $10,000 to cover some of the expenses of this series.[12] In fact, according to a letter to Thomas Glynn the following year, the production costs of the novel were not met. Major did not put up any of his own money to finance the publication but relied on the university and the collective to meet the expenses.[13] It is doubtful that the costs were ever recovered; sales were apparently very low, even for a Fiction Collective book.

The reason for the long gestation and the high expenses appears to be the complexity of the task of creating the novel. Major hoped to achieve "a fragmented form that was essentially a unified, coherent entity" (Bunge, *Conversations*, 65). In his doctoral proposal, he states: "There are no central characters but many characters who will turn up again and again and many others who will not. It is an atmospheric novel rather than a novel of plot and characters. Plot does exist but only in its deepest and truest sense: as a secret design that, finally, is not so secret anymore."[14] Like *Reflex and Bone Structure*, it made use of short passages surrounded by white space, but also added longer episodes, which are sometimes commented on in the text as the "realistic" material that readers expect. It also incorporated imagistic writing and concrete poetry; lists of books, objects, and dialogue; news items; fictive charts and graphs, a photograph, and twenty-six plates of the author's paintings. Major's primary goal seems to have been to exercise as much artistic freedom as possible with the material and still give it form. He indicates his uncertainty and his expectations for his audience with two epigraphs, among several that appear in the book. The first sounds almost defensive: "'. . . if you try to do something different in this country, people put you down for it'—Eric Dolphy" (*Emergency*, viii). Dolphy was a jazz instrumentalist who performed on a variety of wind instruments, worked in several genres, including bebop, free jazz, and Third Stream, and recorded with a number of major artists, including John Coltrane and Major's high-school friend Herbie Hancock.[15] He is, in other words, much like Major in his eclecticism; his statement, then, reflects not only the writer's sense of his difference from others but also his view that yet again his work will not be appreciated. The second epigraph is from painter and sculptor Willem de Kooning: "Art never seems to make me peaceful or pure" (viii). Since the novel that follows this statement is about contamination, violation, anxieties, and frustrations, Major appears to use de Kooning's words as a means of putting his own art in a radical tradition. It is worth noting that de Kooning's comment is subjective; it is the experience, not the definition, of art that matters to him. The book itself reinforces this notion; it not only concerns the emotions and feelings of the characters but also the author's impressions of his activity. While this aspect is less apparent in *Emergency Exit* than in *Reflex and Bone Structure*, it is nonetheless certainly evident. Part of what he undertakes here, as will become clear, is the breaking down of genre boundaries as part of the effort to reinvent the novel.

The solution is similar to that of *Reflex and Bone Structure*: make use of a generic frame that then can be manipulated for experimental purposes. Rather than the mystery, the choice here is the domestic novel; Major even has one character say to another that she wishes he were Henry James. But what is needed is more than a narrative of manners and relationships, since these are limited in their variations. To complicate the story, Major introduces the concept of the threshold and specifically a fictional threshold law that requires that men must carry women through doorways in the town of Inlet, Connecticut. The author has little interest in exploring the politics of this rule, though he does occasionally mention defense of or violations of the law. Rather, it operates as a master conceit that enables virtually unlimited play with boundaries, liminality, transgressions, intersections, relationships, transitions, miscegenation, "passing," rituals, and sexuality. Klinkowitz suggests that it is framed by an anthropological perspective that allows for a range of symbolic possibilities.[16] Indeed, the novel opens with a commentary on the ancient Jewish practice of the groom carrying the bride across the threshold, which Major links to the mysteries of blood, especially as expressed in menstruation and childbirth. Blood was the sacred sign of life and women's "wasting" of it demonstrated their sinfulness. Thus, the doorway, the boundary between domestic and public space, between the self and the world, had to be protected from female contamination. Inlet's law invokes two key elements—women must be carried and they cannot touch doorways—from the ancient practices. At various places in the text, Major provides definitions of thresholds and doors, as well as providing examples of related practices from different cultures.

In an interview with Nancy Bunge, he connected the imagery here to ideas about the emergence of civilization:

> CM: I think that probably men set up systems in which they were able to gain some security at the expense of women. They had to establish their relationship with their god and in order to build that and to sustain that, they had to subject women to a kind of servitude; they had to create a distance between themselves and women in order to sustain their own identities and to create the false security that has always underscored their existence. And I think this happened because women were mysterious; they were associated with all those mysterious things like blood and birth . . .
>
> NB: I think I read this in *Emergency Exit*.
>
> CM: Oh, was this in *Emergency Exit*? Yeah, well I think that's where it all stemmed from. I think it all came out of that need to put that mystery at a distance and keep it under control. And in order to keep it under control, women had to be reduced socially. (Bunge, *Conversations*, 45)

He went on to define this suppression as a conspiracy, a common trend among postmodern writers. Significantly, he also tied it to the emergence of language and writing. Given Major's career-long effort to validate the body and physical reality, in opposition to ideological and religious efforts to control and define them, the attempts to subvert conventional verbal practices in *Emergency Exit* should not be surprising. Like the female characters in the novel urinating on the diamond-studded threshold of city hall, he sets out to shock our sense of order.

Beyond the threshold motif, the narrative offers the story of the Ingram family, upper-middle-class blacks who have settled in the seaside community of Inlet. Jim and Deborah have three children—Julie, Barbara, and Oscar. Jim now works in an office but was once in the American Information Service (and perhaps the CIA) in Kenya. The storyline follows the growing distance between the parents and Jim's affair with his white secretary, Roslyn. It also describes Julie's relationship with Al, who is from a poor family in Harlem, has been in prison, and occasionally deals drugs. Other characters from the community also have their stories told. There is considerable dialogue and indirect discourse about the desires, frustrations, and psychological needs of all of them. Moreover, the narrative develops in approximately chronological order. To this extent, the book resembles work by John Cheever or John Updike in chronicling contemporary U.S. society, with the added element of race.

But of course the novel reads nothing like mainstream fiction, though its connection to it is absolutely essential. Major requires a foundation in the realistic tradition in order to demonstrate his variations on it. He tells Alice Scharper, "As William Carlos Williams said, 'There is no such thing as free verse.' There is really no such thing as a free novel; it's not like life. Life is kind of formless and pointless at times, but a novel really can't be that way" (Bunge, *Conversations*, 65). He says this specifically with regard to the dedication of the book: "To the people whose stories do not hold together" (*Emergency*, vii). His goal then is to coherently present a narrative of incoherence, not only in terms of what happens to people in their lives, but also in terms of our false assumptions about how stories cohere with life. His goal is a new thing, a new object in the world to be understood the way we understand other objects, including ourselves; at the same time, he wants to suggest the inherent mystery, the ultimate unknowability that is part of the world and part of such a text.

The novel opens, not with the rituals of thresholds, but rather with an abstract phallic image (see fig. 16) in gray tones against a white curved space, both set on a black background. It suggests a sexual threshold. The foregrounding of the phallus reinforces the argument on the right-hand

FIGURE 16. Opening image in *Emergency Exit*

facing page about male dominance without reducing it to ideology. Because of its abstraction, the image also cannot be said to "illustrate" such an argument. This combination of image and text demonstrates Major's method in *Emergency Exit*: each part enhances, connects to other parts without being reducible to explicit assertion. It works, as the earlier title of the book stated, as metaphor. The image can also be seen as a prologue to the text, since it depicts the moment of the threshold, both of text and intercourse. It implies the reader's movement into the text as penetration, the act of reading as sensual pleasure. It suggests that reading this work is to be an erotic act, a polymorphously perverse engagement.

The second part of the opening textual passage serves as a parody of acknowledgments: "Emergency Exit. Standing in the blood on the holy threshold right now are so many friends and enemies I'd be up all night trying to remember their names" (2). He then offers a catalog that includes names of characters and authors from fiction and popular culture in which the names are sometimes deliberately mixed up, as in David Dickens, Kar-

enina Tolstoy, Stephen Courage, and Emily Wurther. While the list generally includes classical works and authors of the nineteenth century, with
which presumably readers would be familiar, it also makes references that
the primarily white audience of Fiction Collective works would find especially obscure: Cross Damon, Johnny Beetlecreek, Doris Catacombs, Helga
Crane, Toomer Cane, and "Charlie Messenger in his yellow wig." All of the
references are to African American novels, but they are ones that challenge
the social realism of that tradition. Cross Damon is the protagonist of *The
Outsider*, the Richard Wright work that Major has said he most admires.
The Beetlecreek and Catacombs references are to the writing of William
Demby, an experimental writer of a slightly earlier generation who, like
Major, studied painting; later, as an expatriate, he became a filmmaker.
Helga Crane is the central character in Nella Larsen's *Quicksand*. Her trag-
edy is that she succumbs to the need to have a fixed racial identity. "Toomer
Cane" is, of course, Jean Toomer, whose experimental narrative *Cane* questions any fixed notions of identity, as did the author in his own life. At the
end of the opening, Major parodies Melville: "Call me Dracaena Messan-
geana. I don't mind" (3). This act of self-naming is both a performative act
and one that subverts our connection to the narrator. What he calls himself
is the scientific name of the corn plant (Dracaena fragans Massangeana),
a tropical used in interior decoration. Thus, he begins by proclaiming his
own freedom from the conventions of naming.

   This deliberate misdirection continues a few pages later with the following passage: "I (your narrator) parked my car on the road went down to say
hello to thirty cows eating grass they all came to the fence to greet me. I cut
the fence and they stepped across the threshold into the ditch followed me
up to the car we went down to the local beer pub and got smashed" (10).
On the facing page is a photograph of Major in a field with cows. A few
months before the book was published, a special issue of *Black American
Literature Forum* devoted to Major used the same photograph, with the
caption, "Clarence Major in New Hampshire."[17] Thus, readers are invited
to merge the narrator with the author (or at least merge their images), even
though the narrator is a character within the narrative clearly distinct from
the author. Unlike *Reflex and Bone Structure*, where narrator, protagonist,
and author are unitary, here the point seems to be the assertion of artistic
freedom for its own sake, a form of narrative play. The nature of the play
is transgression, as Major uses a wide range of devices to frustrate readers'
expectations about his text.

Structurally, *Emergency Exit* makes use of the same brief passages surrounded by white space as *Reflex and Bone Structure*. Groups of such passages are broken into untitled chapters. Pages 31 to 33, for example, contain seventeen distinct sections that range from one to nine lines. None are
sequential, some are descriptive, some are small scenes, some are dream
sequences, one is unassigned dialogue, one is a list, some are told in first
person (either singular or plural), though most are omnisciently narrated.
These are contrasted with chapters that are narrated in a straightforward
manner. even when there are visual breaks on the page. Thus, pages 47 to
50 tell of an evening at the Ingram home while Al is visiting. Al and Julie's
relationship is discussed among the party, and Deborah shows home movies about the family's time in Kenya, where Jim worked for the American
Information Service. Barbara, who had left earlier in the evening because
she was uncomfortable, since she once had a relationship with Al, returns at
the end of the scene. The characters all speak and behave in ways consistent
with what we have been told about them previously, and the episode serves
to advance "plot" by revealing family dynamics and attitudes.

There are seventeen such chapters in the book; they generally serve the
same realistic purpose. Even one that is largely abstract provides a storyline. It opens with a comment on narrative: "This realism is my darkest
light" (*Emergency*, 24). The narrator goes on to describe the unnamed protagonist of the section: "He was a man huge and brutal. Believed in himself
and even if he was a character you still had to deal with the reality of him
as a character. Call him Hal call him Ron Barry Dick Al. Call him your best
friend yourself" (24). What makes him remarkable, according to the narrator, is that, unlike the "Inlet characters," he can change, "but did he change
that is the question" (24). He meets a woman—"Stella Cora Rea Cindy Julie
Barbara Deborah Gertrude Janice Sandy Marcia Sharon Cynthia Nikki
Christer Gail Rose Marie Gloria Alla, you name her"—and they begin an
intense relationship. But the very intensity seems to exhaust their love. They
enter routines of middle-class life: "there he was, broken, crawling through
credit cards, Sears catalogues, babyshit, Kenmore washers, hope" (25). The
narrator makes a distinction between art and reality: "Everything comes
together in a novel—life is another matter" (26), but the action of this episode disputes that. Despite the couple's difficulties, the narrator says that
they are "easy and natural." They win the lottery, which allows them a freedom they had lost. But then the text reverts again: "But the smart woman
begins to see her dumbness and there is an ache in her head she must come

to terms with. A scream of pleasure in the middle of madness and night does not release her" (26). The episode ends in what appears to be triumph but is in fact deeply ambiguous: "Even when a composition by the woman and the man is apparently working against conventional composition, with their luck, and the good spirits of Inlet, it comes together. Ain't nothing on earth nearly half as beautiful. Let it continue. The last of the moments. The first of the slow middle. Let it all continue!" (26). If these are characters that are supposed to be different, then is it in fact a good thing that their "composition" comes together? That would suggest, given the comment on life's disorder, that they have lost their vital energy and become like the rest of Inlet. That means that they become part of the art and thus beautiful in that sense. But, of course, they were always only words on the novel's page and so the belief in change, in a different set of options, was always an illusion. The episode serves, it would seem, as a metafictional practical joke, reminding us of the games Major is playing.

Adding to the gamesmanship is a series of inside jokes running through the text. Al is said to be an "all-night visitor." A young Jewish man named Barry Sands hypnotizes Julie and tells her to fall in love with a young Jewish man; instead, she repeats the nonsense phrase "Pax sax sarax afra afca nostra," which comes in part from a fortune-telling game called Ka-Bala. In what could be a reference to the Fiction Collective, the town is said to have had only one published writer; "the other sixty writers in town are unpublished and unknown they get together and exchange rejection slips" (17). When Al returns to New York, he gets off the bus at a hotel called the Other Side, which appeared in *All-Night Visitors*. In "A Selection of Names from the Inlet Telephone Directory," Major includes, among versions of African American folk figures, black media characters, and others, "Alex Roots," a reference to Alex Haley, author of *Roots*, the popular book and television miniseries of the mid-1970s. In another instance, the narrator/author reports that a scholar once asked him if he was trying to write like John Barth: "you know Barth in his stories always sounds like he's teaching a creative writing class I don't like that kind of stuff I think it's misdirected it's just a gimmick" (145). The narrator says that he could not answer the question of the scholar (possibly Klinkowitz in real life, given his views on John Barth), but he then proceeds to create "gimmick" as a character. His gimmick, he says, is language, thus signifying on both Barth and the scholar. A sampling of materials from the Inlet Public Library includes *A Psycho-Analytical Interpretation of the Novel "Emergency Exit" by Clarence*

*Major*, authored by "John S. Narcissism," and tapes, *Why Not Use the Shifting Method of NO?*, narrated by Jerry K. Smith, and *Why Not Throw in a Poem or Two*, narrated by Jonathan B. Zolar. The latter two names refer to Jerome Klinkowitz and Jonathan Baumbach, who may well have asked such questions at the doctoral defense of the novel.

Further devices reinforce the artifice. Some sections of dialogue blend words with random typing:

> "Hugfdswo," said Julie
>
> "Jkwsaopvcxzwerfg then fghksdaw afd bvc asdfghjkl."
>
> "But my dear thfdsg wedpfaszxmn. Then you must understand that hgfd-swpfk bvcsq dfs kjh jhgfyu rewop. Viocp." (140)

It is the substance of statements here that is rendered nonsensical; the introductory and connecting terms are perfectly clear. Similarly, some dialogue is rendered as ellipses:

> "................." said Julie.
>
> "............."
>
> She looked at him. "But .................................."
>
> He avoided her eyes. "............... "
>
> A twig snapped somewhere. (*Emergency*, 132)

In both these quotations, communication has been emptied of its content, in part because, as the narrator states at various points in the text, nothing new can be said by fictional characters. As readers, we can fill in the language because we already know what characters in novels say in these situations. Similarly, characters or situations are shown as generic. Al may be said to be just like a figure in a Richard Wright novel, or Julie to be acting in a soap opera. At times the characters say this about themselves; at others they simply perform the role. The narrator may decide that it is time for a flashback and so tells us about something from Julie's childhood that has no clear relevance to the story. Or he may state that novels are usually naturalistic and then depict a situation in which he repeatedly uses the word "naturalistically." When James Polk of *Newsday* commented that Major tried too hard to draw attention to the fictiveness of this work, it was these gimmicks that concerned him.

A more significant aspect of the radical nature of the work is its employment of multiple genres and discourses. Major uses the languages of journalism, sociology, anthropology, law, history, advertising, and folklore, as well as romance, realism, and naturalism. Added to these are passages that are dreamlike or surreal, poetic, and painterly. These constant shifts destabilize the text far beyond anything done in his previous fiction. The effect is comparable to a collage. But the distinct pieces also invite readers to construct meaning within the narrative. The various discourses reveal something about the community, relationships, or individual characters. The anthropological passages offer symbolic readings of the linked motifs of thresholds and doorways; the news stories provide ongoing reports of the responses of women to the threshold law; and the advertising material exposes consumer impulses (for even more elaborate thresholds) and forbidden desires (for artificial vaginas and penises). Each part, no matter how outlandish in mimetic terms, contributes to the larger design.

The dreams and surreal images function similarly. The dreams generally reveal character. Barry, who is obsessed with Julie, meets her in a dream, but she always leaves, just as in the waking world. Jim imagines himself back in Africa, designing the American Dream; he has created 327 versions of it. However, "In the back seat of each dream Deborah was always making love to a snapshot of Booker T. Washington" (92). His other problem is that the Africans are becoming upset with U.S. policies. "To distract himself he builds model slaveships with matchsticks and glue" (92). Each man is expressing some aspect of his character with the stories he constructs while asleep. Major additionally uses the idea of dreams as a metaphor for his artistic process: "Messengers, on horseback, ride through the cold night, death and leather held in firm embrace. Each section of the dream shifts turns. The disruption comes at the moment when nothing can hold back the blood chilled flowing down out of the body as the eyes close, heavy. And unless the body is held in a great embrace everything—really everything—goes down" (97). The artist is the messenger, who must not only deliver his vision but also hold his invented world together as he does so. In making a text that manifests his aesthetic freedom, it is his skill and vision that keep it from falling into chaos. As the dedication indicates, the lives of people do not cohere; only art can do that. And an art that deliberately breaks apart the conventions of its form is always threatened with disorder.

The surrealistic material would seem by its nature to work against that coherence. At times it involves relatively simple physical transformation of characters, as when a doctor becomes a werewolf, or Jim becomes extremely tall and his wife extremely short, or Jomo becomes a "devil man who sucks a snake deep into his belly. His feet are claws his breasts are like a woman's" (134). At other times, the changes appear designed to break the pattern of narrative through a quick series of images. In one sequence, the Black Professor, with scales rather than skin, cuts opens a giant fish and "a pack of tiny brown and yellow people slide out like sardines, a mob of naked women rush them with giant bunches of grapes prying open their mouths forcing them to eat" (71). This is followed by "Piles of rotten fruit lie wasted along the edge of the river while overhead dragons float complete with seats and seatbelts and passengers secure with credit cards." On the same page, a man gets caught in a seashell, and nobody pays any attention until he begins to decompose. "He looked like Jim." And finally, "A pig-like creature runs about trying to dislodge a bird-like thing clinging to its back. There's nothing I can do to help it" (71–72). The episodes do nothing to advance plot or elucidate character; they are there because they can be in this novel. They are generally offered in the same straightforward manner as the more conventional narrative elements.

The novel ends with an apocalyptic scene, which takes on aspects of the surreal because it is totally unmotivated. It is told as a sequence of numbered short paragraphs, some only a sentence long. Included is a very detailed, "realistic" scene from the bedroom: "Beyond the window of the bedroom where he spent all his time there was a row of pecan trees and beyond it an apple orchard with honeysuckle at the far side. Bees and flies and birds and chickens and dogs made their sounds all day and at night frogs and crickets and other night callers were heard" (255). "The author," said to be married to Deborah, has recovered from a near-fatal illness. One day he decides to go out into the sunlight. Deborah, who calls her husband Drama, refuses to allow him to wear his "Sunday" shoes outside. "So he made his way across the threshold not only barefoot but half naked" (256). The scene is made more strange when we are told that "a few hundred interested characters in this very novel" were watching him emerge. He discovers that a war is being fought in front of his house, though neither he nor the soldiers understand why. As he crawls toward the sunlight, he finds in the street dead soldiers to whom the narrator has given the names of characters in the novel. Later, when he looks back, they have rejoined the fight. "Perhaps they were all using blanks. Just playing a game of fiction" (257). He ignores the call of his wife and steps into the light: "The minute he reached the warm light of the sun he began to burn. First the right arm then his face and left arm. Also the part of his chest not covered by the nightgown. Little flames began to leap from his face and arms. But he did not stop" (258). The immolation of "the author" is the ultimate act of fictional play in the text.

He can kill off characters and bring them back to life; he can change their shapes and sizes, bestow or take away personality traits. What he does here is turn himself into a hero and saint; he takes on tongues of fire and goes forth into the light. The game here, of course, is that someone has to tell this to the reader. The narrative of his gesture must be recorded by a narrative voice, which means that the author in the novel cannot be the author of the novel. The scene is not a grand act of writerly egotism but simply the last of the gimmicks.

Two other aspects of the book require comment. The first is the tendency toward poetic discourse, what Klinkowitz calls "pure writing," as a means of disrupting narrative.[18] At times this amounts to allusions or epigraphs. Jim is said to have "measured out his life with peanut-butter spoons" (*Emergency*, 92), and he is compared to a crab. Another line parodies William Carlos Williams: "The moon is a red broken car fender in the black sky. What else is new?" (52). Lines are quoted from Williams, Kenneth Patchen, and Ezra Pound. At other times, such language serves to satirize characters. Janice says to Barry, whom she wants to make her lover:

> "You look like a man who easily possesses the terrible and sensuous authoritative presence we all envy, like a windstorm and a disruptor of the sunrise on the flatlands of some unnamed planet. So far out are you—yet you're not the Ultimate Prince. Confronting you some immodest desires have set up housekeeping in the attic of my being."
>
> He smiled, "You should be a poet." (201)

Since Janice nowhere else speaks so eloquently, and since Barry demonstrates no sensitivity to language, the passage points to a conventional literary discourse, though the fact that it is inspired by sexual desire does in fact suggest its roots in Major's belief in the connection between the body and the word.

The allusions, citations, and character statements are functional in the text in expressing motifs or advancing character or story and thus are not what Klinkowitz had in mind with "pure writing." Other instances create images or produce word combinations for their own sake. Some suggest haiku in their simplicity and physicality: "on the pier the boat turned over to dry in the sun. Sunlight falls straight down on rooftops" (31). We also have "Windows still damp from recent rain" (52). Human beings and emotion are absent from these images, though the human world is implied in "boat" and "windows." The lines, however, are set apart by white space from anything related to the narrative. Others do express feeling but nothing that is specific to the narrative; they are more like material from the earlier books of poetry. For example, "Inleters' lips were sealed and their stable doors locked. Others ate grapes of pain and slept in deep beds" (37). Similarly, "If the night is cold hard and surrounds us with blue muddy rain, take me by the hand. So strong has been my thrust that at the moment when a single tear leaves me, expressing my fear, suspecting not so much that I am now ready to die, but that I am losing yet another large space in myself" (189). The last sentence could easily be taken from *Swallow the Lake*. The sense of isolation and loss of self are not expressed in such a concentrated manner and with such directness in the main narrative. Surrounding these passages are sections that remind us of the artificiality of the novel, but these have no irony.

The second unusual aspect of the novel is linked to the poetic through a statement made by Jim. He seems to speak for the author at a moment early in the novel: "This situation we're in is being rendered in terms of images, and dramatic description. I am using very few things to represent other things. I think the metaphor has its place but the place is historical. Yet I love the metaphor. I love its *visual* tendency. I want you, Julie, to understand that the ultimate *thingness* of our lives operates as a sort of *extended* metaphor" (55, original emphasis). The claim here is that figurative language has been used as a means of representation; that it works by having one thing stand in for another. What Major through Jim suggests is a desire to make the fiction itself a thing rather than a representation. Language achieves through metaphor opacity rather than the transparency needed for mimesis. The word, the image, the narrative constructed of words and images does not become a mirror for some aspect of life but rather an object that has a mysterious connection to life, just as the tenor and vehicle of metaphor exist simultaneously as similarity and difference. What is also important for Major in this process is the emphasis on the visual in making that happen.

Like the poetic, the visual serves different purposes in *Emergency Exit*. It can serve as a source of humor, as when Julie and Al go for a picnic with a "green blanket and a white basket of fresh sandwiches and a dark red bottle of Italian wine"; the colors, of course, are those of the Italian flag (111). A running joke in the novel is phone calls with strange messages or callers; in one, Norman Rockwell answers and the caller asks for Grandma Moses (101). Another passage satirizes artists:

You know the painters you met at my house? They all live here in town. One is very well known outside the area. The one who does the Absolute Threshold over and over has no name beyond the state highway out there. Eh? When asked what it means she says it's the level of stimulus required for her sense of herself to rise, to surface. One of the others paints a thing she calls The Gateway of Life. The final one spends most of his time doing himself standing in the doorway of his home. They smoke grass while they work and in most of their paintings you can see smoke. (36)

Readers learn nothing about the artist who has some reputation. Instead, we find out that all of them are obsessed with thresholds but represent different approaches to the subject. One is expressionist, the second allegorical, and the third self-referential. Despite these differences, they remain representational, suggested by the appearance of smoke from their marijuana cigarettes in each painting. Their lack of reputation and the obviousness of their work are evidence of Major's contempt for certain forms of expression. Nonetheless, a self-criticism may be implied, since he himself, as shall be seen, often took up in writing or painting the same subject repeatedly or worked and reworked the same canvas for years.

A third example describes art as consumer object: "The Threshold Print Shop and Art Gallery: Canvas thirty-two by twenty-four vase of chrysanthemums, shows influence of French Impressionist. In background a doorway with sunset. Canvas forty-eight by thirty: young woman bather. Shows influence of Renoir. Large soft pink breasts blue eyes heavy hips careless sky and sea meeting at the threshold of a blond wooded area" (65). The art described does not "show influence" but instead slavishly imitates the originals. What presumably are informational tags for the paintings emphasize practical matters: the size, the subject, and the generic style. The identity of the artist is irrelevant because the point is to have something in your house that displays your acquisition of culture, not your appreciation of art. Nonetheless, the choice of subjects also implicates Major himself, since he painted nudes and vases of chrysanthemums. Early in the book, an unnamed character asks, "Have you seen the painting by Morris Hirschfield (1872–1946) called 'Nude on Sofa with Three Pussies'? Quite an accomplishment!" (13). Two pages later, the text reads, "The new apartment is full of empty milk cartons Julie walks around naked all day pressing the kittens to her breasts" (15).

Art also serves as allusion in the text. References are made to Van Gogh, Goya, Renoir, Dali, and *The Last Supper*, as well as the previously mentioned de Kooning, Rockwell, and Grandma Moses. The novel has almost a didactic function in mentioning Deborah Goldsmith, an early nineteenth-century portraitist from Upstate New York; Julien Hudson, a free man of color in antebellum New Orleans who was a successful miniaturist and portrait painter; and Henry Ossawa Tanner, an African American artist of the late nineteenth and early twentieth centuries whose work *The Banjo Lesson* is specifically mentioned. One verbal image re-creates a Hieronymous Bosch painting: "A giant bird with the head of Elmer Blake is eating a naked man. The pink legs dangle from Blake's mouth. The bird is chained to a large platform controlled by tiny workmen. They constantly fork 'sinners' through the back and feed them to Blake who chews them like apples crunch crunch" (109–10). The narrator also makes repeated reference to the nightwatchman, which is the title of a painting Major did during this period, even though it does not appear in the text.

At other points, characters are either creating art or are created within a composition intended to be pictorial. Jim is twice described as painting. The first instance is part of a surreal scene: "Jim is caught through the stomach by the blade of a giant knife. He is busy painting his self portrait. The face is not his. Perhaps the painter is deranged. Below on the street the celebration goes on. Bulls are being chased through the streets. One splits a door and enters a living room where a family is eating supper. Piles of mulch enrich the air" (182). In the second instance, Major seems to be connecting Jim to Gauguin: "First a woman is sitting in the dim doorway of a thatched roof house. Jim is painting her as part of the background for The Great Tree. On closer inspection I realize the woman is Julie's mother and she is in a trance" (233). In both cases, an exotic quality is apparent. The settings are foreign, especially for a resident of Inlet. If we are to take Jim as a stand-in for Major as artist, then the passages also carry a sense of the irrational as valuable in art; in the first scene the painter may be "deranged," and in the second, the woman is in a trance. In both writing and painting, Major has contended for the place of intuition, dream, and the subconscious as fundamental to the imagination and the creative process.

Within the text, visual compositions are built with words, again with little regard for whether or not they contribute to the narrative. They are the verbal version of Major's interest in the technical problems of constructing an image: "Julie in a long white dress running across thick dark grass

and children playing tag screaming. Three ladies sitting in a circle knit-
ting. The old man slices the bread and pours the wine. Above, the clouds
are scattered and moving fast. The smell of steak burning over coals" (64).
While the scene obviously involves more than just the visual sense, it is
constructed within a single narrative frame and thus invites thinking of it
in pictorial terms. In his doctoral statement, Major pointed out the importance of this aspect of the text:

> There will be a great deal of description, direct and simple; I am trying
> to pay particular attention to minute details of place and time; how light
> falls through a window along a floor, for example. I think it is through the
> cumulative effect of clusters of such detail that imaginative reality in fic-
> tion is created. I do not want to simply give the reader information. I want
> to create a sense of *presence*, an imaginative space in which there are "actual"
> things and characters trying to work out the problems and dreams of their
> existence.[19]

In interviewing Jacob Lawrence while writing *Emergency Exit*, Major
complimented the older artist for his "democratic" manner of composition
("Clarence Major Interviews," 16). A similar issue is apparent here. What is
the focus of the scene—Julie, the children, the ladies, the old man? What
is foreground and what background? How are the three acts of motion—
Julie, the children, the clouds—related? Where are the elements in relation to each other? Beginning around this time, Major became interested
in portraying groups of figures and experimented with different combinations. In this scene, he plays with that problem.

Another example offers a completed composition, in this case as
landscape:

> Not far from the mouth of the river a man wearing a red cap and a blue
> plaid shirt sat quietly in a silver rowboat, his fishing line lingering calmly
> in the water. Now the narrow low waterway was crowded on both sides by
> an awesome profusion of trees and shrubs and their twigs buds seed tassels ·
> floated on the moving water around them. Around rocks and beneath vines
> growing out from the riverbed which in this shallow area was so clear you
> could see every inch of its bottom complete with beer cans, ancient rock and
> soggy wood. (*Emergency*, 117–18)

The image is nearly photographic instead of Major's usual impressionistic
renderings. It is a fully integrated picture, unlike the previous example. It

FIGURE 17. *Emergency Exit*, 50

does not present a problem so much as a solution to compositional issues. In both cases, however, we have set pieces unrelated to the storyline. In fact, in the second case, the narrative stops in order to provide the image and then resumes. Verbal images, then, are another means of disrupting rather than enhancing the reading of the novel.

The most important visual aspect is, of course, the set of Major's own paintings that are reproduced within the text. As Lisa Roney has noted, he has been very clear that these images are not to be taken as illustrative of the written text.[20] In fact the evidence on that issue is not so clear. For example, following a section in which the narrator says, "I follow myself across selected landscapes where the self searches for the self," we have Janice commenting to Barry on the nature of the self and its relationship to the world. This is followed by an image of a woman with large eyes looking directly at the observer (42–43; see fig. 17). A few pages later, Julie speaks to Barbara: "The message is here and it's always the same" (50), followed by the same image, though cropped differently. In both instances the art does seem to illustrate the idea of the assertive, seeking woman. Shortly after this, the narration reads: "Jim and Al stand talking with each other holding glasses containing liquor. The room is full of people who are not quite focused: one man's body suggests the need to be filled in with a pencil tracing the dots" (60). The facing page reproduces two figures with only vague markings for facial features. Similarly, a series of enumerated comments by a woman (Roslyn) about her relationship with Jim is accompanied by an impressionist image of a female figure in a room with a bed (76–78). In most instances, however, there is no obvious connection between the visual and verbal expressions. For example, *Grief*, discussed in chapter 4, is reproduced in *Emergency Exit* yet has no relationship to the verbal material surrounding the image. It seems, instead, to be another of the nonsequential juxtapositions in the text designed to disorient the reader, to disrupt any conventional "sense" of the narrative.

Finally, the visual material in the novel must be understood as something different from either the written text or the paintings. These are, after all, only black-and-white reproductions of original canvases. They are not identified, credited, or titled anywhere in the book. Since the originals were not created to be part of *Emergency Exit*, and since they were not (and generally still are not) available to be viewed other than within the book, they exist for readers *as* text, to be read in conjunction with the words. They cannot be viewed as distinct pieces of art because what makes them paintings—color, media, brushstrokes—cannot be seen because of the reproduction process. While they point to something outside the text—the original artwork—that "something" is not accessible directly, just as the characters that the author has invented are not available to us as real people. They are pieces of the whole, like the combinations of words. Just as certain verbal constructs here make conventional sense while others serve to violate novelistic practices, so the visual art sometimes "illustrates" some story point and sometimes subverts the narrative. They work essentially as another set of metaphors whose referents are not something in the "real" world but rather the compositional process by which the artist makes a new object. Major has said that the novel itself "is composed like a group of paintings," but that claim is itself somewhat metaphorical, since such paintings would all fit into the same category (paintings), unlike the materials of the novel.[21] At one point, the narrator mentions a man who owns the Patchwork Store and makes quilts while his wife repairs cars. I would suggest that *Emergency Exit* can be understood as a verbal and visual quilt that uses materials from various sources; the artist shapes these materials to fit his design, regardless of their original purpose. What holds the book together is not some preexisting form but the skill of the maker in putting the parts together. What results is a new thing, made of what already existed refashioned to be a unique creation. The metaphor is imperfect; quilts, at least those made by folk artists, were functional, intended to provide warmth. This novel comes closer to the contemporary decorative use of quilts; they are to be displayed and admired for their craftsmanship, not, as Alice Walker has noted, for "everyday use." Major has consistently rejected any obvious practical function for his work; his novels and poetry, we are repeatedly told, have no ideological, political, or social purpose. They are articulations of the artist's vision, which often, as in this case, is expressed through representations of the creative process itself rather than the end product of that process. Whatever figurative language we use to describe it, *Emergency Exit* stands as Major's most radical experiment in fiction making.

Especially in a work as experimental as this, reading aspects of the life into it is problematic. However, two experiences are clearly relevant. The first was suggested by Klinkowitz: "Clarence's marriage with Sharyn had broken up; indeed, his previous novel with the Collective, *Reflex and Bone Structure* (1975), had been generated by imagining what losing her might be like. Now she was gone, and in her absence Clarence reimagined what their situation had been: he, from a lower-middle-class neighborhood on Chicago's south side, having been involved with a glamorous young woman from the black haute-bourgeoisie."[22] Major has asserted that Klinkowitz is incorrect in his identification, that in fact the model for Julie was Nancy Pettingill, a young white woman he met after his breakup with Sheila and with whom he lived for several weeks in Lee, Massachusetts. That relationship ended, and he met Sharyn some months later.[23] We can in these terms see Clarence as Al and Nancy as Julie. This point is confirmed by comments Al makes about their different backgrounds, and his story of feeling ashamed of his family, his decision to enter the military, and his limited college education (*Emergency*, 227–28). But the situation is more complex than this, since Major had devoted years to refashioning himself as thoroughly distinct from those young men in his old neighborhood. Al is much more one of them, with his Harlem background and petty-criminal life. Even if Major were attracted to Nancy based in part on her social status, what attracted her would be his achievements, not his background. By 1971, when they met, he had published books of poetry and fiction. If we read Julie's interest in Al as a desire to "go ghetto," that was not Major's identity. More likely, Nancy was drawn to his bohemian style and perhaps his race, which would have been a source of awkwardness for him, since he consistently resisted any essentialist identification. Also, the very short duration of the fictional relationship does not correspond to the several years Sharyn and Clarence spent together.

A more complex dynamic may be at work, in which Nancy and Clarence are a model for Julie and Al, and Clarence and Sharyn for Jim and Deborah. Al finds himself annoyed by what he sees as Julie's superficiality; the narrator never accuses Deborah of a lack of substance. Like her, Sharyn was a person of considerable elegance and grace. While the sensuality of the younger couple may come from a casual relationship, the distance that develops between the older couple after being together for years would appear to be based on the distance that developed between Clarence and Sharyn. Given her life and work in New York, one area of tension would have been the move to Boulder. Her life was disrupted by his ambitions. Similarly, Deborah is expected to live in a small Connecticut town after her husband gives up the diplomatic life in order to work for an insignificant company. Her reward for this is a spouse who has an affair with his white secretary. It is noteworthy in this regard that, shortly after his and Sharyn's separation, Major began living with a white woman.

Perhaps more to the point of the fiction are the psychological issues made apparent by this connection. First, a generational crossover occurs that confuses the relationships. Julie comments that she does not think that her father loves her, but her phrasing implies more: "He should *expose* himself to me but he's afraid of me I can feel it he doesn't want me to get too close to him even the few times we've danced together he was uneasy." The statement is sufficiently ambiguous that Al has to ask, "Why do you want him I mean *what* do you want from him?" (191, original emphasis). Similarly, Al finds himself attracted to Deborah, and the feeling seems mutual. He fantasizes having sex with her, and she insists on kissing him one day before she leaves the house. To add further complexity, the narrator describes having sex with her. If Klinkowitz is right about the biographical source of the storyline, then this entanglement can be read as Major's interpretation of his marriage as a situation in which each spouse saw the other as both parent and child. Sharyn is the educated, sophisticated one who nonetheless is accustomed to getting attention and having things provided for her. Clarence, the older one, also does not especially like to take adult responsibility; he is the artist-genius who others take care of. Sharyn holds the substantial job, while Clar-

ence, until Boulder, was always scrambling for work. Clarence is the published writer; Sharyn seeks some similar recognition. Thus, desire is linked
to very instinctual need, which in the text becomes eroticized.

A second point is that mother and daughter in the novel are both presented as promiscuous, though in Deborah's case this comes after Jim's
affair has begun. Julie has sexual relationships with several men, and
she likes flaunting her liaison with Al in front of her family. Her mother,
though highly respectable, has a tryst with an unnamed man in a "fleabag" hotel. As mentioned above, she has sex with the narrator. Neither of
them expresses any qualms about their experiences. In contrast, Al feels
awkward when he sees Barbara again, and he tries to reconnect with Gail,
an earlier partner, who had been living in his apartment even after their
breakup. Likewise, Jim's relationship with Roslyn is apparently his first infidelity, and he tortures himself about it. He can neither give it up nor settle
into it. Thus, Major would appear to grant to the male characters a moral
sensibility that the women lack, which may be a subconscious effort to hold
Sharyn responsible for their separation. At the same time, the men seem to
be far less substantial than the women. Al is an occasional drug dealer and
a college dropout and has a sinecure in a poverty program; this last post is
comparable to Major's work with school children in Harlem. Jim had been
a minor government bureaucrat for the American Information Service, a
painter whose work is never described, and a maker of slave ship models
out of matchsticks. They represent a version of the author that is less than
admirable and perhaps deserving of the failure of his marriage. To return
to Klinkowitz's initial observation, Major may well see himself as a poseur.

The final point about *Emergency Exit* is its possible source in a controversy over a reading Major gave in Falls Village, Connecticut. He had been
invited to Housatonic Valley Regional High School to read some of his
poems in February 1972. A woman was offended by "American Setup" and
left immediately after he finished reciting it. She wrote a letter to the local
newspaper the following week describing the "filth" that she had been subjected to. A series of responses followed over several weeks. Since a video-
tape had been made of the event, a meeting was held to watch it and debate
the presentation. The last story on the subject appeared in the *Connecticut
Western* three months after the reading (*Dark and Feeling*, 151–52).

Major sets *Emergency Exit* in a small Connecticut town, though in a
different part of the state from Falls Village. The Threshold Law, which is
designed to control female bodies and thus create moral order, is a meta-

PLATE 1. *The Long Road* (1976), oil on Canvas, 30×20 inches

PLATE 2. *Yellow Chair* (1976), acrylic, 20×16 inches

PLATE 3. *Grief* (1976), acrylic, 24×32 inches

PLATE 4. *Dream of Escape* (1976), acrylic, 18×24 inches

PLATE 5. *Samona* (2003), acrylic, 30×30 inches

PLATE 6. *Family Togetherness* (1976), acrylic, 32×24 inches

PLATE 7. *Rhythm of Life* (1978), acrylic, 32×26 inches

PLATE 8. *Nightwatchman #2* (1978–91), acrylic, 32×20 inches

PLATE 9. *Country Boogie* (1993), acrylic, 26×32 inches

PLATE 10. *Checkers* (2000), acrylic, 46-inch diameter

PLATE 11. *Saturday Afternoon #1* (1992), acrylic, 44×36 inches

PLATE 12. *Rebecca, My Great-Grandmother* (2005), acrylic, 30×24 inches

PLATE 13. *Blue City* (1999), acrylic, 30×36 inches

PLATE 14. *The Woman Who Danced Once with Dustin Hoffman* (2004), acrylic, 12×9 inches

PLATE 15. *Two Sisters* (2009), acrylic, 36×40 inches

PLATE 16. *Joan* (2010), acrylic, 60×36 inches

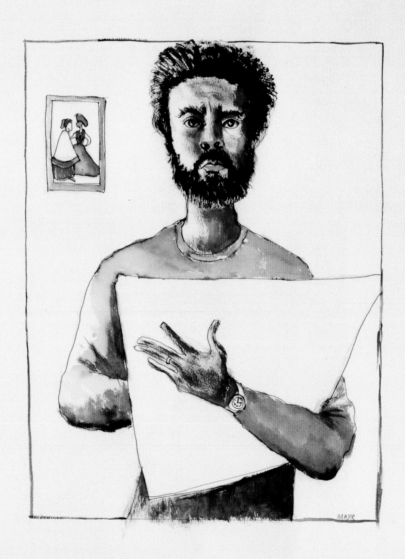

PLATE 17. *The Mirror* (1984), watercolor, 20×14 inches

phor for the kind of closed-mindedness Major encountered because of the subject matter and language of his early works. But he goes further by making the community a site of endless sexual desire and activity, by incorporating paintings of nudes and descriptions of naked bodies, by having women respond to the law by "pissing" and "shitting" on the city hall threshold, and by creating businesses such as the Ritual of the Foreskin massage parlor, the Glans Removal pornography shop, and the Corked Pussy Cat nightclub and strip joint. Most important is the Superior Pussy Company, for which the narrator works as a salesman. It manufactures and sells artificial vaginas and penises. Advertisements for its products appear in the text. Since Major began work on the novel around the time of the Falls Village incident and since he published an article about the event in *American Poetry Review* a year later, it provides a specific context and occasion for his claims for personal and artistic freedom that are central to the novel.

While Major was disappointed by the reviews and sales of *Emergency Exit*, the initial comments were generally positive. Inga Judd observes that he "forces language to its breaking point, ignores rules and conventions, and creates a truly intelligent, genuinely innovative piece of fiction that will fascinate those in love with pure language." Michel Fabre, in *Afram Newsletter*, compares the novel to René Magritte's painting. In a special issue of *Black American Literature Forum* on Major, published the summer before the novel came out, Jerry Klinkowitz offers detailed praise for what he calls the work's "pure writing," by which he means language not tied to narrative or representational functions. Almost three years after publication, Sarah Lauzen wrote a long review for *American Book Review*. She calls it "a celebration: a vibrant assemblage of discrete bits of fantasy, dream, images, definitions, anecdotes, surrealism, and story." Like Fabre, she suggests a painting analogy, this time Jackson Pollock; curiously, neither of them discusses the place of actual paintings in the novel. Positive reviews from Klinkowitz and *American Book Review* should not be surprising, since both are directly connected to the novelist, but they are both detailed in their commentary. One of the few negative reviews came from James Polk in *Newsday*. He comments that, among other things, the author is sometimes "guilty of graduate-school finger exercises," by which he presumably means that the writing falls to the level of creative writing classes. He concludes, "The trouble is that Major tries to give us a textbook on the craft of fiction. *Emergency Exit* would have been more successful if he had just concentrated on giving us a novel."

Peter Quartermain, in a long review of several Fiction Collective works, selects Major's novel as representative of the strengths and weaknesses of the collective's efforts. In doing so, he poses the most serious challenge to the principles of fiction writing practiced by the group. The desire to create art that is nonlinear, that lacks tidy resolution, has been defended by Major and others as following the truth of life itself. But the means by which this new object comes into being is through words rather than through paint or musical notes, and thus it is inherently referential. Because of this problem, the writer has to constantly make the point that the work is *not* mimetic. Additionally, since the work is not about the world but about the writer's creative effort, the author often intrudes in ways Quartermain finds troublesome in all of this fiction, though he again focuses on *Emergency Exit*: "It is very much a part of the book's purpose that the author be present, but the means Major has chosen are rather labored, and give the book an occasional air of coy self-consciousness that, irritating as it is, on the one hand suggests that he trusts neither his material nor his reader, and on the other severely undercuts the unusual excellence of the book by dissipating its energy and muddying its perception."[24]

An unexpectedly negative reaction to the book came several years later from Joe Weixlmann, who, as editor of both *Black American Literature Forum* and, later, *African American Review*, published special issues on Major, both of which featured articles by Klinkowitz. Nonetheless, in his essay for *Melus*, in the midst of a survey of the postmodernism of Major and Ishmael Reed, Weixlmann makes this comment: "The least satisfying of Major's seven novels, *Emergency Exit* nonetheless has its moments."[25] Along with the somewhat mixed commentaries, the novel has garnered little critical attention. The online MLA Bibliography lists only three articles ever published on it. While this number is inaccurately low, it does indicate a problem of attention. The collection of essays edited by Bernard Bell, which was based on the *African American Review* special issue, does not include an essay on the novel, though other works are given individual attention. All of this may suggest that the very radicalism of *Emergency Exit* was a dead end for the creation of fiction. Major has talked throughout his career of his interest in setting and solving technical problems in his art. This novel is an instance where no further solution seems possible, and even though his next work of fiction, *My Amputations*, has some similar characteristics, it ultimately moves in a different direction.

PAINTING IN THE LATE 1970S

Several of the works included in *Emergency Exit* were being painted during the time of the novel's composition. Not surprisingly, they reflect the same interest in identity and relationships. *Family Togetherness*, done in 1976 (plate 6), depicts a family grouping, but the figures are done with slashes of strong color that make them abstract. The dominant color is purple broken with green and light brown; the strong effect of the palette is strengthened by the blank white background. The female figure's face is indicated by an ovoid of pink and the baby's a circle of brown. The male has no recognizable human features; rather his head would appear to be that of a purple cat. The two large figures are facing each other, with a thin line suggesting his arm extending toward her. The violence implied in the color combination and the brush strokes is reinforced by a section of her dress in the shape of a knife aimed in the direction of his groin. The covering on the woman's head suggests that this may be a version of the Holy Family. If so, it functions as a parody, with a half-man, half-animal Joseph and a Mary prepared to castrate him. Moreover, the infant has no special significance within the frame, which is consistent with Major's largely negative view toward Christianity, which he has expressed at various times over his career. In *The Dark and Feeling*, "This was Jesus the Christ, who, by the way, was constantly being put to death everywhere he could be found—both in fantasy and in reality. This act attempted to meet the unconscious need to challenge and if necessary destroy the father figure so the male ego could burst forth and make felt its own presence in the world, as man, not boy" (13). It is Christ the Son, not God the Father, who poses the threat to manhood. Therefore, making the child in the painting insignificant is the artist's way of reducing that threat.

Another painting reproduced in the novel is typical of a pattern of works Major began doing during this time and continued over several years. In it, two figures, one male and one female, are shown (plate 7). What is noteworthy is that the male is upside down, though his head is right-side up. This pattern is typical of most of these works. The limbs of the man are elongated, thin, and outlined in red; he has no genitalia. The body itself is very pale, and his body reaches from the top to the bottom of the canvas. His face is brown, perhaps an African mask, with a yellow T centered on it. The effect is to suggest the head of a bull. One arm is bent at the elbow so as to curl under the woman's belly. One of her arms bends down to meet his, while the other reaches toward his waist. The effect is to encircle the belly and make it a focal point. While most of her body is also white, the belly is yellow moving into green. This emphasis and the shape of her midsection suggests pregnancy. Her head, which is partly separated from the body by a line of blue matching the background, is covered with deep red hair. Her face looks like a helmet or mask. Her limbs are much sturdier than his, and her feet are firmly planted at the bottom of the canvas.

Major has said that this painting and the others like it represent a struggle for identity and a place in the world.[26] The masks symbolize the creation of a persona that can conceal and protect the self, even in intimate relationships. The gender aspects of the composition give us an earth mother committed to reproduction and stability. In contrast, the male is both assertive of his masculinity and alienated in the world. However, the positioning of his head in relation to his body suggests a bifurcated self, in which the mind and body lack coherence. The absence of his genitalia implies the emasculating effects of such a condition. This work can be interpreted as a statement on Major's life in the sense that he, in all his relationships up to 1980, was the one floating through the world, always seeking a firm place and recognition of his achievements. He moved from woman to woman but never established a home. He perceived any restriction on him, whether by wives or girlfriends, publishers, audiences, racial assumptions, or artistic conventions, as threats to his being. This point is made again and again in Major's poetry, fiction, and, in this case, painting.

A variation on the composition is found in a painting that is something of a transitional work, though from the same period (fig. 18). Some of Major's later work moves in the direction of folk art, while retaining experimental qualities. This particular work again shows two figures with the male body upside down with the head right-side up. In this instance, however, both are dancing, with their arms extended and their hips turned. Moreover, both are clearly African American, without any form of masking. The curved lines of the figures are parallel, suggesting coordination and agreement. In addition, the garish colors of the other work are replaced with subtle, neutral tones for both figures and background, implying characters at home in their environment. While it is important to be careful in offering any reading of Major's work involving race, it is possible to conclude that some form of essentialism is at work that sees African Americans who accept their identity as more at home in their bodies and in the world than are either whites or blacks who take their sense of self from the white world.

FIGURE 18. Untitled (1978), acrylic

The interconnection of written and visual art can be seen in a painting that is not included in the novel but which was being composed at the same time. A character known as the Nightwatchman is mentioned three times, though he does not participate in the action and is given no other qualities than the loneliness of his job (*Emergency*, 104). It would seem that the creation of the character generated the image, and in fact a second painting was done several years later, at the time Major published his next novel. The first painting, called *Nightwatchman #2* (1978), employs geometric shapes, predominantly triangles, for the composition (plate 8). The face is an inverted African mask with three rounded sides; it is pink with an elongated light-green nose, with round red eyes and a red oval mouth; all the features are outlined in white. The neck, another triangle, is also pink. A red collar is on one side of the neck, apparently attached to a brown shirt. Over this, or attached to it, is a bluish jacket. The lines of the clothing work with the edges of the frame to produce a series of triangles. The background of deep purple provides strong contrast to the figure. Most important, however, is the brown oval behind the mask; it has the shape and position of a head for the body. However, it has no features—not hair, not ears, not wrinkles.

The effect is to make the mask more human than the head, and because the neck has the same coloration as the mask, it appears to be a more "natural" part of the body. The image can be read as a play on Franz Fanon's *Black Skin, White Masks*, in which the mask has merged with the skin. If so, then Major is asserting a political critique of those blacks who have thoroughly identified themselves with the values of the dominant culture, much like Jim in the novel, who once worked for the CIA and thus was a national nightwatchman. He seeks to become one with the white world, and that desire can be manipulated by those in power, who want to know what is hidden and thus require watchers in the night. But the point of the painting is that such desires are absurd; in U.S. society, blacks cannot become white, just as the inverted white triangle cannot conceal the brown oval in the painting.

In January 1977, during this period of intensive writing and painting, Major conducted an interview with painter Jacob Lawrence, who was then at the University of Washington. The interview was published later that year in *Black Scholar*, a journal that built its reputation on diversity of views. The striking thing about the interview is the extent to which Major uses it to align the older artist with his own theories and practices of art. At times, he makes a statement and then expects Lawrence to find something to respond to:

> MAJOR: It seems to me you have developed a highly effective style with
> certain kinds of distortions. I want to emphasize the word "distortions."
> I don't think of your work as primitive nor neo-primitive. Like certain
> experimental writers, you have, in your own medium, discovered a
> stronger sense of realism, in the truest sense of that word. You've done
> this by not trying to create the *illusion* of so-called reality. Instead, the
> surface, the design creates its own reality. I see this in your work and
> I appreciate it.
>
> LAWRENCE: I think you're asking here . . . ("Clarence Major Interviews," 16)

Among the experimental writers, of course, would be Major himself. They go on to talk about art generating new reality, about universality versus race-based art, about the relationship between art and propaganda, and about the Americanness of African American art. In much of the conversation, the questions are longer than the answers, and it is not because Lawrence is particularly reticent as an informant. Major often pulls out long statements by critics, adds his own thoughts, and then invites Lawrence to say something. The goal here would seem to be to gain an ally in the struggle against artistic conventions and at the same time to create a tradition of experimentation, specifically one that is African American. By claiming Lawrence, a renowned and respected artist, for his cause, he could continue to make the case that his own work was not a compromise of his identity as a black man but rather an expression of it. The decision to publish the interview in *Black Scholar* indicates his continuing desire to be part of a racial community, even as his professional and social connections were primarily white.

# CHAPTER SEVEN

# Finding a New Life

Major and Pamela Ritter met in the fall of 1979 at a party in Boulder given by Diane Johnson, Major's girlfriend at the time. Pam was with her husband, Robert Steiner, who had just been hired by the English Department at the University of Colorado. Born in Iowa, she had attended the University of Iowa and Bowling Green University before entering the doctoral program at the University of Massachusetts Amherst, where Steiner also studied. The relationship with Major developed very quickly; they started living together on 22 December 1979. They were married on 8 May 1980, with Clarence's mother and sister in attendance. Shortly after, Major took a leave from the university, and they moved to Bernardston in northwestern Massachusetts, so that Pam could continue work on her dissertation on Robert Coover. They remained there until December. Major spent the time writing poetry and giving readings of his work. He saw the town as racist, as he did other parts of New England they visited ("Licking Stamps," 194). He later published a poem simply titled "Bernardston" about the community in *Literary Review*. In it, the place is represented as lacking the possibilities of poetry:

> The mythic figures of literature are far
> away . . .
>
> .   .   .   .   .   .   .   .   .   .   .   [
>
> Epics have no place
> here. (*Configurations*, 198)

Yet the apparent deadness of the fall conceals life and motion:

> The white Fittonia veins in the green surface
> seem even but they are not. A profusion of leaves
> in the shade, by the window, seem still
> but the steam is moving them. The long shadows
> of Fall—in here and out there—are cool
> and vacant yet I *know* them, as I know Cezanne,
> to contain life! The sun on the Fittonias—
> it is moving fast. Their veins glow white! (199)

Despite the mysteries, dreams, and artistic possibilities he discovers, there remains a need to be self-protective. After a trip to the coast, he feels the need to dress in "blue armor" and charge into the town "with my sword out before me, ready to strike!" (554). But the world is too mundane: he ends up standing "at the intersection of Five and Ten" (554). The poem ends in a moment of death:

> Five figures
> carry a dead cat on a stretcher
> between the olive trees. (203)

The poem suggests that it is the ability of the artist to respond to his experience of the world rather than its reality or quality that produces art. The poem does not so much represent Bernardston as it demonstrates the sensitivity and aesthetic feelings of the poet.

## NICE AND BEYOND

After Pamela finished her work in Massachusetts, they returned to Boulder for the spring 1981 semester. But Major soon arranged to leave yet again. One of the reasons was the difficulty with his application for promotion to professor. It was opposed by the English Department, though approved by higher-level administrators. While the documents related to the decision are confidential, it is reasonable to assume that once again problems with his teaching and his editorial responsibilities played a significant role. The rejection by his colleagues caused some bitterness.[1] But he received a Fulbright Fellowship to teach at the University of Nice and thus was able to leave the situation behind. After Pam defended her dissertation, they left for France in September 1981. In Nice, Major taught modern and contemporary poetry and fiction, as well as a course on literary magazines. Pamela was invited to teach writing courses. A member of the faculty was Maurice Courturier, who had translated *Reflex and Bone Structure*. They also met James Baldwin, who lived nearby in Saint-Paul de Vence.

In addition to teaching, the time was filled with travel to lecture in England and Germany. The trip to England in late November was sponsored by the British-American Commission for Educational and Cultural Exchange and hosted by Eric Mottram, whom Major had met in the home of Ted Wilentz years earlier in New York. He spoke on African American literature at King's College and then gave a reading at the University of East Anglia. Later, they met up with David Henderson, another acquaintance from the Lower East Side, and the two men gave a joint reading at the Young Vic Theater in London. Major reports the event this way: "David had an Italian woman belly dancing while he read his poetry. The audience loved him. The next day a newspaper said he was the real stuff of Afro-America and that I was too academic" ("Licking Stamps," 195).

Major and Pam returned to Nice for the Christmas holidays. They made friends and traveled with their neighbors, who took them to the Alps. They also became acquainted with Muriel Lacotte, who was writing her dissertation on Major. She took them to jazz clubs and, on one occasion, to a nude beach near Monte Carlo.

The trip to Germany began on 10 January 1982, in Nuremberg. The next day, he spoke at the University of Erlangen on the problems of literary publishing. On 12 January, they arrived in West Berlin, and he spoke at the Kennedy Institute of the Free University on African American literature. The next day he gave a reading at Amerika Haus, followed by an interview and reading on Armed Forces Radio. The tour continued through Frankfurt, Mainz, Aachen, Bonn, Tübingen, and Munich. He notes in "Licking Stamps" that the trip offered little in the way of tourist occasions, which was a problem for Pam (195).

In late March, another tour was arranged, this time to Italy. It began with a drive from Nice to Genoa, where they boarded a ship to Sicily. Major spoke at the University of Catania. They then drove up to Florence and stayed at the Hotel Argentina, a three-star hotel in the historic area of the city. He delivered a lecture at the University of Florence on postmodernism. They then moved on to Milan and ended back in Genoa, where he repeated the postmodernism talk.

They returned to Nice at the beginning of April. Later that month, Major participated in an international conference organized by Maurice Couturier at the university. Titled "Representation and Performance in Postmodern Literature," it included William Gass, Stanley Elkin, Malcolm Bradbury, Tony Tanner, Ihab Hassan, and Klinkowitz. His talk was an effort to connect to the intellectual side of the fiction-making process. The published version, in Couturier's collection of the proceedings, was titled "A Meditation on Time and Space in Bamism." It is an attempt to give his experimental approach to fiction an African American grounding. The term *bamism* is a neologism he constructs from the Dizzy Gillespie scat "Obopshebamobbleeop." He contends that the central syllable is the downbeat and thus the heart of the innovation that is jazz. "The aesthetics of jazz, after all, are not so different from those of innovative fiction" (163). Just as he had made Jacob Lawrence's paintings analogous to his writing, he does the same here. The difference is that he makes little attempt to actually construct the analogy with music. Instead, he creates another term—*intertexmime*—that is derived from "inter-textual mime," or the "echo of the lineage of innovative techniques embodied in such work."[2] This language enables him to create a literary tradition for experimentation that validates his approach to fiction. He creates nine stages of fiction making dating from the earliest human beings. He offers no evidence or examples for these stages. Instead, he moves to a discussion of space and time and the relation between the known and the visible world. The space of a text can be broken up, as he did in *Reflex and Bone Structure* and *Emergency Exit*, much like a cubist painting. The time can be an endless present rather than a carefully plotted development leading to resolution, much like the lives readers and writers live. The problem for the innovative author is how to stop a text without such resolution. He notes here, as elsewhere, that realism "has too long been associated with totalitarian regimes to still have its virginity" (176). The goal of realism is to bring order, to embrace the End. Such writing makes readers comfortable, even happy. This is why innovators have small audiences; they disrupt, cause dis-ease.

Thus, we can read this presentation as not merely a manifesto but also as a gospel. Major's response to critics of his work and of a whole body of contemporary writing, including some African American and African authors, is to posit a species-long tradition of the approach he takes to storytelling. In effect, he construes the idea of the universal not in the conventional terms of a Eurocentric model but rather as a practice inherent in human nature. In an ironic twist, that which is most avant-garde is most traditional.

A few weeks after the conference, 30 May to 10 June 1982, Major went alone to Africa, sponsored by the U.S. International Communication Agency (the successor to the U.S. Information Agency). He traveled first to Ghana for four days, where he spoke at the American Cultural Center on 1 June and at the University of Ghana, near Accra, on 2 June. While the talk at the university was a standard one on African American fiction, the one at the Cultural Center was a version of his "Bamism" presentation, probably because he wanted in some way to differentiate himself from expectations about what African Americans writers are and do. He added specific references to African writers to make the local connection.

On that trip he was also reunited with Kofi Awoonor, who had earned his doctorate in comparative literature at SUNY–Stony Brook and was part of Major's New York circle. Awoonor had been imprisoned upon his return to Ghana in 1975, on grounds related to political unrest. He was held for a year without trial. Major discussed the case in an interview with Maury Povich and Geraldo Rivera on WTTG in Washington, D.C., on 19 April 1976. By the time the two friends met again, Awoonor had become a significant figure in politics and two years after this meeting, he would become the ambassador to Brazil and later the representative to the United Nations. Major also had the opportunity to meet several other Ghanaian writers.

After Accra, he stopped over in the Ivory Coast on his way to Liberia, where he received considerable press attention. He initially was invited to a reading by Liberian poets, organized by Greg Lynch of the U.S. International Communication Agency and held in the auditorium of the agency on 4 June. Major read a number of his works at the end of the evening. The next day, he participated in a writers' workshop at the University of Liberia. He engaged in a debate with some of the attendees over the question of universalism. They were concerned both about the standards that were used by Western critics and publishers to dismiss African authors and about the need to maintain cultural authenticity through the use of vernacular materials. Major responded that universal literary qualities must always be the standard for judging art ("American Author Speaks"). He spoke at the University of Liberia in Monrovia twice, once on Faulkner's short fiction and once on Gertrude Stein and Richard Brautigan. At Cuttington University College in Suakoko, he discussed the work of Faulkner and Flannery

FIGURE 19. Major at the Parthenon

O'Connor. As a result of a suggestion made during a reception after the workshop, he was also instrumental in forming a Liberian writers' association: his comments about the talent of local writers created an impetus that led to the founding of the Liberian Association of Writers, with the support of the university English Department and the Ministry of Culture. The organization continues to exist. Major returned to Nice on June 10.

He also arranged to stay in France for an extended period. Originally, he had hoped for an additional year in Nice, but in fact he remained there only until February 1983. In the fall of 1982, he and Pam went to Greece for a vacation, arriving in Athens on 17 September. Renting a car there, they traveled to the Acropolis, Plaka, Volos, Kalambaka, Delphi, Clovino, Olympia, and Tolon before returning to Athens. The photo of him at the Parthenon (see fig. 19) reveals a man trying to appear at home in the heart of Western civilization. The angularity of his posture reflects the geometry of the setting. He, in effect, claims this space for his own purposes. The image signifies on James Baldwin's assertion that those of African descent will always be outsiders in the European world. Here Major takes a defiant stand, a tourist perhaps, but one who has as much right to the space as anyone else. He and Pam then returned to Nice, where he completed the fall semester, though not without controversy. After they left in February, Michel Bandry, a young faculty member at the university, wrote to Major to complain that he had left without assigning grades to his students.

## ART FROM FRANCE

In addition to several paintings, two literary works come out of this experience, *Inside Diameter: The France Poems* (1985) and *My Amputations* (1986). Michel Fabre has cited these two books as ones that make extensive use of the author's experience in France.[3] The book of poetry, consistent with the pattern of Major's work in this area, was published by Permanent Press, a London company that specializes in books of verse. Only five hundred copies were printed.[4] Possibly because of its non-U.S. publication, it received minimal reviews. *Inside Diameter* focuses on Major's experience in the area around Nice. The opening piece, "At Pointe de Rompe Talon," is set on the coast near Beaulieu. Fabre suggests that the poem is a metaphor for peace, but it more specifically continues the exploration of how to present the "thing itself," in this case a woman sitting on a rock.[5] The persona tells us what she is not:

> not a hysterical uterine, not
> Leda peaceful after fucking
> the swan. (*Inside*, 7)

Moreover, "Sea form is not her counterpoint. Sea motion is not / her metaphor" (7). She is something beyond both poetry and music; the closest the speaker can come is painting:

> She gazes out
> to the tuna fishing silence of the early morning watercolor
> with its slushing and response. (7)

This piece demonstrates a pattern that runs through the collection. On one hand is the dissociation of geography from experience. While most of the poems designate specific places in their titles, they seldom have much to do with those locations. "Beaulieu," for example, describes in detail the way to eat a red mullet, while "Revelation at Cap Ferrat" attempts to locate the divine in mundane activities, rather than in the contemplation of place, as the title would suggest. On the other hand, over half of the poems refer to a painting, to an artist, or to the process of visual creation. Unlike some of the earlier poetry and fiction, there is relatively little creation of detailed images, either landscapes or portraits. "On Promenade des Anglais" suggests the figure of a woman, but instead of depicting her, the speaker offers options:

> How would you have her?
> In a metal dress
> With strapped legs, hugging her neck
>
> .   .   .   .   .   .   .   .   .   .   .
>
> or would you have her
> wear a left-arm full of bracelets
> that click as she walks.
> Perhaps on the floor
> with her arms locked around her
> neck, gazing suspiciously
> out of the corners of her
> unbearably bright eyes.
> Go on! Dance her in a Russian army
> suit or skip her high in velvet
> and wool while her hair flops
> about her shoulders. (*Inside*, 24)

Finally, the speaker gives up this effort and just assigns her possible names: Bardot, Lena Horne, Lauren Bacall, the Duchess of Alba, Barbrielle Chanel. The point is that the artist is free to do what he or she pleases with the subject. In the case of this poem, of course, he is free to ignore the subject of his title. Presumably the stimulus was something seen on the beachfront walk in Nice, but it could have occurred anywhere and have been any woman. As in earlier work, what is real is what the artist generates, not what the world presents to him or her.

"Over Drinks at Café du Charbonnage" constructs a brief episode situated in a café that Van Gogh painted early in his career. The speaker imagines meeting there with the artist as he does a variety of sketches. Three are specifically indicated: *Old Man with His Head in His Hands* (1882), *Winter Garden* (1884), and *Old Man in a Tail-Coat* (1882). The speaker asks questions that seek to get the artist to engage with his subjects and not merely draw them. An irony of the poem is that the speaker feels somewhat insecure in his own position:

> it's important that I
> hold my glass with as much
> skill as you hold your pencil.
> Otherwise they will notice. (28)

The narrator seems a version of the art critic, who raises issues about the art but lacks the talent to create himself. He worries that the patrons, mostly coal miners, will tell him to go do something useful.

Two other poems, which Major later combined, focus on Cézanne's house near Aix-en-Provence. The first is a tourist-artist view of the interior:

> Blue chair.
> We whisper.
> Blue chest. We whisper here.
> Dresser.
> Here's the green apple. (33)

The space is a shrine in which the simple act of naming confers sacred status on objects. But it is also important to note that the speaker comments on color and invites us to construct a composition through his detailing of the room. He concludes by mentioning Mont Sainte Victoire, the mountain Cézanne saw and drew from outside his house. Major italicizes the name of the mountain, which suggests that he is deliberately blending the actual view (which would not be italicized) with the artist's rendering of it (which would be italicized), as he once again posits the linkages between art and the world.

The second poem concerns what the speaker refers to as the artist's "frozen garden." The reference is to Carrière de Bibémus, a quarry that Cézanne painted obsessively at the end of his life. In fact, the pneumonia that killed him developed after he was caught in a rainstorm at the site.[6] The point is important because the poem is in fact about the relationship of art and death:

> I may die as you are dying.
> Will I choose, at the last moment,
> To see death in everything: in corn,
> In flowers, in birds and bats?

Your frozen garden is close
To the skyline that we call
Its edge: we do not plan
To eat its food: as disease,
It eats at you, and me
    and Vincent, too. (34)

Each artist, whether those of the late nineteenth century or the late twentieth, has obsessions that can both make possible the art and overwhelm the
artist. Major seeks here, as in "Over Drinks," to understand the deep necessity to create at all costs.

Two additional themes run through this collection, spirituality and identity. Given Major's long-standing critique of Christianity, it is not surprising that none of these pieces directly engage that faith. "Divine Law: A Blue
Beach Sermon" depicts a group of Muslim women from Algiers who "sit /
like white marble on top of their darkness" (9). To the speaker in the poem,
they are Other, though he claims to know something about them:

Women from Algiers stand
in intersecting triangles
trusting the light of creation
to follow—shining through their dresses
toward the world of Emanation.

Their devotion may be of value to them, but the speaker has his doubts:

The upper world
may open its gates. But will the light
shine down? (9)

They are silent, submissive, and patient, artifacts of a different world; they
remain for him objects he can compose into art but not subjects he can
meaningfully interrogate.

"In Absence of the Sefirotic Tree (or Divine Unity)" plays with the language of the Kabbalah in order to define a secular consciousness. The
Sefirotic Tree is a figure from Jewish mystical tradition that provides a
means of elucidating the emanations of the divine.[7] Although YHWH is
always one, He manifests himself in a variety of ways, which are structured
according to importance. Major immediately breaks with the discourse of
spirituality with his informal style:

> sure, there is a hierarchy
> of worlds: here, one place
> is above or below another. (18)

He then removes us from mystical territory, by making the hierarchy literal and mundane:

> Cap Roux is up the coast
> beyond, say, Beaulieu
> and below Eze. (18)

Even the art of the churches along the way provide no counter to his non-belief:

> angels with dog-
> faces float in chariots
> spinning through clouds
> on golden wheels. The divine
> world? Not likely: more
> likely: the carriages on
> their way to that place
> where earth meets the world
> of action. (18)

Religion cannot do anything for him: he cannot consult Ezekiel, Jacob's Ladder will not support him, and he has no skill at "spiritual cyclic systems." What engages him instead is the realm of sensation: speeding along the *autoroute* above the coast, smelling the tire rubber burn, or being rubbed with "erotic oils." He is a material being in a material world: "I am mineral, molecular. / Cells." The wisdom he seeks comes from Rimbaud and Baudelaire. The world of physical experience is his spiritual home:

> I am already in the highest place:
> Roll me in the sand at Monte Carlo,
> In my own hallucinations. (18)

He does not claim for himself a superior knowledge; his insights and visions are, after all, "hallucinations." But the implication is that all other forms of wisdom are equally fictive.

The third poem on this topic appears to work in the tradition of Wallace Stevens in "Sunday Morning," though Major offers no sense of the pull of "that old catastrophe." Rather, he seems to reveal the same delight in and devotion to the present moment and physical reality. In both, however, it is something behind or within that reality that is crucial. For Stevens, it is the fact of death that creates beauty. For Major it is something like *élan vital*:

> It's not solely the dance
> of the juggler but his spirit:
> with its turkey wings, perfect thighs,
> sensuous hips, large round flat eye.
> This eye smiles like lips.
> Watch this eye; it is not a donkey-eye. (12)

But this commitment is deceiving; the poem in fact explores the matter, not through reality, but through art, for the poem is a verbal rendering of Marc Chagall's *The Juggler*. The painting, which also contains elements associated with the Kabbalah, depicts a dancing figure with the body of a woman and the head of a bird. Major misdirects us by labeling the wings those of a turkey rather than an angel. Otherwise, a number of allusions extend the image. Major mentions a girl in a swing, a circus animal, a clock, the village square, and a violin, all of which are part of Chagall's work. The 1943 painting was acquired by the Art Institute of Chicago in 1952 and so would have been seen by Major.

The connection of the painting to the location—Cap Ferrat—is not immediately apparent. The cape, a small peninsula that extends into the Mediterranean not far from Nice, offers some privacy to the rich and famous who have villas there. Perhaps it was the joining of land, sea, and sky that produced the image of a creature tied to earth and air. Moreover, while Chagall's work has a dreamlike quality, it achieves that through the blending of disparate figures and objects, much like aspects of Major's writing, including the novel he was writing while in France. If the emphasis is to be on spirit, then the French-Russian artist may be the way to it.

> It's not even the village square
> with its musicians and happy faces
> that makes the difference: no,
> because if it were, weddings with
> violins, harps, flutes, would have
> settled the question; no, it is
> the rising and lifting, falling and

catching of the spirit before
it crashes, that matters. (12)

Werner Haftmann has said of *The Juggler* that the central figure is "woman, man, animal, demon, and angel, all at the same time, comprising all manifestations of humanity." If the previous poem signified on the emanations of the divine, then this one speaks, through its referent, to those of the creative individual, for as Haftmann adds, the figure is most specifically the artist: "The figure that appears as an animal-headed Egyptian deity is an interpretation of the artist, not of his ego but of the id which stands behind all individual expressions of creative art, the personified genius itself."[8] This aspect serves Major's purposes, as he links the spiritual to the erotic. Not only do we have the "perfect thighs, / sensuous hips," but also a reference to the nipple that is an eye. Moreover, the rising and falling of the poem's conclusion is the rhythm of sexuality. A more subtle allusion in the first stanza is the donkey's eye, one name for the seed of the mucuna pruriens, a tropical legume said to be an aphrodisiac. Thus, the poem brings together nature and art, the spiritual and the sensual, in a statement about what matters in life.

The last motif is the problem of identity that has shaped Major's art throughout his career. The titles of some of the poems demonstrate this concern: "Seine Split," "Losing Control at Nice," "Selected Moments in France—In Memory of My Illusions," and "Last Days in France." One that is not immediately obvious as part of this category is "Bouquet for Lovers." The title is ironic and even sarcastic, since the speaker repeatedly tells us what he does not like about lovers. His underlying complaint is that lovers fear their individuality:

lovers avoid night
clowns, pretend
it's not possible
to go one's own secure
way, or to find refuge
in a self-portrait. (*Inside*, 22)

They refuse to take chances or do anything out of the ordinary. Again, art becomes the standard by which judgments are made. In the third stanza, the speaker says

I am quietly finished
with lovers, with their

inability to make love
in the farmyard,
in the picture window,
where Monique sat,
with her hand-made hats. (23)

The allusion here is to Henri Matisse, who lived much of his life in the environs of Nice. One of his important early works was *Woman Sitting before the Window*, which was done in 1905. Major takes license with history, however, since Matisse did not meet Monique Bourgeois until the 1940s. The "mistake" is likely the result of, first, the sound of her name, and, second, the story of that relationship, which offers an alternative to the lovers of the poem. Bourgeois was a student nurse who agreed to care for the artist during his convalescence from surgery. At the time, she was in her twenties and he in his seventies. She became a model for four paintings. She shortly after became a Dominican nun, despite his protestations. They remained friends and later collaborated on the Chapel of the Rosary at Vence. By following their individual callings, they were able to create something that neither could have accomplished alone.[9]

It is somewhat surprising that the recently married Major would produce such a deprecating comment on lovers. Despite his longstanding use of personal material in his art, there are no poems in the collection that refer to Pam, either directly or indirectly. There are various calls for passion in the abstract but nothing that can be read as directly connected to their lives together, which seem to be happy. Instead, we get the opposite of love and contentment.

In fact, in several instances, he returns to versions of the divided self that has been prominent throughout his career. At the end of "Bouquet for Lovers," he states

There is an afterbirth
of shame on both sides
of their minds. (*Inside*, 23)

This notion becomes literal in "Seine Split," when he mentions the corpus callosum, that part of the brain that enables communication between the left and right hemispheres. He records, in essence, the failure of that connection, through a variety of images of splitting:

Remember, at that moment of waking, your
swimming body divided into irritated halves,

one
floated up,
The other, nude and under-nurtured,
scattered as it fell down
insane and guilty,
pretending to be the lower twin
with the welded-eyes of Gemini. (13)

The self not only divides but also partially disintegrates into madness. "Swimming" suggests the emergence from a dream state in which the speaker has returned to the womb and the "lost twin."

A key issue is the source of this disintegration; the answer seems in part to be the city itself:

Paris had a way: it came
together as *content* in one
of you (which one "I don't know")
and the merged, reflected image
of Castor and Pollux. (13)

If we can take art as the central concern of the collection, regardless of the specific motif at work, then it might be said that, for Major, the problem is finding a form for the content that is Paris. The need is to bring them together; that is, how does one make artistic sense of Paris? The inability to do so is nightmarish for him: "*If color were sound you'd hear / the bleak screaming of green*" (13, original emphasis). He insists that the problem exists at a fundamental, physical level:

When you tried to silence the conflict,
to yellow-and-blue it in dream
it burned an orange hole
in your corpus collosum.
The brackets beneath your vermis
broke. Silence itself
reached its maximum
in your central nervous system. (13)

The corpus callosum and the vermis make connections between the brain hemispheres, the first to allow communication between the intuitive and logical functions and the second to provide awareness of the body's internal performance. The references to Castor and Pollux indicate that the two parts of the self, while different, are mutually necessary. The part that experiences must be balanced by the part that provides structure. But for the speaker of the poem, who tries to distance himself from the problem by using second person, Paris, with its storied connections to history and art, is too much experience. Without form, the artist doubly drowns:

> The Seine flowing through Paris
> was a braille-spine: your two
> floating bodies, bloated, bobbed
> in its stormy vomit. (14)

The image, like that of "screaming green," is surreal and nightmarish. The verbal play of alliteration and internal rhyme, along with the shifting metaphors of "braille-spine" and vomit, add to the disruption of meaning. The poem concludes with the repeated word "Remember," which echoes the first word. But *what* is to be remembered? Is it the collapsing of artistic identity and the source of that dissolution? If so, who or what remembers? Memory here can serve as the means by which shape is given to the chaos described. The self is saved because it can give verbal form to the experience of formlessness.

Given the range of experiences and responses registered in the collection, the closing poem, "Last Days in France," is surprisingly sentimental. As in other pieces, Major relies on a series of images rather than a fully developed conceit. The verbal play is either flat or merely strange:

> My days are falling
> stars: with numbers
> on them. I smelled
> the Nice beach, freshly
> cut rabbits suspended
> up-side-down from hooks
> got my goat. Old Town
> bins of spongy tripe
> were the larva of Crispus
> Attucks brains. (36)

The days as numbered falling stars seems easy, and we are not told what the smell of the beach is. The reference to Crispus Attucks, while consistent with other surreal images in the book, seems to be merely random. The closing lines of the poem, "A sadness / clouded my coronas," seem clichéd. The final word appears to be an error, since "corneas" would be more logical. Nostalgia is not the author's long suit.

## MY AMPUTATIONS

The problem of providing form to a divided identity is given semicomic treatment in *My Amputations* (1986), Major's third novel to be published by the Fiction Collective. The novel originated in a bizarre event in 1971. A parolee from a prison hospital went to the offices of International Publishers, claiming to be the author of *The New Black Poetry* and demanding royalty checks. The secretary knew Major and so refused to hand over funds. The man was eventually subdued. He apparently believed that Major had stolen his identity (Bunge, *Conversations*, 48, 51). The story did not become possible as part of a fiction until 1982, when the author suddenly knew its form: "In the case of *My Amputations*, I remember the very day the book came to me. Pamela and I were walking up a hill to the Jewish cemetery in Nice, and I said, 'I'm going to write a book in blocks of prose. Just panels. Not paragraphs'" (89). In another interview, he referred to "long Faulknerian blocs of prose" (52). Joe Weixlmann has verified the structure, counting 112 blocks of from a hundred to two thousand words.[10] Much of the novel was written during Major's time in France and completed after his return to Boulder in 1983. While the initial writing went well, despite the fact that Major was uncertain about sequencing, it was another three years before the novel came out. One of the reasons for this was that it was rejected by six publishing houses, though it was consistently praised.[11] He obviously remained committed to the idea that experimental fiction was commercially viable and turned to the collective as a final resort.

The underlying structure is a quest-picaresque. Mason Ellis, who has the letters ME tattooed on his chest, lives in poverty in Chicago until he abandons his families and responsibilities to go to New York. He ends up in Attica Prison, where he reads the works of an author named Clarence McKay. He comes to believe that he is the actual author of the works and, when he is released, becomes obsessed with finding the man he calls The Imposter and reclaiming his literary identity. He eventually kidnaps McKay, robs a bank, and convinces the Magnan Rockford Foundation, which had given the author a perpetual grant, that he is the real McKay. In the meantime, he arranges for a tour of U.S. universities giving readings and having sex and eventually moves to Europe, where he engages in similar behavior. He is last seen in Africa, where he delivers an envelope containing the message "*Keep* this nigger," an act of signifying on Ralph Ellison's *Invisible Man*. The novel makes use of spy stories, slapstick comedy, pornography, academic fiction, satirical scenes, dream sequences, and slave narratives along the way. Mason Ellis seeks to find his identity by taking on that of someone else. In the process, he begins working on his own novel, a story of the desire to find an identity. At the same time, he worries that his true identity has in fact been uncovered and that his scam will be revealed. The narrator sometimes refers to him as a madman, and his paranoia seems to reinforce that view, though acts of violence in his presence and his repeated problems with the police in various countries would suggest that there is a basis for his fears.

Moreover, while Major has said that the work is not autobiographical, most of the details of Mason's life are variations or exaggerations of the author's own experiences. The character is born in Georgia, goes to Chicago to live with his mother, and tries to deal with a stepfather who owns a dry cleaning business. He seeks to become a writer; "he claims he swallowed the lake" (*Amputations*, 2). He joins the military, is sent out west and then to Valdosta, Georgia. In the military, he spends much of his time reading modern literature. After his discharge, he returns to Chicago, where he marries and has six children. He abandons them but takes up with another woman in the neighborhood by whom he has more children than he can count. This is a fairly straightforward parody of Major's own life, with his six children by two women, all of whom he eventually left. Even the uncountable progeny has a basis in the story he tells in "Licking Stamps" of responding to an old woman's query about his offspring by claiming that he "had about fifty-seven children in and out of wedlock" (194). Moreover, Mason's U.S. tour includes only the institutions where Major taught, his international lectures are given in the places where Major had spoken at that point, and his tourist activities occur in the places Major visited. The author goes so far as to give Mason one of his own literary agents, Howard Moorepark (with a minor spelling change).

The book thus takes on the qualities of a roman à clef, giving Major the opportunity to satirize or, perhaps, fantasize about his colleagues at various universities. Among his archived papers is a set of pages in which he lays out the list of characters for what apparently would have been an academic novel. In it, he matches the characters with real people, both family and colleagues, mostly from Sarah Lawrence and Brooklyn colleges. Internal evidence suggests that the document was created around 1973, indicating that this use of personal material had been incubating for several years.[12] By displacing the experiences in *My Amputations* onto the life of a possible madman, Major is free to comment any way he chooses on individuals. So the women in some instances can be promiscuous, the men can be pompous, and many of the faculty drunkards or drug users. He makes no effort to disguise the schools, thus inviting speculation about who the characters might be in real life.

The text also makes reference to many of the artists that had interested Major in his apprentice years: Verlaine, Genet, Wilde, Himes, and Cervantes, among others. Two citations early in the book suggest the theme of the work. The first is from Nietzsche: "'Aren't books written precisely to hide what is in us?" The second, naturally more diffuse, comes from Jack Kerouac: "'I'll . . . get to believe . . . I'm not . . . Jack . . . at all and that my birth records . . . published books, are not real . . . that my own dreams . . . are not dreams . . . that I am not "I am" but just a spy in somebody's body pretending . . .'" (*Amputations*, 42; ellipses in original). With a protagonist who needs to literally brand himself ME, it is not hard to see this as a text in which the ability to affirm the self is the central issue, especially when he seeks to impersonate a writer with the initials C.M. So the question comes down to, in the folk expression that led to the Aretha Franklin song, "Who's Zoomin' Who?" We have layer upon layer of Nietzschean "hiding" and page after page of dreams that may or may not be dreams. Mason Ellis, after all, claims his identity by taking on someone else's and then spends the novel obsessing over whether his disguise is a disguise at all or part of an elaborate ruse about which he has no knowledge. Moreover, the person from whom he has stolen his identity is himself borrowing his name from another writer, Claude McKay. Of course, this device serves to allow Clarence Major to both reveal and conceal himself in a text he claims is not about himself, even though all the textual "facts" point to him. So who is the spy and who the spied-upon?

One way to think about the issue is to consider the role of race in the text. While the topic is one Major generally resists, it is in many ways most manifest in this novel. By the time he is writing this book, the notion of the criminal, irresponsible black man had become commonplace in public discourse. The Moynihan Report of 1965, a study of black poverty written by Assistant Secretary of Labor (later Senator) Daniel Patrick Moynihan, had defined the black family as matriarchal and thus dysfunctional; it became the conventional wisdom of sociology and political debate that black men were irrelevant to modern society. The image of the Bad Nigger became a form of self-representation in the Black Power and Black Arts movements. The Welfare Queen, a stereotype of black women that emerged in the public assistance debates of the Reagan era, when Major was writing the novel, is the flip side of the construction of black masculinity as violent and detached from institutions and relationships.

Despite the postmodern aspects of the book, which are similar to those in earlier works, Major is careful to create his protagonist within the social reality of U.S. racial practices and African American culture. Joe Weixl-mann has called this the "blackest" of Major's postmodern works.[13] This aspect of the text is apparent from the beginning: "Did his mother Melba love him? She was certainly not his muse. Look at her apron: too clean: something is wrong. Is it that she doesn't like him much but loves . . . ? Her eyes: unfriendly—yet she's a person of responsibility as big as the Atlantic. Small, tight mouth—Anglosaxon. her skin was lighter than his. He was—in color—between her and his father Chiro: nutmeg. Her Irish-African eyes? His were more in the tradition of Chiro's" (*Amputations*, 2). While some aspects of the description fit Inez and Clarence Major Sr., what is important here is the emphasis on color and race/ethnicity. The linking of identity with these categories has not been readily apparent in previous narratives. It is noteworthy that the distinction between "like" and "love" in the mother's relationship to her child is found in another African American text, Toni Morrison's *Sula* (1973). Here, unlike Morrison's story, that distinction seems at least partially to be based on the child's racial similarity to the darker father. Shortly after, Mason's initial efforts at fiction are associated with narratives about "yella" girls; he notes that he could "hear" such stories, not just because of the writers—Faulkner, Stein, Toomer—but because "his mother was one too" (6).

Race reenters when Mason is stationed in Valdosta. First, he wonders why the military insists on putting black men from the North in small southern communities, a comment similar to Major's own description of his experience ("Licking Stamps," 179). He then tells the story of a group of black airmen going to a barbecue in the black part of town. The first thing they encounter is a black man crying over his daughter, who has been gang-raped by city policemen and dumped on the street. They then arrive at the festivities, which are presented in detail, including the food, the music, the smells, the tastes, the color. He mentions specific songs and performers, and ties them all to Toomer's rendering of Georgia culture. He concludes the episode with the intrusion of the police as the airmen are running to catch the bus. While the narrator foregrounds fictionality by questioning the realism of the scene, it is in fact precise and realistic: "Now folks, you know brown or black folk running *had* to be guilty. They'd forgotten— in their haste: with only five minutes. ('I know I'm guilty but what is my crime?') The cops, with their huge pistols already drawn, got out. 'Against the wall, niggers.' The heroes obeyed. Were these the rapists? With hands against cold glass, legs spread, Mason felt his balls swing inside his Jockey shorts" (10). Nothing in this scene suggests anything other than the harsh reality of the midcentury American South. Its surrealism (the police, we know, were the actual rapists) has more to do with racism than with dream psychology or aesthetic theories. It is a scene that could come out of Richard Wright with little modification.

An additional element is the incorporation of aspects of African American folk culture. From the first page, we find references to blues performers and blues songs. While in some instances, such as the barbecue scene, it is an expected part of the setting, elsewhere it serves the same function as literary allusion; that is, it reveals an aspect of character or situation. As an example, when the officers stop the airmen, the radio in the police car is playing "Au Leu Cha," a Charlie Parker bebop classic. This information, which the narrator refers to as "profound irony" (10), not only works in terms of the African American source of the music but also because the very name of the genre comes from "bop," which was the sound of a policeman's nightstick on the head of a black person.[14]

At other times, the narrator launches into a speech performance putting on display black vernacular speech:

> And here is Mason's father as Red Charleston with a history of backdooring, listening to Duke Ellington in Kansas City directing his band through "Chocolate Shake." Cats outside in the alley gambling. . . . Many of the lames in the turnout are talking trash; trotters angling for attention. Duke keeps on keeping on. Up there—big smile. It's Saturday night: somebody feels mellow, somebody else feels deadly. Frankie and Johnnie meet C.C. Rider. Coppers are pulling coats, police swinging billysticks. Some up on china white, others down on sneaky pete. (*Amputations*, 18)

In fact, such performances run throughout the text, making use of various discourses, much like Ellison's *Invisible Man* or the novels of Leon Forrest, which were contemporaneous with Major's work. These performances include not only Mason's riffs on academic lectures and selections from his work-in-progress but also monologues by other characters, such as the Nigerian woman in Nice who gives him a "body reading" that blends psychobabble with folklore: "She grinned. And grabbed his cock again. She shook it as she spoke. 'This majestic thing is a crab apple one day, a black locust another, a Hercules Club. It has bark. And history. It has fast-moving guys behind it. Nicodemus from Detroit might know more about it than I. Yet, there are times, in the Blues, when the slaveholder gets the better of good old John or Moe or Moses'" (95). A key question is why Major would build into his text such a significant level of African American material. While it appeared in some way in all the earlier novels, here it is much more a part of the design. Stuart Klawans has suggested that it might have emerged from the immersion in postimpressionist art, and especially the connection of Cézanne to cubism. The movement, drawing on African practices, was intended as a shock to European aesthetics and, Klawans argues, that shock depended on offending the Western sense of racial superiority. Picasso and others needed racism to produce their effects: "The very term for tribal art adopted by artists and critics before the First World War—*art negre*—tells us something about the nature of the insult to Europeans."[15] The phrase was often rendered as "Negro art," but in fact it was more accurately "Nigger art." Klawans speculates on the response of someone who was such a careful student of this art:

> How would a young African American have felt when he realized that the most adventurous, most revolutionary art movement of his time derived part of its appeal from calling him a "nigger"? How would he have felt when he learned that the century's most exciting art had borrowed something from African sculpture, but nobody could say what? Was there room for the likes of Clarence Major in Cubism? If so, would he be the unrecognized hero of this artistic movement, or its buffoon—the "I" [narrator], or the "ME"?[16]

Klawans goes on to argue that *My Amputations* is a cubist fiction with its blocks of prose and multiple versions of the self, as well as its use of elements of collage.

This perspective would suggest that the presence of African American materials is an act of signifying on cubism and perhaps the whole Western artistic tradition by making overt the "nigger" materials that had been relegated to secondary status and manipulated for the purposes of aesthetic politics. The problem with this view is that Major had in fact been using this "block" approach to storytelling from the beginning, whether or not there was a noticeable African American content. Moreover, this new novel is the one most like traditional fiction in the sense that it follows a linear pattern to a much greater extent than the earlier works. While it does include dream sequences and hallucinatory episodes, even these tend to occur in chronological order. Material that belongs to earlier time periods tends to be presented as conventional flashbacks rather than the disruptions of time found in *Emergency Exit*. In addition, the offense to Major's sensibilities that Klawans argues for logically would have occurred much earlier than this novel, since by the time of composition, he would have been studying and practicing painting for thirty years.

I want to propose a different source for the "blackness" of this text. It has to do with an incident that Klinkowitz describes in *Keeping Literary Company*. One evening the Fiction Collective group had gathered for food and drink at a restaurant near Washington Square. He is not specific about the date, but it would have been in the mid-1970s. Raymond Federman told a story about playing saxophone with Charlie Parker and later sitting in with John Barth, his colleague at Buffalo. Various members of the group then told their own stories of playing musical instruments. When it was Major's turn, he had nothing to say.

And so Ron Sukenick began to prompt him.

"Come on, Clarence," Ron chided, "what did you play? You must have played something!"

Clarence had already shaken his head to indicate *no*, but now, under pressure, became visibly angry. "I didn't play anything," he said, quietly but firmly, and then withdrew from the conversation. For the next hour, he kept to himself, but afterwards, as he drove me back to my hotel . . . he revealed what had been on his mind.

"I really didn't like Ron's comment," he said, and when I asked him why replied that he thought it was "racially motivated." In all the years I'd known Clarence, this was the first time the subject had come up; but even as I tried to argue against Ron's intention, I could feel Clarence stiffening further. Then I realized that he'd been the only black person there. That was almost always the case; but then again, all the subjects discussed in this crowd were white, or at least nonracial. Jazz had racial overtones, tones Ron Sukenick had elected to stress. And for that Clarence could not forgive him.[17]

Klinkowitz goes on to observe that the episode revealed to him that Major's fictional practice incorporated race without ever being about it.[18] But a somewhat different conclusion can also be drawn: that race is the repressed subject of the early novels that is finally expressed in *My Amputations*. Major's ties to the Fiction Collective were an effort, in part, to evade race as a defining factor in his art and his status as an artist. One could be the only black member of the group if nobody ever mentioned that fact. Regardless of Sukenick's intentions, the insistence that Major "must have" performed jazz calls him back to his difference.

The novel then can be read as a postmodern response to the condition of difference. Nobody can tell Mason Ellis and Clarence McKay apart. Mason's claim of uncountable children is not challenged by the narrator because everyone "knows" that black men are promiscuous and irresponsible. His anxieties about being discovered have no basis, not because of luck or talent, but because no one cares. No matter what he does or writes or becomes, he will still be labeled on the basis of race. He can even brand himself "me," but that physical sign cannot override the social one of "Black Man." In the final scene of the book, as already mentioned, he delivers the message that signifies on Ellison: "*Keep* this nigger!" (*Amputations*, 204), but Major has changed the message by shortening the command and adding italics. The Invisible Man was to be kept running, and the message is delivered early in that novel to announce a key theme. Mason is to be *kept*, to be fixed by his African ancestry. The mad pursuit of self ends in the prison house of race. It tells us something about Major's views on the subject that this novel is linear; what such a text can do is create a sense of inevitability. All the experiences, the shape shifting, the performances, the recognition, the money, the notoriety lead only to this dead end. Similarly, no matter his achievements within the avant-garde, Major will always be expected to do a "black thing," such as playing jazz. It should not be surprising that this is his last publication with the Fiction Collective and his last effort at truly experimental writing. Though he will claim that his later work is a continuation of his postmodern approach, in fact it becomes more realistic and more specifically racial in its approach.

*My Amputations* received far more mainstream reviews than any of his previous works, and these were consistently positive. In addition to the standard notices in *Book List*, *Kirkus Review*, *Publishers Weekly*, and *Library Journal*, there were comments in a number of newspapers as well as *American Book Review*, *Review of Contemporary Fiction*, and *Callaloo*. One of the reasons for its critical success appears to be the fact that it is on recognizable racial territory. It is "about" the black writer, even if the story of that subject is done in a highly experimental way. In fact, part of its virtue can be seen as its move beyond what readers had come to expect of African American fiction. The complex of references and the uses of black cultural materials reassure reviewers. Also, it seems to be a work more easily placed in categories, even if it crosses generic lines. It can be talked about as satire, picaresque, bildungsroman; it can be compared to the work of Ralph Ellison or Thomas Pynchon. Unlike the earlier fictions, which tended to be seen as sui generis, this one "belongs" somewhere, even if the fit is not perfect. Consistent with the positive evaluations, *My Amputations* earned the 1986 Western States Book Award, sponsored by the Western States Arts Federation. The award, granted since 1984, is given in poetry, creative nonfiction, and fiction. It recognizes authors and publishers primarily located in the west. The fact that much of the work of the collective now took place in Boulder thus aided Major's nomination.

PAINTING FROM FRANCE

Some of the painting that comes out of the time in Nice reflects, as did some of the poems, an interest in spirituality. His travels produced a desire to try his hand at traditional images, but naturally with his own postmodern perspective. He does a series of works that depicts nuns, saints, or madonnas. These include *Mother and Child* (1983), which has a silver-gray background done very roughly, without facial features for the figures, and without limbs for the mother. The child, in contrast, is depicted as a miniature adult, standing on the mother's lap. The work seems modeled on medieval representations, with the traditional colors associated with each figure: blue for the Madonna and red for the Christ child. But her blue is a shade virtually never seen in Western religious art, and the bottom of the child's attire is black. As an additional act of signifying, the child appears to point toward the mother rather than the reverse. The mother's facial features appear to be covered by a fold of cloth close to the color of her skin. If so, this would suggest a lack of spiritual vision on the part of the Madonna.

Two works from the same year are both titled *Sister*. They are identical in many ways: shoulder portrait, starched white wimple, deep-cut neckline with cleavage apparent, clasped hands at the bodice, head tilted, and the background a muddied blend of neutral colors. What is striking, however, are the differences. In one the skin is an intense pink, and the features are very simple lines and circles. In the other, the skin tone is mixed red and brown, but most important, the head is inverted. The eyes are outlined in blue, with white centers, and only one has an iris. A blue line extends down to the nose, which otherwise is an inverted L shape. The mouth, disproportionately large, is open with a row of teeth visible. The differences in skin color imply racial differences, with the implication that light-skinned women are passive and silent, while women of color, even in traditional roles, are more expressive. But the inversion of the head (or the body) in Major's painting consistently signals a problem of identity. This work, then, suggests a double consciousness in the tension between devotion to Western values of the Roman Catholic Church specifically and Christianity more generally and one's ethnic heritage. Whether this "sister" is African in ancestry or simply part of another non–Western European group, her sense of self is problematic.

A final painting in this tradition, *Blue Love*, is a version of the Adoration. In it, a shepherd kneels before the Madonna. The elements of the work are outlined in ink, and the figures are rather crude. The face of the shepherd is inverted, but otherwise these two figures are stylized. While the straw color of the floor indicates a setting in the stable, what is striking is the absence of the Christ child. The love of the title seems directed at the woman; moreover the lines make her face the focal point. Thus, Major plays with the Catholic tendency toward Mariolatry. But a further disruption of convention is caused by the third figure, a rambunctious cherub that has the musculature of a Michelangelo angel. He appears to be leaping off the head of the shepherd. Moreover, he has the wings of a monarch butterfly and the only color associated with him is the red and blue of his genital area. He becomes the center of attention both by his position in the upper center of the canvas and by his disruption of the composition. He is the artist's impish response to the seriousness of religious iconography and belief. Despite his interest in the art as art, Major makes it clear that he has no use for Christianity.

# CHAPTER EIGHT

# Back to America, Back to Europe

Major notes that their return to the United States in the spring of 1983 was especially difficult for Pam, but he clearly had some ambivalence about returning to Boulder ("Licking Stamps," 197). This is evident in their almost perpetual movement over the next two years. Soon after he returned to Colorado, he began making arrangements to take a visiting position at the University of California at San Diego for the following spring. That appointment was arranged by Sherley Anne Williams and Jerry Rothenberg. At the end of the 1982–83 academic year, he had received a sabbatical leave from Colorado that enabled him to go from San Diego in 1984 almost directly to Venice. It was this constant movement, rather than editorial or financial considerations, that led to the delay by the Fiction Collective in publishing *My Amputations*, which was released 12 March 1986. After its completion, he immediately began work on the manuscript for *Painted Turtle*, the story of one of the minor characters he had introduced in *My Amputations*.

Before going to California, however, he made a sojourn to Georgia; he had been invited to be a short-term writer-in-residence at Albany State University in January 1984. This job enabled him to visit relatives in Atlanta, which provided the basis for *Such Was the Season*. He conducted workshops, did readings, and visited local music clubs while in Albany and Atlanta.

Within a short time after his return to Boulder from Georgia, he and Pam began the drive to San Diego. On the way, they visited Mesa Verde, site of the Anazazi cliff dwellings. They then drove to Gallup, New Mexico, and then to the Zuni reservation, which is key to the setting of *Painted Turtle*. They moved on to San Diego, and a week later celebrated Pam's birthday by going to Tijuana. They had difficulty finding a place to stay. The experience was so unpleasant that they did not cross the border again until accompanied by a colleague with significant experience.

The trip to Venice began late in August 1984 with a flight to Rome, where they stayed at the Hotel Sitea. Two days later, they moved on to Venice. They were met at the airport by the friend of a scholar who was doing an Italian translation of *Reflex and Bone Structure*, a work that was never published. Their apartment at Fondamenta Tolentini 170 was not yet ready, so they spent a few nights at the two-star Hotel Tivoli nearby. The time in Venice was spent very quietly and involved a daily routine of food shopping, walking around the city, and occasional trips to the countryside with William and Franca Boelhower; William was a U.S. scholar who taught primarily at universities in Venice and Padua. There were no lecture tours or tourist trips to major European sites for the first six months. Instead, Major prepared *My Amputations* for publication (Fannie Howe was his editor), worked on the manuscript of what became *Painted Turtle*, produced a set of poems related to the material of that novel, developed ideas for a novel about Venice, wrote a long poem about the city that was later published as *Surfaces and Masks*, and did a large number of pen-and-ink drawings and watercolors. It was one of the most productive periods of his career. Even the leisure time was used creatively. He describes their morning practice of getting coffee in the Campo Santa Margherita: "Across the *campo* was a building which became one of the main settings for my Venice novel. Many of the people we saw daily became models for its minor characters. When I needed a face to go on a character, I often found one in the newspaper. I'd cut it out and pin it to the sheet with the character's history" ("Licking Stamps," 199). This passage not only suggests the integration of everyday life into his artistic work but also the orderliness that he had introduced into his creative process. The young writer who put things down with minimal revision or who employed rolls of paper à la Kerouac has now become the calm craftsman methodically going about his business.

It was only in April 1985 that he felt the need to hit the road again. The justification for the trip was research that Pamela wanted to do for a novel she was writing set in medieval Italy.[1] They rented a car and drove to Monte Cassino and then farther south to Salerno, and, from that base to Paestum,

Amalfi, and Ravello. At each stop, Major would do watercolors, keeping, he has suggested, a visual "diary" of the trip ("Licking Stamps," 200). After visiting museums in Naples, they drove east to Melfi, Venosa, Canosa di Puglia, and Trani, then north to Monte Sant'Angelo and Urbino, where they visited the childhood home of Raphael. Soon after this trip, he was asked to go to the University of Algiers to serve on a doctoral committee; he was there for a very brief time and was not impressed with the people or the country ("Licking Stamps," 200). By the time of his return, he was ready to leave Venice, which they arranged to do quickly.

He and Pamela moved to Paris in June, having exchanged apartments with a Parisian couple. Their residence was near Pére Lachaise Cemetery, but in the Eleventh Arrondissement, far from the main tourist areas. They were socially active, meeting with previous acquaintances from the earlier visit to the city and from their time in Nice. The Boelhowers and Muriel Lacotte also came to visit. Time was also spent visiting artistic sites. They went to Auvers-sur-Oise to see the site of Van Gogh's death and the graves of Vincent and Theo. Back in the city, Major visited the Montmartre apartment of Theo. More conventionally, they went to the museums, with multiple trips to the Jeu de Paume to view the Impressionist and Postimpressionist collection. In these activities, we see the contradiction that Major embodies: the conventional overlaid with the consciously unconventional.

In early July, they traveled to Warsaw. Major had been given an International Research Exchange Board grant to go to Lublin at the invitation of Jerzy Kutnik, a critic who had written on Sukenick and Federman, and who later participated with Larry McCaffery in a frequently published interview with Major. He was introduced to several Polish academics, including the editors of *Literatura na Swiecie*, who had published two of his poems, and Zbigniew Lewicki, who published translations of contemporary U.S. fiction. Even here, we see examples of Major's network. One of the journal editors, Anna Kolyszko, later visited Boulder, and Lewicki had taught at SUNY Buffalo, where Federman was on the faculty.

The time in Lublin, which lies in southeastern Poland, was spent with faculty from the university, but Major did not give readings or lectures. They toured the university and visited the museums, the cathedral, the castle, and the old city area. One of the things Pamela and then Clarence noted was the attention he attracted from people on the street. Though there were a few African students in the area, the presence of darker-skinned people was both exotic and, Pam believed, threatening for local residents ("Licking Stamps," 201). The issue became more serious when they were leaving the country. Pam went through the passport check without difficulty and boarded the plane. Major, however, was detained and sent to a waiting area with two dark-skinned Arabs. Officials claimed that the passports were improperly stamped. Pamela returned and demanded an explanation. Major commented, "Isn't it obvious?" The official explanation was clearly one the Americans found unacceptable. As a kind of bureaucratic revenge, the three men were then required to go through the complete boarding procedure again and finally allowed to board. Given Major's sensitivity to any form of racial distinction, the event must have been infuriating ("Licking Stamps," 201–2).

They left Paris on 11 August 1985 to return to Boulder. The coming months included a series of recognitions. In November, he was notified that *My Amputations* had won the Western States Book Award. In January, the First National Bank Gallery in Boulder hosted a one-person show of the watercolors he had produced while in Italy. In 1986, he was awarded a grant from the university to support publication of *My Amputations.* Around the same time, he became fiction editor of *High Plains Literary Review*, which was based in Denver. In May 1986, he and Pam went to the Western States Awards ceremony, which was held in New Orleans at the home of Congresswoman Lindy Boggs. Because it was held in conjunction with the American Booksellers Association conference, Major was expected to participate in a number of events. Nonetheless, he and Pam also managed to visit many of the tourist spots in the city.

## THE ART OF VENICE

The visual art that came out of the time in Venice, and Italy more generally, was initially in the form of pen-and-ink drawings and watercolors; he later redid a number of these as acrylic paintings. They were almost entirely landscapes, a new genre for Major. He created two views from the Hotel Riato in Vietri, on the Amalfi Coast. One is a large perspective that looks down onto the town and also across the bay to Salerno. The second turns away from the water and, unlike the first, places figures at the center. The view is more limited, reaching only to the bay, and the two figures appear to be looking away from it. In both cases, the colors are pastel, with a contrast of dark green for foliage. The acrylic version of the second image, produced ten years later, uses stronger colors, with the bay, for example, replaced with a pink sky. Interestingly, while he is very coy about Ravenna in his autobiographical statement—"I have no memory of what we did there. I could ask,

FIGURE 20. *Communist Party Headquarters, Venice* (1985)

couldn't I? I have chosen not to. So that's that" ("Licking Stamps," 200)—it was a productive artistic resource for him. He created a pen-and-ink drawing of a large view of the city, which later became a colorful acrylic, as well as a pen-and-ink rendering of the old city, which would be useful for Pamela's fictional project.

The pen-and-ink drawings of Venice mark a departure from Major's earlier work in that they attempt to record with some precision external reality. The Giardini Papadopoli, the Basegio restaurant at one of the bridges, and the Communist Party headquarters are all very precise representations of locations in the city. Each offers a clear focal point, though not necessarily one directly connected to the title of the drawing. Thus, *Communist Party Headquarters, Venice* (1985) has as its center a hay wagon, with the office itself cut off by the frame. In this sense, Major still refuses a full commitment to representational art.

## SURFACES AND MASKS

*Surfaces and Masks*, like the visual art, was intended as a version of a journal of Major's experience in Venice. It is, in fact, in many ways more detailed about that experience than the actual journal he kept, which blends commentaries with sketches in such a way that the text often becomes illegible. Moreover, the journal seldom offers details about the city, its art, or sojourns to other sites.

In contrast, the "long poem" that constitutes the book provides observations on history, literary renderings of the city, artwork, everyday life, residents, and the general ambiance of the city. The book is broken into forty-four cantos of varying lengths. One source for several of them is the commentary on the city by earlier literary visitors. The opening canto, for example, begins by engaging Mark Twain's *Innocents Abroad,* which famously undertakes to demystify Venice. Major takes note of that author's linkage of "unlovely" Byzantine art and the presence of a cultivated black man originally from South Carolina. It is, for Twain, in Major's reading, a place whose difference and cultural richness is associated with disease. Likewise, Thomas Mann is taken to task for disliking closed windows and apparently undernourished people. The speaker not only disagrees with these provincial views but condemns the writers of such views:

> Left to rifle the situation
> I'd hang them all in San Marco
> like the French conspirators
> > were hanged
> after the plot of 1618
> > was uncovered . . .
> Then console myself with the music
> > of Schubert and Miles. (*Surfaces,* 4)

Lumping writers with those alleged to have plotted the overthrow of the city-state suggests an underlying anger at Westerners who cannot tolerate the very thing that for the speaker is the city's virtue: its cosmopolitanism and diversity. In response to their complaints, he offers a portrait:

> Her face was framed by
> > a halo of thick dark hair
> she was no doubt a contessa (they
> > all are!)
> > and you could see the distant signs
> of the Orient around her African eyes,
> > the Middle East
> in the slope of her nose.

She was the summation of the human race?
    Her seriousness was Greek.
There was no way to point
       a reckless finger
at any part of her. (5)

She is then linked to the dama Veneziana of the early eighteenth century, thus making the cultural and racial hybridity of the city essential to its identity. In fact, as Linda Selzer has argued, this essence is at the heart of the criticisms of literary visitors and at the core of Major's embrace of the city.[2] His attack extends to Disraeli, Dickens, Shelley, Henry James, and Browning.

In place of these dismissive attitudes, Major describes visits to cultural and artistic sites that display the range of Venice's history, and he depicts everyday life in a way that undermines notions of a decaying and dying city. We also see, early in the poem, how the concept of "surfaces and masks" can enhance the poet's own experience. In canto 3, he and Pamela enact some of the classic roles associated with the city:

She takes him into "The Rape
         of Europe"—
He takes her by surprise
       by playing the Avocadore
         di Comun.
She delights him as Puttana
    then again as Odalisca.
He scares her as Nobilgiovine
        Veneziano
and again as Cuoco
       of the Hotel Saturnia.
He scares her nearly out
    of her senses
when he does his Compagno
        della Buona Morte
       act.
He is her cavalier-servant.
    He helps her lace
her underclothes,
     to take off her tight
        corset. (*Surfaces*, 7)

The emblems of death and corruption become the source of erotic play, a form of personal theater. Many of the parts are associated with Carnevale and specifically with prostitution and death. He celebrates precisely what other visitors have condemned.

The representation of art here is different from that of *Inside Diameter*. In that earlier work, Major entered imaginatively into the life and work of individual artists, such as Van Gogh and Cézanne. In *Surfaces and Masks*, he is more focused on the tradition, especially of religious expression. He counters Twain's disdain for the Byzantine by visiting the Istituto Ellenica with its image of the Hodigitria, the Virgin Mary as first depicted in Constantinople. In this setting, the "you" of the poem becomes the Christ Child:

> As though you really were her child,
>     she makes you
>             look
> toward the camera, tickles your belly,
> tries to make you smile
>             but too many centuries
> of suffering the sins
>         of Judeo-Christian heartbeat
> have turned your little head
>             and its quite odd face
> to metal quickly painted brown. (40)

The hardness of the image is not from the formality of the Byzantine artists but rather from what Western religious dogma and practice have done to the mother and child. The two have been victimized by claims of moral and cultural superiority put forth by the writers and intellectuals of the modern age.

He also takes interest in ordinary life in the city and its environs. They cross one day to Vignole to eat at the trattoria. What he finds just across from the city is "A wonderful wilderness!" (47). What emerges is a painting in words:

>     —While waiting for ribs
> on grill, we kick our way
> Down to the shore where
>         fishing boats are moored
> in stillness and a fat old woman

in a red bathing suit
            and a little fat girl
in one blue with white flowers
            hold their hands
                        over their eyes
            shielding them from the sun
to see better
                        these strangers—here
            where strangers are rare . . .

The shirtless men with their big red
            bellies, sun themselves
            after lunch—
                        smoking and drinking coffee (*Surfaces*, 47–48)

We have entered a world of simple people indulging in simple pleasures, a world that the poet-painter seeks to capture for itself and not for any judgments to be made about it.

Even the most conventional tourist activity can become an almost sacred moment. In cantos 22 to 24, he takes a tour on the canals. From a gondola, he sees

Green ducks fly up
                        against the light,
electric as shock,
                        from some invisible crevice,
and they are caught
                        in midair
by my own wonderment. (49)

The rows of houses along the canals are

a reality uncelebrated
except
in bad photographs
by determined tourists.

Nonetheless, there is the possibility of epiphany:

That's how important
                        the long dark point

of this simplicity is.
   Is there progress?
Do you mean, uh, toward recognition?
       Yes, eyes about to open up to
the occasion, and it is
       bending with the wind,
where everything suddenly
          might be seen,
as it breaks with a snap,
         and the joy of it,
transformed as understanding
      stays on clearly
centered and smelling
       like say
from a young branch. (50–51)

Finally, canto 24 echoes William Carlos Williams:

Nothing else
matters more
than the light, sparked as that light
from rowing,
and that light from blades,
and I could go on. (52)

The old city mingles with regenerative nature, as do land and water, and light and darkness, as well as external reality and the artist's eye and mind. In such moments, Major functions as both verbal and visual artist. He moves away from the self-referential expression of his earlier work to something like a Romantic sensibility that finds significance in the mundane. While he still draws some attention to himself ("I could go on"), it is a self integrated into the reality it depicts and not ironically distanced from it.

## ZUNI WRITINGS

The third project to come out of Venice was the novel *Painted Turtle*, the first work of fiction to be clearly distinct from Major's personal experience. He conducted three years of research on Zuni history and culture in preparation for the writing. It had its origins in a completely different work, a novel based on the life of African American actress and singer Dorothy Dandridge. The completed work was consistently rejected by publishers. What emerged was a decision to take a different approach to creating the story of a woman artist, one that would have more distance from its subject. While living in Boulder, he had become interested in Native American cultures; in particular, he was intrigued by the role of Estavanico, an African slave who traveled with the Spanish explorer Cabeza de Vaca to the Southwest. He was killed by the Zuni but entered their mythology. Major's original plan had been to make him a central figure in the narrative, but as he revised the text, he kept reducing Estavanico's role until it disappeared altogether (Bunge, *Conversations*, 69, 78–79). He then undertook to tell the story from Painted Turtle's point of view but was unable to get it right. What worked instead was the creation of a male observer, a fellow Native American and artist, who becomes her lover.

It is useful to keep in mind the subtitle, *Woman with Guitar*, an allusion to important cubist works by Braque and Picasso, though the image is much older. The reference would suggest that Major returns here to the fractured narrative of his earlier fiction, but that is not the case. Although the short book (157 pages) is broken into forty-eight chapters (plus prologue and epilogue), the narrative follows the chronological order of Painted Turtle's life, with occasional flashbacks that are easily identifiable as such. The "experimental" quality of the text is in its effort to render a protagonist far removed culturally from the world of the author and his audience and not in its storytelling technique. To create this narrative, however, Major does introduce a distinct element: he incorporates short poems or songs that are the art of the protagonist and, he has said, consistent with the cultural expression of the Zuni (Bunge, *Conversations*, 69).

The narrative is straightforward; in the prologue, the narrator, a Navajo-Hopi musician, has been sent by his agent to try to convince the folk-singer Painted Turtle, another of his clients, to switch from acoustic to electric guitar. From this point, the story moves back to her childhood in a traditional Zuni community; as it moves forward, the narrator virtually disappears and the narration becomes third-person. In chapter 36, the narrator is reintroduced and this time named: Baldwin Saiyataca. We gradually learn of his background, including his alienation as one considered a "halfbreed" by the Hopi, because of his Navajo father. He identifies with Painted Turtle, and they become lovers because of their shared isolation from community and tradition.

Her story is one of violence, rejection, and perhaps madness. She is raped by a young neighbor and gives birth to twins. During the birth, she refuses to accept the traditional Zuni posture for delivery; she insists on modern methods. This section of the narrative moves in and out of dream states, as she experiences pain and the humiliation of being forced to her knees for the delivery. The ritual also normally included the participation of the father's mother, but since the children were the result of rape, that part of the tradition was also broken. Nonetheless, Painted Turtle is expected to be a good mother to her sons. Instead, she attempts to drown the boys. She fails to do so and as a result is sent to a mental hospital. When she returns, she is no longer trusted by the community, and her sons do not undergo initiation rituals. She seeks work away from the reservation and for a short period becomes a prostitute. Whenever she returns, she is told that she is not a good Zuni and must return to the community on their terms. Each time she leaves again and returns to singing traditional songs about the world from which she has been excluded.

One theme running through the text, as in many of Major's works, is the shaping of art. Here this is done in multiple ways. One is through the experiences of Painted Turtle that she shapes into song. In some cases, this happens even before she has become a singer. When she is still a small child, she goes with her mother to gather clay for pottery making. This narrative event is followed by a verse:

> Soaked in water
> then ground between rocks
> The hand-shaped surface
> made into a spiral
> Mudfrog handles, one
> on each side; dung-covered
> Fired in hive-shaped oven
> Olla carried to the goat-
> owner for milk. (*Painted*, 10)

After she is raped near Corn Mountain, she returns home but does not tell anyone of her experience. Instead, she goes out to hide in a derelict car and creates a song:

> When I was a little girl
> I ran around Corn Mountain

early morning at sunrise
When I was just a little girl
I ran around Corn Mountain
My hornbells woke Tarantula
When I was a little girl
Tarantula caught me
he split me open
When I was just a little girl
Tarantula took my moccasins
He tried to wear my leggins (31)

The poem takes a Zuni legend and modifies it to fit the circumstances of Painted Turtle. In the legend, Tarantula tricks a young man into giving up his sacred costume; the people, nature, and the gods work together to restore order and punish the trickster. In the song, the girl is "split open" and must face the situation alone. As is often the case in Major's work, the materials of cultural tradition, whether themes or artistic conventions, are adapted to the reality of the individual.

At other times, the songs express private feeling, with no cultural reference:

Reality is losing touch
with the pain
caused by the nail
driven into the crutch
you use to prop up your soul. (40)

Such a verse is little different from the work Major presented in his early collections of poetry. The self is alone and troubled. Connected to this are moments of self-assertion; we learn, for example, that she becomes a prostitute in part because the alternatives are unacceptable:

Some things I will do
Some things I won't
I won't change the beds
at a fleabag
I won't wash windows
I won't scrub floors
Some things I will do
Some things I won't. (71)

The narrative does not offer a motive for Painted Turtle's choice of the sex trade as a way to make money, but the song suggests that it may have to do with agency and pride, as in the verse that follows on the same page:

I come from the Zuni Reservation
but not my lipstick
I come from the Zuni Reservation
but not my highheels
I come from the Zuni Reservation
but not my sweet smell. (71)

What emerges is the sense of an individual who respects the old stories and many of the traditions but insists on living as a modern woman. Like Major, she cannot accept the restrictions imposed by social conventions. So she comes and goes with the Zuni community, neither inside nor fully outside its boundaries.

The last category are those songs constructed from within the cultural tradition but truly modern, since they have been made into verses to be performed for an external audience. They are, in other words, purely art, regardless of their source. One about clown figures, for example, opens with Painted Turtle holding a corncob between her legs, waving it from side to side:

Koyemci, are you Wantateu
or Awanpekwin
or Posuki or Nalaci?
Koyemci, did you plant
the seeds for the crops
and create your own soul
from the footprints
I left in your dust?
Koyemci, lift your kilt
and show us your lack
of lust, your limpness
Koyemci, I sing
your innocence, I dance
your blessing. (127)

The Koyemci are both the clowns and the priests of the Zuni and serve a similar function for the Hopi. While their behavior is often outrageous in pointing out the absurdity of human behavior, they also speak wisdom to the people. They stand as the intermediaries between humans and kachinas, or spirit figures. They go by different names but perform the same functions.[3] Thus, the Koyemci may be seen as artists whose play is serious business. In Zuni and Hopi traditions, the spirits never speak; it is the Koyemci, though in many ways disreputable, who have the power of language; they give meaning to human existence. In this novel, Painted Turtle, cast out of the community, is the one who can speak its reality to a larger audience. She accepts finally her status and, like her creator, turns that alienated condition to aesthetic purpose.

*Some Observations of a Stranger at Zuni in the Latter Part of the Century*, published the following year, serves in essence as a poetic coda to the novel. Having created songs for his character out of her fictive experience, Major wrote verses of his own about the indigenous culture. He even provides a glossary at the end that serves in part to demonstrate his knowledge of the society. The voices of the poems are often first person, but the "stranger" of the title is never specified. This male voice is not clearly that of the author, since the figure at times has close ties to the Zuni characters and factors such as race and origins are never mentioned. In some instances, Major reworked material from the novel. The rape of Painted Turtle is changed to the legend of the girl who is assaulted by kachinas so that she may produce a god. There are stanzas in the same poem that describe what is required of the "good" Zuni girl, thus detailing the kinds of actions the novel's protagonist either failed to do or did inadequately.

One poem, "In Hollywood with the Zuni God of War," is a critique of popular culture representations of Native Americans. The speaker works as an extra in movies about Indians and is constantly attempting to sell versions of western stories in which there are more accurate historical points of view taken. Every time, he and his friends are ignored and wind up in films where all the Indians are killed or disgraced. They continue to do the work because it pays much better than any other jobs they could do. The critique is reinforced by giving the white director the only dialect speech in the book:

> what ya guys want?
> Ya got Studio City by da balls!
> Ya got all the blondes
> in the District hot fa ya
> 'cause ya got dok skin and ah— (*Observations*, 18)

Since *Painted Turtle* is, as some critics have noted, a lyrical text, not only because of the main character's songs but also because of the short chapters and spiritual aspects of the narrative and poetic qualities, it is not surprising that Major would make use of the stories, names, and beliefs of the Zuni and Hopi to create an additional text that did not require narrative. In both works, he gives primary attention to female figures, though he largely ignores the matrifocal character of those societies. Instead, he critiques their social orders both because they are traditional and thus do not allow for modern individuality and because they are dominated by men and male spirits and thus do not allow for female self-expression.

After several months of inquiries and rejections by major publishers, both books were accepted by Sun and Moon Press and appeared after additional delays. Sun and Moon had been established in 1976 by Douglas Messerli as an alternative publisher. By the early 1980s, it already had a significant reputation in fiction, poetry, and drama. Most important for Major, it had become Russell Banks's publisher and had put out work by Walter Abish, Steve Katz, and Fanny Howe. It was a way for Major to move beyond the Fiction Collective but still remain in the company of his earlier collaborators. *Painted Turtle* received consistently positive reviews and was selected by the *New York Times Book Review* as a Notable Book of the Year. Critics saw the text as lyrical and as a welcome break from his earlier, experimental work, especially *My Amputations*, in which the character Painted Turtle made an appearance.[4]

## BACK IN THE UNITED STATES

While there was much activity on Major and Pamela's return to Boulder in August 1985, with final preparations of *My Amputations* for publication, the art exhibition, the final work on the Zuni manuscripts, work on a new novel, and university responsibilities, it was clear that he still was not quite at home in Boulder. A little over a year after his return, he began making arrangements to be gone again, an effort that would eventually lead to his permanent departure. In the spring of 1988, he took a position as visiting professor at SUNY Binghamton and in the fall as distinguished visiting writer at Temple University in Philadelphia.

He was invited to Binghamton through the efforts of Jerry Rothenberg, who had earlier arranged for his visit to UC San Diego. He was the first visiting professor of creative writing at the SUNY school. He taught a graduate course in poetry and an undergraduate workshop in experimental prose.

He also did two public readings during the semester and gave interviews to the student and local newspapers. For *Inside SUNY-Binghamton*, he constructs a version of the past that makes him very much an isolated artist. He contends that his parents saw his interest in reading and daydreaming as "bad signs," suggesting an overall laziness; he also describes the need to keep his writing and painting a secret while growing up in Chicago. Somewhat contradictorily, he says that his mother encouraged him "as much as her understanding permitted."[5]

From Binghamton, he and Pam moved to Philadelphia for his visiting writer appointment at Temple. His teaching load was even less than at Binghamton; here he was only in charge of a graduate creative writing course. His time was used to complete his novel about Venice, whose working title had changed from "A Boatman's Tenure" to "Solid Ground." By November, it was being shopped to publishers by his agent, Susan Bergholtz. It is described as a 675-page novel within a novel, the story of a young black professor trying to write a biography of a famous black journalist who died in Venice (Alexis Moore). This work remains unpublished. He also completed work on the short-story collection that was published in 1990 as *Fun and Games*. While at Temple, he also did a number of watercolors at his home in Elkins Park, a suburban neighborhood several miles from the university. He also delivered a public lecture, "Necessary Distance," which became the title piece of his second collection of essays.

## SUCH WAS THE SEASON

Major's most popular novel was started after his return from Venice but was published before the work that he had written on that trip. The speed of writing and of publication is in part the result of the subject matter and the style of the book. *Such Was the Season* is the most traditional work of his career. In interviews, he bristles at the notion that it is not experimental, but he defines its difference in terms of the voice rather than the structure (Bunge, *Conversations*, 75). The idea of the novel began with a visit to family in Atlanta, where he listened to his female relatives tell stories. He has said that the voice is drawn from the voices of his mother and her sister (115). As usual, he discourages tight connections between his life and the narrative but does admit that he and the character Juneboy, who was originally going to be the central figure, share some qualities, such as their early departure from the South. Though the manuscript originally ran to over two thousand pages, both composition and revisions went quickly. He started work on the book in late 1985, and it was published in September 1987. He chose Mercury House because, after making inquiries among commercial presses, he met Alev Lytle, who was the editor and a founder of the nonprofit press in San Francisco, at the Western States Awards ceremony. She invited him to send her his next novel and accepted it quickly.[6]

While Major has insisted that Annie Eliza's narration made the work experimental, readers of African American fiction would have become familiar with the construction of such voices through Ernest Gaines's *The Autobiography of Miss Jane Pittman* (1971), Alice Walker's *The Color Purple* (1982), the novels of Gayl Jones, and the short fiction of Toni Cade Bambara. SallyAnn Ferguson reviewed the novel jointly with Gloria Naylor's *Mama Day* (1988), which uses a different narrative voice but a similarly strong, elderly black woman as the central character. Moreover, during this period of the flowering of black women's writing, there was also the recovery of Zora Neale Hurston's *Their Eyes Were Watching God* (1937), which blends folk and standard English voices in the narrative. Instead of these black models, Major tells Larry McCaffery and Jerzy Kutnik in a 1992 interview that he had been rereading *Huck Finn* and found himself intrigued by the creation of such a distinctive voice (Bunge, *Conversations*, 82). The best explanation for what is undertaken is a combination of technical and market concerns. The mid- to late 1980s was the high point of popularity for black women's writing. The film of *The Color Purple* came out while Major was in Venice, and Toni Morrison's *Beloved* was published the same year as *Such Was the Season*. Unlike Ishmael Reed and other male authors and critics, who launched both fictional and nonfictional attacks on Walker, Morrison, and others, Major chose to see the situation as an opportunity to do what he had not been able to do with *Painted Turtle*: create a credible female storyteller. The effort succeeded because he had living models to work from, because he had command of black vernacular speech through his work on the *Dictionary of Afro-American Slang* (which he would reissue in an expanded form as *Juba to Jive* in 1994), and because he did not feel compelled to produce an "authentic" black folk figure, which was another trend of the post–civil rights period. In place of that, he offers an urban narrative inflected with the language of televisual culture, the black church, politics, and southern black speech patterns.

Annie Eliza Hicks is the matriarch of a prominent Atlanta family, though her speech retains the flavor of her rural Georgia upbringing. One of her sons is the minister of one of the largest churches in the city, and his wife, Renee, is involved in local and state politics. The focus of the narrative is the return of her nephew, who does research in sickle cell anemia. He moved to Chicago with his mother when his parents divorced during his childhood. After his father was killed by a white man, he vowed never to return to the South. He comes back to speak at Spelman College and to reacquaint himself with the family. Major's original idea for the novel had been to focus on the idea of return, thus making this a "roots" narrative. But the shift to Annie Eliza produced a digressive approach consistent with his earlier fiction. So even though the story takes place within the confines of a one-week visit, we learn about the soap operas that are so important to the narrator's daily life, the political machinations that Renee gets involved in as part of her political campaign, the scandal associated with her husband's church, and the desire of Juneboy to connect to the places and memories linked to his father. Despite the shifting concerns, the novel is much more plotted than Major's other fiction; this is necessitated by his decision to incorporate political conflict, which must be resolved within the time frame.

While the novel can generally be read as celebratory, given Annie Eliza's commonsensical approach to the world and her ability to deal with any situation, the book does involve some aspects of social critique. The depiction of Jeremiah, the preacher, is consistent with the author's negative view of religion in general and Christianity in particular. He is nearly a caricature of the black preacher, with his emphasis on material possessions, his power over his congregation (and its women), and his underlying corruption. As his mother understands, he loves to be the center of attention. She is aware of his serial infidelities and, when he is shot by his latest mistress, her only reaction is to be curious about how he will explain the situation to his wife. The wife, I would suggest, is Major's subtle attack on black feminism. Annie Eliza sees Renee as pampered, self-absorbed, and materialistic. But when Renee decides to run for a state senate seat against a popular incumbent, her mother-in-law supports her out of a sense of family loyalty. However, Renee's ambition leads her to uncover a produce scandal, in which her husband, unbeknownst to her, is deeply involved. The matter explodes in her face as one man commits suicide and Jeremiah is faced with a prison sentence. Thus, the modern self-assertive woman is set against the traditional enduring mother figure and made to look foolish. In effect, Major uses a version of the idealized wise woman of black women's fiction (Baby Suggs in *Beloved* and Pilate in Morrison's *Song of Solomon*, Shug Avery in *The*

*Color Purple*, and Gloria Naylor's lead character in *Mama Day*) as a means of subverting the womanist and feminist impulses of those very writers. Unlike Reed, however, he does not do this in the service of a masculinist alternative but rather as part of his lifelong resistance to using the arts for ideological purposes.

Reviews of *Such Was the Season* were generally very positive. Critics seemed happy that Major had broken away from his experimental practices. As he wished, they saw Annie Eliza's voice as the main feature of the text. SallyAnn Ferguson, for example, compares the narrative to Robert Browning's dramatic monologues, without the ironic exposure of the speaker. Al Young expresses the consensus: "Unlike his previous fiction, which was unstintingly experimental, 'Such Was the Season' is an old fashioned, straight-ahead narrative crammed with action, a dramatic storyline and meaty characterization. But it's the widow Annie Eliza's melodic voice, by turns lilting and gruff, that salts and peppers and sweetens this story, enriching its flavor and meaning." A dissenting voice was offered by Julie Washington, who argues that the narrator is "exactly the kind of clichéd character one expects to find in a book about southern blacks. She is the stereotypical salt-of-the-earth, spunky mother, uneducated but wiser than her book-learned offspring." Nonetheless, the *New York Times Book Review* included it in the "And Bear in Mind" column and its "Summer Reading" list, and it was made an alternative selection for the Literary Guild. Mercury House issued it in paperback in 1989, and Louisiana State University Press reissued it in 2003.

# CHAPTER NINE

# Consolidating a Career

The often-difficult but also productive sojourn in Colorado ended in 1989, when Major accepted a position at the University of California Davis as a professor of English and creative writing. The opportunity developed in 1987 when he served as a panelist for the National Endowment for the Arts with Will Baker, a fictionist and essayist who had joined the faculty at Davis in 1969. The two remained in contact and discussed the move in late 1988. An interview was arranged for February 1989, which meant that Major returned from his visiting positions at Binghamton and Temple and almost immediately went out to California. The creative writing program at the time included Baker, Sandra MacPherson, and Jack Hicks, who was one of its founders, though he was known primarily as a critic. The readings, social events, and meetings with faculty and students went very well. Both the chair of the department and the dean were supportive of the appointment. While the open position was for a writer, Major had the advantage of being able to teach both poetry and fiction, as well as American and African American literature. An offer was officially made in the late spring, and he and Pam moved to Davis for the beginning of the fall term. While looking for a house to buy they stayed first at the Aggie Inn adjacent to campus. Within a couple of weeks, they acquired a ranch-style house at Toyon and Villanova streets, where they lived until moving to their current home on Wren Street in suburban Davis in the spring of 1992.[1] Around this time, he also

FIGURE 21. Major's Davis home at 3510 Wren Street

briefly considered another professional move. At the time of the Davis interview, there was some effort to get him to take a position at Binghamton. A job did not materialize then, but the possibility reoccurred in 1992. As part of his thinking about this, he sent out letters of inquiry to several universities to test the waters. Based on documents in the archives, these queries produced no results, and he finally decided to remain in Davis.[2]

When UC Davis was established in the early twentieth century as the agricultural campus of the University of California system, the College of Letters and Sciences was created, and the English Department later set up a graduate program in creative writing. Though the program did not have the kind of commitment to experimentation found at Colorado, it was clear that Major had already moved to a different kind of writing. Among his new colleagues were Baker, who published fiction and nonfiction, primarily about the American West; MacPherson, who had established herself as a poet several years before coming to Davis; Alan Williamson, known for both his poetry and poetry criticism; and Sandra Gilbert, a nationally known feminist scholar and poet. Thus, Major's new situation was one in which critical and creative training were integrated.

It is perhaps not surprising that the shift in environment was accompanied by a hiatus in literary publication, with only a collection of stories and a chapbook in the seven years following the move. After all, between 1985 and 1989, he had produced three novels (*My Amputations, Such Was the Season*, and *Painted Turtle*) and three books of poetry (*Inside Diameter, Surfaces and Masks*, and *Some Observations*). What happened during this period was the beginning of his effort to solidify his reputation as a significant figure in contemporary American literature generally and African American literature specifically. He continued to publish poems and short fiction, but now more often in *Black American Literature Forum* (later *African American Review*) and *Callaloo*, both major academic journals, rather than little magazines. His essays tended to appear in anthologies and general circulation magazines. In addition, he wrote reviews for the *Washington Post* and the *Los Angeles Times*. He also did dust-jacket blurbs for novels published by major commercial houses; the irony here, of course, is that virtually all of these houses had rejected his work earlier in his career.

## "REACHING AND LEAVING THE POINT"

As part of the effort to define his career, Major published "Reaching and Leaving the Point," an essay on perspective and point of view that appeared in 1989 in *High Plains Literary Review*. The journal itself is evidence of his networking skills; he served as its fiction editor from its founding in 1986 until it ceased publication in 2002. Also listed on the masthead were his friends and acquaintances Fanny Howe, Charles Johnson, Joe Weixlmann, Maurice Couturier, and Bill Boelhower.

The essay itself draws connections between writing and painting that Major has been emphasizing in his writing and interviews for a number of years. He is consistent with that pattern in focusing on the technical aspects of art, in this case on how the artist controls the perceptions of his audience. In doing so, he considers matters of history and anthropology as well as aesthetic theory. Also typical of his work is the blending of the subjective and imaginative with the expository in his discussion. Rather than make use of sources in academic disciplines to construct the context for his argument, he relies on himself: "To begin my investigation, I tried to *imagine* the earliest humans, just beginning to stand upright and to look about. I *thought* that at that point a sense of space—different from the one likely generated by searching the earth's floor for food—*might* have begun to evolve" ("Reaching," 28, emphasis added). To this is added, within a page, "I speculated," "it hit me," "I began to think," and "For me, the real eye-opening revelation." Major represents himself here as an original thinker rather than one who is building on the insights and analyses of generations of intellectuals. In this sense, it is an exercise in point of view as much as it is a disquisition on its subject.

It serves as an ex post facto defense of the artistic practice of his career, especially in its emphasis on the arbitrariness of representation. Ironically, he does this at the moment when he is shifting in both fiction and painting to a more mimetic style. This is what he means by the "revelation": "[It] was the sudden realization that *real* space—even in a tracing of a shadow on the ground—could not be transferred to a two-dimensional surface. In other words, all uses of any degree of perspective in painting were based on deception. Three-dimensional space could not be rendered on a two-dimensional surface.... So, in a similar manner, point of view itself— I thought—had to be some sort of literary slight-of-hand" (29, original emphasis and spelling). Added to this notion of art as artifice or game is the related claim that the observer of the work is limited and controlled by what the artist has done. The audience always comes to the work belatedly and can see it only in the ways established by the creator; even if these ways are flexible, the flexibility itself is determined by the design (30). This assertion helps to explain Major's persistent view, expressed in both fiction and commentary about his art, that he wants to suggest an element of mystery in his work, something that puzzles the audience but cannot be grasped. That "something more" is an illusion constructed by the artist's manipulation of our perception of the art object. It is a means of enticing and frustrating us at the same time, giving the work an erotic quality that Major also often seeks.

To develop his case, Major invents a figure to serve as a "research tool." In other words, he offers a story as a means of analysis. This character is a writer of fiction, a term the author defines from a legal dictionary as "'An assumption or supposition of law that something which is or may be false is true, or that a state of facts exists which has never really taken place'" (31). He prefers this definition because it allows the artistic invention to be a "new reality." The question is what is needed to give the figure a story. "He" requires time and space, a frame and a landscape. Here Major returns to the subjective aspect of his argument, as he claims that these things come out of himself: "whatever will take place, in a sense, has already taken place in me first" (32). Having taken this step, he then must return to the question of representation. If the figure is not merely words on a page or strokes of a brush but an expression of the experience of the artist, then is "he" truly a new reality?

Interestingly, Major evades this question by shifting to another aspect of the problem: perspective. He comes back to artistic control by show- ing how the writer or painter decides where and how to place the figure. Its relative importance is determined by whether it is in the foreground or background; moreover, different choices produce shifts in the nature of art itself. Modern art emerges, in part, from the breakdown of certain assump- tions about the certainty of perspective and point of view and the ways to present them. But this breakdown liberates the artist by giving him or her greater freedom to create. But this freedom does not lead to an open-ended work: "Because perspective exists only in a *closed* scheme the elements in the frame are much like those created by Nature in, say, the formation of a leaf. My figure—or character—is therefore the agent of a *constructed* reality, signifying primarily within the context of that closed scheme" (34). In a sense, Major here answers the previous question. Whatever the sources of the figure, his story, and his context, they have meaning almost entirely within the frame of the object created. Their sources and their references to the world outside the object, including the being of the artist, are inciden- tal. It is in this sense that Major could claim that *Such Was the Season*, for example, was experimental, despite the claims of critics otherwise. Annie Eliza, regardless of her origins in the family, was a tool that allowed the story to be told; discovering her point of view made possible the art object that is the novel.

While the essay generally joins perspective to point of view, a conjunc- tion that explains the coherence of his different aesthetic endeavors, he also wants to differentiate them, in part to explain why he needs to do both writ- ing and painting:

> It seemed the most important difference was this: fiction was essentially *temporal* in nature; it was also sequential and linear—because that was how writing worked. Point of view was about how the writer chose to *understand* things.
>
> On the other hand, perspective was, in perhaps the most important sense, about *how* the artist chose to *see* things. When I remembered these differ- ences I thought I could see why I might not always recognize my figure as the agent of essentially the same functions though transformed by the par- ticular frame he happened to be part of. (35, original emphasis)

Noteworthy in this passage is the emphasis on *how* the artist sees. Despite his commitment to subjectivity, Major ultimately presents himself as a technician rather than as a romantic. He goes so far as to say that "point of view and perspective were basic elements, both having beginnings in 'the smallest constituent element,' in writing and painting and were *engineering* devices aimed at, among other objectives, establishing balance—and distance—between model and object created" (39, original emphasis).

Art, by this argument, is a form of technology; it makes use of various mechanisms to construct objects. While it is not part of the essay to determine the need or value of such objects, it does tell us how some of the tools for building it operate. While the source is somewhere within the creator, getting it from that source into the world is a matter not of inspiration but rather practical decision making. One of the goals of this process is the liberation of the thing created from whatever models for it already existed. This separation is important to Major, in part perhaps it defines his own body of work as belonging to modernism and postmodernism; perhaps more important, it provides him cover as he moves toward a more traditional aesthetic in both writing and painting.

## *FUN AND GAMES* AND *PARKING LOTS*: THE LAST EXPERIMENTS

*Fun and Games*, Major's only collection of short fiction, brings together experimental and traditional works from the full range of his career. The book is divided into five sections, with only the last having a title. Major wrote the story "Old" when he was twenty-five and "My Mother and Mitch" (which won a Pushcart Prize) appeared in *Boulevard* just months before *Fun and Games* came out. "Ten Pecan Pies" uses characters that appeared in *NO*, "Letters" contains correspondence between Julie and Al of *Emergency Exit*, and "Saving the Children" draws on the childhood of Juneboy from *Such Was the Season*. About half of the stories had been previously published. The collection was issued by Holy Cow! Press, created and run by Jim Perlman in Minnesota. Major comments in an interview that Perlman was in touch with him virtually every day during the production (Bunge, *Conversations*, 69).

"My Mother and Mitch" is the core of what Major at one point thought might become a novel (Bunge, *Conversations*, 120). It tells the story of a young boy living with his mother in Chicago. It is based in part on a summer around 1950 when Serena went by herself back to Georgia, and Clarence stayed with his mother. "[My] mother and I were alone together and *it felt so different. It felt so different.* It was a new experience: I'd never, never felt that way before, didn't feel that way after she returned and I had the kind of experience with my mother that maybe I preferred. I don't know. It was a wonderful experience and we were friends for about a month. It was great, it was great, it was great" (121, original emphasis). The repetitions and emphasis suggest the psychological importance of this memory. The boy Clarence, who felt abandoned by his mother in Georgia and then betrayed by her when she remarried, but nonetheless filled her house with his art-work, is recalled by the nearly sixty-year-old man as having this one special moment when life was perfect, when he was the center of attention. Major never wrote the novel, probably because, as he also says in the interview, he was concerned with it becoming a "happy, happy book" (121). Instead, he later wrote *Come by Here* (2002), a somewhat fictionalized story of his mother's life based on extensive interviews with her.

The short story is a coming-of-age narrative in which the boy comes to understand the limits of adult wisdom. The mother and son have lived together in Chicago since the parents separated twelve years earlier; it is now 1951. A misdialed phone call from a stranger leads to the mother hav-ing a series of conversations with Mitch Kribbs, a white man who keeps calling her. The mother makes it clear to Kribbs that she is not white, but the calls continue. What is crucial is that the child is given considerable responsibility in the situation as it develops. The mother tells her son the details of the phone calls. When the adults finally arrange a meeting, she consults with the son on the dress that she will wear. He takes on the ar-rangements for the meeting, choosing a café nearby; he also intends to be there as an observer, though keeping his distance. This last, he says, is so that he can be in a position to "protect" her. In effect, he takes on the role of his mother's father or older brother. The relation with Kribbs does not develop, though the reason is not made clear; Major does not, for example, indicate that it has to do with racial difference. The real point is the wisdom gained by the child:

> I learned for the first time that she did not always know what she was doing.
> It struck me that she was as helpless as I sometimes felt when confronted
> with a math or science problem or a problem about sex and girls and grow-
> ing up and life in general. She didn't know everything. And that made me
> feel closer to her despite the fear it caused. She was there to protect me, I
> thought. But there she was, just finding her way, step by step, like me. It was
> something wonderful, anyway. (*Fun*, 13)

While the story, told "many years" later, centers on the son, we are also asked to trust his childhood perceptions of his mother. What is striking is the amount of control that she cedes to the boy. His involvement is associated with what he describes as her fear: "She was a scared little girl with wild eyes dancing in her head, unable to make up her own mind. I sensed her fear. I resented her for the mess she had gotten herself in. I also resented her for needing my consent" (9). He presents himself as the adult in the situation, trying to make sense of the irrational behavior of a woman-child and needing to be in a position to protect her. He also takes note of her performance in the cafe: "She looked back in that timid way of hers. But she wasn't timid. It was an act and part of her ladylike posture. She used it when she needed it" (12). Here he exposes the artificiality of her engagement with adult men, which is compared to the naturalness of her relationship to him. The end of the "affair," as he refers to it, comes rather quickly and without explanation. Mother and son return to their routine of domestic life, with the woman infrequently going to social events or on dates. They become, in effect, an old married couple.

The fantasy of mastery in the story, in which the child believes that he must take on the role of protector, suggests the complexity of Major's relationship to his mother. In his own childhood, he was the one who needed protection, which came from either his mother or his younger but bigger sister. It was his mother who left an abusive relationship with his father and traveled alone to Chicago and who worked at various jobs to provide for her children, including situations where she had to pass for white in order to get better pay. That narrative is revised into one in which the boy is placed at the center and holds the power over the adults. Instead of the reality, in which Inez marries Halbert Ming just four years after the children come to the city, here the mother abandons a possible adult relationship in favor of life only with her son. In effect, the author turns the memory of a brief episode from his childhood when he had his mother to himself into one in which he not only has her always but is truly the man of the house.

Another piece that deals with the theme of mother and son is "Mother Visiting," which Major has defined as one of three "prose poems" in the collection (Bunge, *Conversations*, 68). (The other two prose poems are "Fun and Games" and "Mobile Axis: A Triptych," the latter of which is discussed below.) This story again takes the point of view of the son, who this time adopts a condescending attitude toward his mother, who comes to New York to see him. He emphasizes her tendency toward repetition of stories and comments, at one point comparing her to Gertrude Stein, whom he emphasizes she had not read. She has to have the notion of therapy explained to her. Even when his roommate "patiently" defines it, we are told that she "still does not understand" (*Fun*, 49). The poetic aspects of the narrative come in the brevity of sentences and the patterns of repetition. We hear, for example, about the cab driver who brought her from the airport, loves Hitler, and wants to kill his own mother. In shops she visits, she retells the story, apparently in the same words. At the end, she is taken to the airport by the same driver, who repeats back to her the words she spoke to him at the beginning. The story also utilizes brief character depictions and images rather than plot development. Mrs. Velma Mae Thompson is an old friend who now lives in Harlem. The only things we learn about her are that she has distinctive views on health and that the mother has dinner with her; she has no other role in the story. Jessica, the roommate, is present several times, but though we learn about her fashion sense, we are told nothing about her relationship to the narrator.

The effect of this fragmented approach to the story is to establish the emotional distance between mother and son. He does not go to the airport to pick her up, he does not accompany her to Harlem, though she has to travel from the Lower East Side to get there, and he does not take her back to the airport at the end of her three-day visit. One evening of her stay, he leaves her alone to go out with a belly dancer they had seen at a Turkish restaurant earlier. They spend several hours together "reading Edith Sitwell" (50). At no point in the tale do mother and son communicate anything about their lives. He emphasizes to us her tendency to live in the past yet tells us nothing of what that past might mean to him. Like the narrator in "My Mother and Mitch," he seems more interested in establishing his control than in understanding her. And, as in the earlier story, the mother can be linked to Inez Major, who, like the mother in this piece, is a habitual smoker and who worked as a dressmaker. In this sense, the narrative records the distance between mother and son that was the actual experience of the two rather than the fantasy of the other short story. Clarence moved on to the world of New York and art, while his mother remained in the working world of Chicago's South Side.

The concluding section of the collection turns to a different concern: visual and literary art. Unlike the other sections, this one is named: "Mobile Axis: A Triptych." Initially, it is difficult to identify the "hinges" that join the three stories into a single work. The first, "Liberties," focuses on Vincent Van Gogh; the second, "Women in Love," suggests a connection to

D. H. Lawrence; the third, "The Ghetto, the Ocean, the Lynching, and the Funeral," seems a pastiche of unrelated events. What holds the three stories in the triptych together is the concern of the author for composition, both visually and literarily. Each story is made up of fragments; there is no attempt to create a coherent narrative in any of them. In this sense, they return to Major's earlier fictional practice, though the triptych was first published only a few months before *Fun and Games* came out. They bring together issues of perspective, structure, the representation of emotion, and the means of depicting sense experience. Major seeks to link together questions of technique with expressions of feeling.

The liberties of the first "panel" of the triptych are those taken by the narrator with the life and work of Van Gogh. One way to read this story is as a prose version of *Inside Diameter*, in which the painter is also imaginatively engaged. Episodes in the narrative are connected to various paintings or are reconstructions of moments in his life, often based on his works. So, for example, the first piece places the narrator in Van Gogh's *Bedroom in Arles*; he simply details what can be seen in the painting: "two chairs, five pictures, a mirror, a washtable, a towel on a nail, two doors, perhaps three" (*Fun*, 113). What interests him are the "tricks" the painting plays, in terms of perspective, proportion, and light. He moves quickly to *The Church at Auvers*, which again is shown to do "impossible" things in relation to reality. This time, we learn of the visual effects as well as the emotional ones. The eyes are compelled to follow certain lines of the image, despite "their own intelligence," and the emotional impact of the work is described: "I notice the brooding blue sky and the blue windows of the church. The angle of the light is brilliantly impossible, compositionally correct: the grass around this—the back side—is partly shaded by the presence of the awesome church. Light falls directly onto the church just above the shaded area. This gives my heart an ache it has never felt before" (113).

The sequence of the work might be said to be an ever-greater imaginative involvement with the painter. From entering the painting to recording one's response to the art, we move to engagement with the artist himself. The third segment discusses one of the self-portraits yet undertakes not to examine the artistry but to understand the subject. While the narrator says, "I still don't know what to make of him," he then describes his feelings and even diagnoses his condition: "Morbid depression and calm scrutiny. I've never seen him smile or even appear to be at peace with himself. Art never makes him happy" (114). The remainder of the story elaborates on this point, as the speaker observes the artist, usually through a window, though there are no paintings that render Van Gogh in this way. He plays with various images that Van Gogh created but generates fictive versions of them so as to create his own images. He takes these "liberties" in order to construct a version of the artist that fits his own understanding and knowledge of the artist's fate. The story, for example, does what a painting of Van Gogh by Major could not: it can offer moments of perception of the subject in rapid succession with clear delineation of the emotion of both the subject and the observer. It is a specific illustration of Major's repeated assertion that he paints what he cannot write and writes what he cannot paint. Here he can say what he needs to say about painting and the painter in ways he could not on a canvas.

"Women in Love," the central "panel," is also the longest, thus making the set consistent with the tradition of painting in the triptych format. The title suggests a link to D. H. Lawrence, though Major is much more self-referential and metafictional. He calls attention to himself as the artist working through the composition and physical description of the characters: "She now appears to be an unmovable mass: made of something other than flesh. There is no way she is ever going to move again. She is one-sided, about to topple but she will never fall. She will continue to lean like this. Her arms are too short for her body. She could never reach her feet with those arms. Her head is also too small for her body" (118). What began as narrative before the quoted passage, a woman bathing and then emerging, is transformed into sculpture in a modernist style, with physical distortions and suggesting a feeling of instability.

He leaves this image to visualize a group of women, one of whom is pregnant. What interests him is their arrangement: "The seated woman would have had more foreground had she felt more important than the standing woman. Yet I do not sense that the woman in the background is actually in the background. . . . There is no background, no foreground. All aspects of the yard are equal. In coming out here under the stars they have chosen also to ignore the rules of retreating-advancing colors" (119). Here the figures become agents in the composition, determining what happens to perspective. The scene recalls the issues about narrative that Major's narrator-author raised as far back as *Reflex and Bone Structure*, when he claimed to struggle with the representation of his characters. Here they are rendered more complex in the sense that he uses one medium to examine technical problems in another.

The text becomes more specifically self-reflexive as the narrator moves, without transition, into a description of "climate" as an aspect of art. His concern here is the effective depiction of emotion. His examples are taken primarily from Munch and Van Gogh, but the references are to works—*The Scream*, *The Sick Room*, *The Miners*—that Major himself had created versions of or had made clear textual comment on. He suggests variations on the works, such as the man screaming without holding his ears or without a town in the background. He also posits the image as nonallegorical: "The screaming man here on the long road does not represent Human Nature but is naturally human" (*Fun*, 120).[3] He rejects abstraction in favor of concreteness, just as in his earlier works he had insisted on his art as extension of rather than imitation of reality.

The connection to Lawrence, beyond the references to coal miners, comes in a vignette in which the narrator has an affair with a married woman, Dagmar. What is emphasized as emotion is the passion of the lovers and the ineffectiveness of the husband, Stanley. Having caught them together, "his body seems limp with the emotion that has suddenly hit it from within" (123). But more important than the feelings involved is the sense of performance. There is an audience, and the setting seems to shift between a theater stage and a movie sequence. But Major then further complicates the presentation: "Despite his [Stanley's] foreground location, he begins to go out of focus and Dagmar and I come into focus. With the emphasis shifting to us, it is like a painting of a cornfield taking up ninety-percent of the canvas with a ten-percent view of a strip of great historical ruins—squares, monuments, signs of Western civilization far off in the background. In this latter view, there is no doubt about the creator's intentions" (123–24). It is not clear how the analogy relates to the narrative since he mixes focus and perspective; moreover, of course, all of this is done with language rather than any of the mediums otherwise mentioned. The net impressions of "Women in Love" are the shifting of foreground and background with words, the problems of composition, and the construction of emotion that are part of modern art and of Major's own practice in painting.

The third panel, "The Ghetto, the Ocean, the Lynching, and the Funeral," involves five—not four, as the title would suggest—brief, unrelated episodes. The first is simply descriptive, offering a verbal variation of a painting from this period titled *Saturday Afternoon* (1992). The narrator initially asserts that this world of stoops is life affirming but concludes that the figures, whom he had called "vibrant," "open," and "regenerating," are in fact "flat, blunt paper cutouts" (129). Likewise, in each episode, we are reminded of the artificiality of what is presented. Even the lynching, the most emotion-laden occurrence represented in African American writing, is here reduced to artifice: "The event will be nonlinear. It is sure to represent selective focus. We will sigh and feel glad it's not us. Someone moving far, far back from the townsquare, might see all of us, and the hanging as a decorative composition, flat figures in a stark space" (130).

The triptych, then, is a tripartite examination of the relationship of art to life. The first panel considers the life of the artist, while the third may be read as studies for such an artist to develop. The center "panel" is the most detailed rendering of the artist engaged with his materials, concerned with composing the material, solving technical problems, and giving the work feeling so as to appeal to readers-viewers. But this effort has the effect of emphasizing the distance from the subject in the act of rendering it. This set of fictions may be seen as the endpoint of Major's career as an experimental writer. He has played out all the variables of self-conscious art. *Such Was the Season* demonstrated his turn to a more traditional form of storytelling, one in which the "experiment" is found in the narrative voice or in the style but not in drawing constant attention to the arbitrariness of narration.

The reviews of *Fun and Games* were generally consistent with Major's own designs for the collection. Merle Rubin observes in the *Los Angeles Times Book Review* that "in Major's hands, straightforward realism has a way of wandering off into the labyrinth of literary self-awareness." This is because "simple realism runs the danger of collapsing into the literary cliché. Major's 'short fictions' remind us that reality is not simply something out there. Ours, as he puts it, is a 'man-made world,' influenced by our ability to reflect, re-imagine, re-interpret and reform it." Commentators consistently note his care with language, with some pointing out the poetic impulse in several of the stories. The sales of the book were good for such a small press, totaling around two thousand.

Like *Fun and Games*, *Parking Lots* (1992) blends tradition with experimentation. In this case, the chapbook's distinction is in its design; it achieves status as an art object in itself. Only 130 copies were done by Perishable Press, located in Mount Horeb, Wisconsin. Walter Hamady, in conjunction with his wife, Mary, began producing books of poetry in 1964. The works are hand-printed on paper made by the Hamadys in their barn. They have produced limited, signed editions by many of the best-known modern poets, including W. S. Merwin, Howard Nemerov, Robert Creeley, Denise Levertov, and W. D. Snodgrass.[4] In the case of *Parking Lots*, Hamady notes in the colophon that he used accordion double-pamphlet binding for the first time and also used a combination of Shadwell and Japanese paper in different colors. It was printed in black and blue inks. The wrappers are maps of the Philadelphia area, the front one of which includes a super-imposed parking stub with the words "Major Parking Lots" followed by a number, probably the individual copy number. There is no pagination. The artwork was done by Laura Dronzek, a Wisconsin artist who earned her MFA at the University of Wisconsin, where Hamady has taught studio art for many years.

The poem itself offers a cultural critique of the contemporary United States through the image of the parking lot. It is set primarily in the Philadelphia area, especially in Elkins Park suburb, where Major and his wife lived during the semester he taught at Temple. Running through the work is a sense of motion as a key to the national character:

> all across America we
> travel, on and on
> and I remember Heather
> saying, All I need
> is a post office
> and a liquor store. (*Parking*, n.p.)

The narrator claims that he is seeking "the essence of parking lots" and associates it with fast-food businesses, which depend on automobile traffic:

> Notice, there are no sidewalks.
> People on foot
> are not welcomed.

Early in the poem, having noted the emptiness of the life in such spaces, he experiences both a loss of identity and the difficulty of sense-response:

> Even the heartache
> of boredom is hard to sustain
>     in any ordinary sense.
> But it's a new perfect response
> to the despair at the graveside
>     of something lost.

The "something lost" is what he seeks but cannot quite locate. He even finds it hard to recognize himself in "this starved imagination" that is contemporary society. Nonetheless, he rejects the idea of chaos. After noting that his commuter train rides into the university take him by empty lots and crumbling buildings, he insists that there must be rules and order. He refuses to believe that pattern would be found only in an "inner landscape," but actually exists as "precious metal, space, intelligent stretches."

He finds possibility, for example, in the ventilation system of a burger joint, which sucks up oily smoke and spins it out and up, and is just the opposite of a flushing toilet. He finds in this comparison "comic relief." In this same space, as elsewhere in the poem, the faces of people can be understood as both guilty and innocent:

> Everybody here looks
> like faces on the Ten
> Most Wanted list, and
> I know they're as innocent
> as I ever was, it's just
> the way they look.

The nature of their innocence is indicated a few pages later when he talks about men in motorcycle gangs, who, though getting old, think of themselves as

> cartoon characters
> who will stay the same
> age always, just like
> in the strip.

This is, in other words, not the innocence of childhood but that of a willful self-ignorance.

The speaker of the poem sees one of his purposes to be to challenge that denial of reality by pointing out to students in his workshops the mistakes that they have made in their writing. He is energized by the gratitude they express for his correction. What he seeks, in effect, is a sense of humanity in the midst of sterility, delusion, and emptiness. He does not even have the expectation that what can be found is natural or tender:

> I'm seriously searching for something
> like a surface, private

and public to the touch, terrible
    too, that's all right,
  as long as it's a true surface,
     metallic is okay,
touchable metallic, engineered
    to fingertip kindness,
    something not exactly
     a totally remote
    source of impersonality.

The speaker has obviously come to a place where his expectations are low; an "engineered" world is now acceptable, as long as there is something recognizably human about its obvious manmadeness. The world of physical reality has always been a significant part of Major's art, but he has tended to emphasize that which is organic: the human body or nature or the aesthetic products of human endeavor. Here, his desire is reduced to that which is not utterly impersonal. In fact, he criticizes those things that simulate rather than embody human creativity:

    Too many art substitutes,
   too many hangdog constructs,
     artificial surfaces touched
       to serve as a link
back to Nature.

He concludes the poem with what can be considered a case study. During the time Major lived in San Diego, a gunman entered a San Ysidro McDonald's restaurant and killed twenty-one people before being shot himself. The speaker tries to puzzle out the connections among madness, the cultural sterility that produces fast food and mobile homes (such as the gunman's), and innocence. He asserts that

Surely,
if psychosis is there,
so is innocence,
so are good intentions.

What is known of the gunman, James Oliver Huberty, is that he was a survivalist who believed that U.S. society was on the verge of a breakdown; thus, he can be seen as someone who sought to bring the apocalypse by his actions. His "good intentions" are to bring quickly the mayhem and chaos that he sees as inevitable; his "innocence" is in believing that he can make such a difference. What troubles the speaker is how little difference Huberty made:

> What still amazes me
> is how quickly the shock
> passes.

In effect, he understands and in some sense agrees with Huberty's perspective; the killer's own "metallic" home, as the poem describes it, was "untouchable at highnoon." It represents, as do the parking lots and the burger joints mentioned earlier, a failed, dehumanized culture. In such a world little can shock any longer. While the speaker has the reasonableness and hopefulness that allows him to continue to believe in human possibility, he cannot be surprised that others have given up. The book itself, of course, embodies this paradox; it is a physically beautiful object that carries a message about the physical, social, and psychological ugliness of the world.

## RACE MATTERS AND "FOLK ART"

One characteristic of this early Davis period was Major's emphasis on African American materials, which began with *Such Was the Season*. He not only turned to African American journals for his short works, but he also produced three books with a specific racial focus. *Juba to Jive* (1994), an expansion of his 1970 *Dictionary of Afro-American Slang*, was published by Viking. In 1993, HarperCollins released the anthology *Calling the Wind: Twentieth Century African-American Short Stories* and followed it three years later with *The Garden Thrives: Twentieth Century African American Poetry*. These have been the only works in his career to come from major commercial publishers. This circumstance suggests that, while Major himself has not achieved canonical status in his own right, his literary standing is such that he could be counted on to produce canonizing works in African American studies. As will be seen, this return to "race matters" also became apparent in the creative work he was doing during this time.

Despite Major's resistance to being defined in terms of race, he turned for a period in the early 1990s to forms of folk expression in both painting and fiction. This emphasis can be seen earlier in the voice of Annie Eliza of *Such*

*Was the Season*. It becomes pronounced in *Dirty Bird Blues* (1996) and a series of paintings begun around 1992. The pattern did not carry over to his poetry, of which there is relatively little for several years after *Parking Lots*.

While Major has denied the connection, the visual work of this period tended to follow the style and content of African American painters such as William H. Johnson and Jacob Lawrence.[5] While creating both rural and urban images, Major often used simplified figures and primary colors. A work such as *Saw*, for example, depicts a female figure without detailed features sawing a log. The canvas is split in half by background colors of dark red and green; the palette is otherwise limited to white, light yellow, and brown. The colors occur in blocks, reinforcing the sense of simplicity.

*Country Boogie* (plate 9), which was the cover art for the hardcover edition of *Dirty Bird Blues*, shows two couples dancing in a open space. Like *Saw*, its background is red and green, though here the green forms a curved area that takes up most of the space, and the red is much lighter. The clothes of three of the four figures are pastel—blue, lavender, pink, and lime— while the fourth figure, in the background, nearly disappears with his dark attire. The limbs of the figures are elongated, which emphasizes motion. It also combines sharp, ninety-degree angles with soft curves. The overall effect is one of festivity, though this is tempered by the figure in the foreground. Though she has no facial features, she seems turned away from the others; one arm is crossed in front of her body, grasping the other one at the elbow as though she is protecting herself. Her lower body is at a forty-five-degree angle to the frame, creating a sense of instability. Her neck is unusually elongated, and her head is turned downward; the line created by her body closes in on itself, in contrast to the other figures, who lead the eye outward. Unlike the others, her skin tone is very light. Thus, what marks her is difference. She seems much like one of Jean Toomer's mysterious women from *Cane*, and in fact the color of the sky in the painting suggests the light in "Blood-Burning Moon," a narrative of cross-racial desire and violence. While the drawing in some ways calls attention to its "primitive" qualities, the artist uses the technique to do what he often does: point to the isolation of the individual in the midst of community.

Another disruptive element in the work is the contrast of simplified and complex composition. The male figure on the right is done with straight lines and associated geometric shapes: triangles and rectangles. There is no sense of a play of light. The female figure in the middle ground seems to come from a different work and is similar to the large number of women

Major painted a few years later. Her feet and hands are in graceful dance positions, almost balletic. Her body is given sensual form, in part through the effects of light on her lime-green dress; the sheen occurs on her breasts and hips. That same light gives her hair a bloodred color and shape that reinforces the curves of the body. The upward thrust of her figure contrasts with the downward pull of the central figure. In this sense, Major is simultaneously making and breaking the composition, both in what the viewer's eye must do and what the viewer would expect from "folk" art. In effect, he moves that tradition in the direction of postmodernism.

His urban portrayals reveal a similar commitment to the folk tradition that is modified over time. *Checkers*, first completed in 1992 (plate 10 is a version from 2000), is a circular painting of what folklorists and sociologists refer to as "street-corner men," those who may or may not have employment but who derive their identity from a homosocial environment. The figures are somewhat crude, with disproportionate body parts; the hands do not have fingers; some of the faces do not have features; and the colors are limited to red, green, and white, with brown for the skin. The figure at the center is less distinct than any of the others, in part because the red is so close in tone to brown. The checkerboard itself is merely a light-gray square. There is no sense of light or shadow, and the figures are not proportional relative to their location in the composition.

Major continued to revise this work over several years; the effect of doing so has been to suggest a modern, trained artist making reference to folk tradition rather than making folk art. The vagueness of the central figure in the 2000 version is magnified because the arrangement of the other men creates a telescopic effect that draws the viewer's eye toward him (plate 10). The two large, foreground figures create a parenthesis with the curvature of the painting, while the four inner figures enclose him from above and on both sides. His shirt is the only clearly patterned clothing in the picture, and its bright green stripes contrast sharply with the bright pink squares of the checkerboard. Thus, the painter draws even more attention to an essentially invisible man. All of the faces except his have become more detailed. The palette has become more subtle, with a wide range of greens. The checkerboard now has squares, which are echoed in the pattern of the floor, which is silver and olive. While the dominant colors are now green, yellow, and white, the pink of the board is reflected above, below, and to the side with flashes of magenta. Four of the figures wear hats or caps, all with brims that tilt toward the board. The figures in the foreground are drawn especially carefully. The draping of their clothing and the effects of light on it are precisely depicted. We see details of their dress and of their hair and faces; their focus and intensity are very clear. Another disjunction in the work is the apparent blending of indoors and outdoors. In the 1992 version, the primary background colors were green in the lower half and violet in the upper, indicating an outdoor setting. In the 2000 revision, the tiled floor suggests the setting of a barbershop, while the upper part of the background is grass-green. The changes suggest an artist backing away from any notion of "primitive" work, as is also the case in the next painting discussed.

*Saturday Afternoon,* variously dated December 1992 (on the back of the painting) and 1993–94 (credits in *African American Review*), is a large work done in acrylic. It appeared as the cover art for the 1994 issue of *African American Review* devoted to Major. In that version, it fit easily into the folk mode. Though complex in composition with groups of figures spread across the canvas, it minimized facial detail, simplified perspective, elongated limbs, and used a limited range of colors. It depicts a street scene in a black neighborhood with blocks of different shades of gray for the background. It can be seen as a positive rendering of community since it presents family and friendship groupings, a range of skin tones, music, and athletics. It is a world without tension, without violence, without apparent oppression. In this sense, it is a city version of Zora Neale Hurston's porch narratives. Clearly what interests the artist is how one composes a busy canvas without losing coherence. Major does this by constructing something like a triptych. The center contains the largest number of figures, arranged in a rough pyramid. The predominance of white clothing outlined in orange allows the focal point to become a figure in a green dress with blond hair. The figures on the left of the painting are drawn in by the use of white and orange again, with green tones used to link them to the center. In addition, the two most substantial figures face toward the center. The right side is not so fully filled. A direct connection to the center is made with a baby carriage, which links the hands of center and right figures. White dominates here as well, with clothes complemented by laundry on lines between the two spaces. The activity of the two boys boxing in the left foreground is balanced by the saxophonist on the lower right. Thus, the apparent simplicity of the painting can also be read as Major's effort to create and resolve a complex compositional problem: how do you incorporate a large number of figures into a painting, individualize them in some way, and yet maintain coherence?

He does so by simplifying the palette, by providing a monochromatic background, and by creating distinctive groupings.

In the revision (plate 11), Major had made radical changes that give the painting a postmodern quality. First, he adds a wider range of color, mostly blues, especially in the background. The effect is to give it more detail and depth. For example, the figure standing in the doorway in the original seemed to be floating in air; in the new version, he is clearly on the doorstep. In addition, some of the clothes that had been white are now given color; in a few instances, he changes colors to provide greater contrast. Major has also added some pattern in that the baby carriage and the sweater of one of the men have been given an argyle design in contrasting colors. The most significant change, however, is in the faces, most of which are actually photographs of faces pasted on top of the canvas. Many of these seem to be from black-and-white magazine photographs that have been lightly washed to add a hint of color. At the same time, the legs and arms have been left in their original tones of brown. The effect is to suggest a multiracial community that has adopted masks that make them racially ambiguous. The artist is no longer simulating folk art; instead, he is emphasizing his freedom as an artist and making a statement through his postmodern pastiche of his preference for individuality over racial identity.

## DIRTY BIRD BLUES

He continues his investigation of folk representation in his 1996 novel *Dirty Bird Blues*. In fact, he has labeled some of the visual art that he was working on simultaneously with the novel "blues paintings" (Bunge, *Conversations*, 161). The hardcover, as mentioned above, incorporated "Country Boogie" in its cover design. The novel was originally published by Mercury House, a nonprofit press in San Francisco. It was brought out in paperback the next year by Berkley Publishing, an imprint of Putnam Books. It tells the story of Manfred Banks, a blues musician from Chicago whose passions are music, his wife, Cleo, and Old Crow bourbon (the "Dirty Bird" of the title). His problem, unsurprisingly, is that the three do not mix well, and he is constantly being told that he must choose. This blues situation constitutes the storyline of the novel; it ends only when Man gives up alcohol. While the book is generally read as an attempt to construct a blues narrative, it is also useful to think of it as a story of alcoholism. As Klinkowitz has pointed out, Major had for a number of years a reputation as a serious drinker.

He recalls a conversation with Sharyn, Major's wife at the time: "'When Clarence drinks too much,' she warned me, 'he doesn't act like others. He doesn't get loud or silly, just even more quietly serious.' Here indeed was a danger, I was told. 'When Clarence seems totally reliable,' she said, 'that's when you have to watch out.'"[6] He eventually had to give up drinking completely for health reasons. Thus, the novel may be read as an exploration of the pleasures and pains associated with this particular addiction. The book also follows the trajectory of Major's early life, from childhood in Lexington and Atlanta to adulthood in Chicago and Omaha. Similarly, it is about the struggles to create and gain respect for one's art in the face of criticism and censure. For both character and author, the difficulty involved a desire on the part of others for him to accept the role of conventional breadwinner, taking whatever work was available for a black man at the time. Both are frustrated by such demands to surrender their artistic passion to moneymaking, and they ultimately fail in those endeavors.

In the novel, Major brings together virtually all the motifs associated with the blues: love, labor, money, racism, violence, alcohol, travel, and music itself. In his rendering, they are linked by the dialectic of trouble and desire. Banks, called Man by the narrator but Fred by his family, moves through a post–World War II landscape that does not yet include civil rights activity. Just as in early novels, Major here takes a basic genre and modifies it for his own purposes. He adapts the naturalistic fiction of Richard Wright and other Chicago writers—some of whom he knew in the 1950s—to create a narrative that never quite surrenders to the pessimism or irony of Wright, Chester Himes, William Gardner Smith, and Willard Motley. Like them, he details the violence associated with a racist legal system, the prejudice found in modern industry, and the resultant frustration and anger found in black men, who often vent their rage on whites or, more often, on other blacks. In these areas, Major produces the most realistic writing of his career. As one example, he describes Man undergoing a test to gain a welding position in the factory:

> He adjusted the rod onto his iron. Then he lowered his face-cover. Took
> a few minutes to adjust to the view. It was hard to see through the plastic.
> Because it was all scratched up and everything. But he got it. Then he could
> see the rail standing there all right, the place where it was resting, the mark-
> ings. Man got himself in position. Okay, don't bluff, do your stuff. Time.
> Take yo time. He pressed the iron, getting it ready. Then he touched the rod

to the crevice where the rail and the beam met, right at the corner marking.
Hoping like hell that the damned rod wouldn't stick. He'd had such a hard
time with that in the beginning, keeping the rod from sticking to the iron.
(*Dirty*, 113)

Major, too, takes his time, using two pages to depict the task. In doing so,
he captures the stress of performing the task under the critical eyes of the
white foreman and other workers, the nervousness of Man in trying to
prove himself, and the linguistic means by which by which the protagonist
maintains control in the situation.

Other details reinforce the connection to the earlier tradition. Both
names used for the main character are associated with figures from Wright's
short fiction: Brother Mann from "Down by the Riverside" and Fred Dan-
iels from "The Man Who Lived Underground." The two violent policemen
who arrest Man and refer to him as Big Boy are reminiscent of Himes's
Coffin Ed and Gravedigger Jones from his Harlem detective series. Finally,
the world of dingy apartments recalls the tenements of the fiction of Ann
Petry and Gwendolyn Brooks. He portrays the racial tension in the factory
setting, as the foreman who promotes Man later causes him to be fired, in
large part because he saw the black man with a white woman outside the
work setting, an event that corresponds exactly to an incident that happened
to Major in Omaha.[7] He also reveals some of the self-destructive behavior
that black men engage in as a result of having few options in their lives.

But unlike the social realists, Major is not interested in exposing the difficulties of African American life. Rather, he uses those conditions to test
the mettle of his artist figure. Throughout the narrative Man faces problems, many of his own making. However, as Michael Harris points out in a
*Los Angeles Times* review, creativity is never a problem for the protagonist.
No matter how much he is antagonized by racist whites, or misled by the
unwise Solomon Thigpen, his musical partner, or frustrated in his marriage,
or enchanted by the Dirty Bird, he can always perform and invent new
material. He thinks and talks in lyrics almost as much as in conversational
English. It is as though Major took the minor figure of the cartman who
calls himself Peetie Wheatstraw in Ellison's *Invisible Man* and made him the
central consciousness of this novel. His discourse is a mixture of blues lyrics and jive talk: "Yeah! I ain't the driver, ain't the driver's son, but I'll do the
driving till the driver comes" (94). Throughout the novel, the author incor-

porates traditional lines from folk material or invents it to sound like such material. Man, who is shown repeatedly to have insight into his own problems and sympathy for the situations of others, primarily uses this mode of communication to make sense of the world. Because the novel is realistic, it is not the language used in ordinary conversation. Rather, it is the means by which Major gives his protagonist an inner self and a performative persona. Unlike other works that have been labeled blues narratives or that include blues characters, *Dirty Bird Blues* reveals the emotional and psychological essence of the blues artist. In this sense, blues is not what Man does, but what he is; in this, he is parallel to Vincent Van Gogh, who exists in Major's poetry as nothing other than artist.

The themes of love and alcoholism in the novel must be understood in this context. Man's drinking is linked to his initial conflict with Cleo and leads to their separation. While the use of alcohol does not impinge on his musical work, that work, in clubs, frequently leads to excessive drinking. In Cleo's mind, especially because of her desire for respectability, the music and the whiskey come to be the same problem. Alcohol also makes it difficult for Man to hold a day job, since he is often unable to go to work after nights of playing and imbibing. It also makes him unable to see the developing problems in their relationship. Her turn to a minister for aid and eventually for sexual comfort demonstrates her belief in blues as the devil's music, since for her it is tied to drunkenness and irresponsibility. In addition, Man himself thinks of his two activities as joined, since drinking is simply part of his musical environment and does not interfere with that work. He sees Cleo's criticisms as an attack not only on his addiction but also on his art. He believes that the solution is in proving himself capable of supporting his family through a conventional job while continuing his old practices.

For a while, this works. He moves to Omaha, obtains employment at a factory, plays at a local club on the weekends, and eventually persuades Cleo to join him. Even when he loses the job, the fact that its termination results from racism rather than drink allows him to continue his old habits, which are reinforced by the appearance of Solomon, who is incapable of responsible behavior. It is only when Man comes home drunk and believes that Cleo has left him for another minister that he finally hits bottom. In an extended scene that combines humor with threat, he journeys through the city seeking her as he drinks more and more. This episode, two-thirds of the way through the novel, concludes not only with his discovery that his wife has only been visiting family but also with a surreal lynching nightmare, similar to ones in *Invisible Man* and Leon Forrest's *There Is a Tree More Ancient than Eden*. Having gone through these experiences, Man vows to quit drinking, a promise he keeps despite temptations.

What he and we discover is that his drinking in fact has no inherent relationship to his music but is related to his fears about his own manhood. His underlying fear is that he cannot be a real man and be an artist, that to provide for his family and to have respect in his community, he must bow to the demands of a conventional life. Some of the men he worked for appear in his nightmare about being lynched in the factory from which he was fired. He is hung from a crane and sees a black child (his daughter) thrown into a shredding machine. The last line of this scene reveals the connection of lynching to black masculinity: "The flames are gaining power, lapping up his pants leg, cutting into his crotch" (235). A few pages later, he has a sudden memory of a childhood experience when light-skinned members of his extended family called him a baboon and ugly because of his dark skin. The scene had ended in violence, with him as the victim. Thus, he learns that his drinking is a way of suppressing fears, and that his true manhood can be asserted by facing them soberly.

Love is a struggle for him as long as the issues of manhood are not addressed. Cleo can leave him, she can cuckold him, she can demand that he give up his music and his friends, as long as he cannot define for himself his masculine integrity. Even when he gets a job in Omaha and brings her there to start a new life, they remain unhappy as long as they both are fundamentally committed to their old ways. Though he demonstrates throughout the book a willingness to take the side of women in their times of need, they cannot be happy until he forsakes the world of money for the world of art. In the penultimate chapter, he is offered his old job cleaning at a Sears department store. He rejects it without a second thought, though he is expecting only one remaining unemployment check. Instead, he relies on the money Cleo makes at the beauty shop and his own pay from the blues club, where his tips depend ironically on how much people have been drinking while listening to his music. At the end of the novel, he has another dream, but this time it is about a man who offers him a record contract. He awakens as Cleo enters the house: "And there she was, smiling and carrying Katrina against her bosom, coming toward the living room.

He got up and met his wife and daughter" (279). In essence, love works when Man can live his dream and not concern himself with money, status, or insecurities.

Major seems to be suggesting here an idealized version of the artist's life. Devotion to one's art solves all problems. It enables one to see beyond race, beyond exploitative labor, beyond personal traumas and the ways of suppressing them. The novel can be read as the author's preferred life: Man, unlike Major, stays with one woman, who finally understands the necessity of his art to not only his but their happiness. She is willing to sacrifice financial security for the pursuit of his dream. In contrast, Major had two wives who seem not to have understood his need for aesthetic expression, and that lack of commitment required him to move on, first to Omaha, then to New York. By the time he wrote the novel, Major had finally entered a relationship in which his art was valued by his beloved, Pam. Ironically, of course, he could only reach that position through a life of labor only secondarily related to the art itself. Teaching and related activities provided the financial foundation for artistic endeavor and led to successful marriage later in life. The argument of the text, to the extent that there is one, is that art conquers all (and results in love). Moreover, Major, by writing the book, can also have it all. He produces a mainstream narrative that takes risks through its blues discourse, that can claim experimental credentials through that discourse, can speak to a black audience, and yet retains a universal theme of love and art redeemed through struggle. It also serves as his *apologia pro vita sua*, justifying and explaining all the problems and complications of his own life in terms of aesthetic quest.

The sales of *Dirty Bird Blues* have been the best of Major's career, with approximately six thousand in hardback and over twenty thousand in paper.[8] The reviews of the book would reinforce his sense of accomplishment. *Publishers Weekly* praised the author's "ear for the music of the American vernacular," though the reviewer found Man's insistent blues discourse "calculated" rather than true.[9] Such a comment reflects the consistent pattern in mainstream commentary throughout Major's career of irritation at elements that suggested experimentation. In this sense, the negative comment may actually have served his self-identification as an avant-garde writer. Critics also gave emphasis to racism, referring to the novel as a story of a black Everyman or of black survival. While there is truth to this observation, it has more to do with historical accuracy and genre conventions than with the author's effort to construct a social critique. The strongest praise was based on the language of the text, not merely the specific patterns of the blues, but also the varieties and patterns of ordinary speech:

> In its unpretentious way, this is a novel about language. Major catches the subtle differences in the ways his characters speak, depending on their company. He listens to characters in bars, assembly lines, blues clubs, beauty parlors and the janitor's break room at Sears.
>
> He also observes the way people use language moment by moment to make sense of their lives. When readers overhear Man as he translates his experience into the rhythm and language of the blues, it sounds entirely natural.[10]

## "THE SLAVE TRADE"

In 1994, Major published "The Slave Trade: View from the Middle Passage" in *African American Review*. It is an extended meditation on, not only the trade, but also the meaning of race in the modern world. It comes on the heels of a series of works designated by Ashraf Rushdy as "neo–slave narratives." These include Toni Morrison's *Beloved* (1987), David Bradley's *The Chaneysville Incident* (1981), Charles Johnson's *Middle Passage* (1990), and the fiction and poetry of Gayl Jones, among others. What distinguishes Major's work, as carefully detailed by Linda Furgerson Selzer a few years later, is his employment of European art as the evidence for his cultural critique. In doing so, he reverses his usual method of referring to artists and their work as a positive means of positioning himself within traditions or of exploring the relationship between art and other aspects of life. In this instance, visual expression is shown to be a means by which racist attitudes and cultural domination are naturalized by whites.

He creates a central consciousness, Mfu, whom he imagines jumped overboard and drowned during the Middle Passage rather than endure a life of enslavement. From his position "where he sleeps free in the deep waves, / free to speak his music" ("Clarence Major Issue," 11), he looks toward the three continents

> for understanding of the white
> men
> who came to the shores
> of his nation. (11)

He wants to grasp the how and why of human exploitation, though not because he really believes it will fundamentally change anything: "Escape? / No such luck then or now" (11). He comprehends the role of greed in the process; Major gives a list of the material explanations for the trade:

> ivory, gold, land, fur, skin, chocolate, cocoa,
> tobacco, palm oil,
> coffee, coconuts, sugar, silk, captured Africans,
> mulatto sex-
> slaves, "exotic" battles, and "divinely ordained
> slavery." (12)

Mfu recognizes that in that historical period, racial domination created wonderful possibilities for the dominant race: a "heaven-on-earth for white men" (12).

But his concerns are really elsewhere. The poem establishes a personal history, as we learn of Mfu's betrayal by his own chief, who sold him for a shaving brush, though, at sixty, he had "never had even one strand of facial hair" (12). Embedded in this comment is the cultural meaning of slavery. Unlike, say, kolanuts, which would be useful and thus a "reasonable" deal to make, the brush serves primarily as a symbol of the acquisition of Western civilization. Europeans assume the superiority of their technology, religion, and humanity; Africans buy into that view. Specifically, what the native population learns is a basic principle of modernity: the value of conspicuous consumption, as the list of European desires suggests. Mfu's goal, and thus that of his creator, is to shape a countermemory to the history defined by whites, to go beyond rationalizations for greed and cruelty to find actual reasons for what has sometimes been referred to as the "black holocaust."

Major even questions the "good" Europeans—those, for example, who wear Josiah Wedgewood's medallion ("Am I Not a Man and a Brother?") as they baptize the local population. Or the monk who rejects white racial superiority and yet cannot resist eroticizing Africans, even if they are biblical figures such as the Ethiopian Eunuch or the Queen of Sheba. Another ambiguous example is John Stedman, who is not mentioned in the poem, but his autobiographical *Narrative of a Five Years Expedition against the Revolted Negroes of Surinam* (1796), with its frontispiece engraving by William Blake, serves as the source for one instance of horrific cruelty in the poem, even though Stedman and Blake were antislavery.

As Selzer points out in detail, Major makes extensive use of European art to make his case. She notes that many of the images offered come directly from specific paintings, such as those of St. Maurice, the Queen of Sheba, and Jean-Baptiste Belley, all black figures who serve in some sense the purposes of Western culture.[11] Because the art to which Major makes reference spans several centuries, he can demonstrate the deep structural significance of race to European identity and culture. And because Africa and the United States are also implicated in this history, it becomes inescapable. As an artist, then, he discovers his own "imprisonment" in racial discourse, which may be why, here and elsewhere, he is so committed to demonstrating its arbitrariness.

### DAVIS AND PARIS

The mid- to late 1990s was a quiet period in which the work of consolidation was going on. The spring 1994 issue of *African American Review* included five poems, eight paintings, two pieces of short fiction, and an essay that became the title piece for the nonfiction collection *Necessary Distance* (2001); it also included six articles about his work, an interview, and a checklist of his books. This material became *Clarence Major and His Art*, published five years later by the University of North Carolina Press, with additional essays, poems, paintings, and excerpts from five of the novels, but no short fiction. The same year (1994) saw the publication of *Juba to Jive*. The previous year HarperCollins had published *Calling the Wind*, which was followed in 1996 by the companion volume *The Garden Thrives: Twentieth Century African American Poetry*, which includes many of the same artists as Major's 1969 anthology. Two years after this, Copper Canyon Press brought out *Configurations: New and Selected Poems, 1958–1998*; it included selections from eight of the earlier books plus fifty-six previously uncollected pieces dating back to 1968. Almost simultaneously, Northeastern University Press released an "unexpurgated edition" of *All-Night Visitors*. This version restores the text as Major had created it, though with some materials that were not part of the original manuscript nor in the first version, as well as deletion of a rape scene that appeared in the first version. The net result is a much more linear narrative that also tells a safer story. He also gave a number of interviews during this time; they constitute nearly half of Nancy Bunge's *Conversations with Clarence Major* (2002). All this work resulted in a much more mainstream, professional identity.

On 21 July 1998, Major and Pam flew from San Francisco to spend about a month in Paris. They chose an apartment in Montparnasse overlooking the cemetery. The journal that Major kept of the trip suggests that this choice was connected to the area's cultural history. He notes on the day of arrival that Josephine Baker had performed nearby on 20 December 1927. The next day, he quotes a passage about the area from Jean Rhys's *Quartet* (1928). He links artists and writers to specific locations, such as La Couploe, a bistro famous in the 1920s but still in business. Similarly, the apartment seems to have been chosen in part because the Montparnasse Cemetery contains the remains of Baudelaire, Maupassant, de Beauvoir, Sartre, Saint-Saens, and Gainsborough.

On the 1998 trip, he was less interested in going to museums, though he visited a few, than in simply walking the streets and sketching people of the area. The journal contains 102 pages; of those, fifteen contain drawings of objects, such as places or animals, while sixty-five present images of people, often occupying the full page. He and Pam went to the building where Theo and Vincent Van Gogh lived but discovered that it was no longer open to the public. In effect, he appears to have situated himself among the artists who lived and worked here, rather than as a pilgrim to sites associated with his heroes or as a tourist come to see their objects. The journal tells us little about their social life in the city, which he had emphasized in previous works on his European travels. They did have dinner with Ron Sukenick and his wife, Julia. Major described the evening as including "much one-upsmanship talk."[12] The tension may have had to do with the choices they had made as writers; both men had continued to produce fiction, though Sukenick had remained committed to experimentation and was eventually recognized for his career of innovation. By this time, he had also developed inclusion body myositis, a rare muscle disease, from which he died six years later.

Major and Pam returned to Davis at the end of August, and he returned to his routine of teaching creative writing and American and African American literature. At the same time she was teaching writing for the university. What is noteworthy about this period is a shift away from the African American material of the early and mid-1990s. In all of his expressive forms, he focuses on "universal" subjects. His painting is primarily devoted to the female figure, with some attention to landscapes. His poetry is largely concerned with art, and his last novel is the story of an African American painter who falls in love with a Chinese American poet. Even his

excursion into memoir, in the form of his mother's life story, is not significantly attentive to race matters.

*ONE FLESH*

His last novel, *One Flesh*, was published in 2003 by the Dafina imprint of
Kensington Books. Dafina was created to market to African American
readers, especially in popular genres; Kensington was primarily known
for romance fiction. Thus, Major was positioning himself in the rapidly
expanding genre-novel field emerging in the 1990s and early new century. Ironically, the choice also returned him to his beginnings as a novelist; much of the list for Dafina includes black erotica. So, despite his long
commitment to small presses, the decision to place his romance novel with
a mass-market publisher made some sense, especially since its publicist
noted in a 2006 interview that it had developed a multicultural line.[13] The
results were disappointing for both author and publisher. *One Flesh* managed sales of around seventeen thousand copies for a press that, according
to Major, considers anything less than fifty thousand to be a failure.[14]

The novel is a distinct departure in multiple ways. It is a straightforward
romance story without any recognizable experimental aspects. It contains
none of the folk elements of the three previous novels (including the Zuni
traditions of *Painted Turtle*). Finally, it is multicultural, as it incorporates a
failed black-white marriage and a Chinese American love interest for the
African American protagonist. It tells the story of a few months in the life
of John Canoe, a black painter in New York City who has reached the age
of thirty-three without being involved in a serious relationship, preferring
to devote himself to his art. He lives in a loft in Soho. Major is very careful
about details, locating parking garages, restaurants, and galleries in the area.
Adding to the apparent realism, he places the loft at 39 Greene Street, at the
corner of Houston Street. Curiously, he gets this detail wrong; number 39
is in fact several blocks south, in the block on which he situates the gallery
where John's work is shown. Since Major had lived a few blocks from this
address when he first was in New York, it is unlikely that he would mistake
the site. This "error" suggests Major's continued willingness to play games
with his readers by constructing rather than reflecting reality. Adding to
the "fun and games" in the text, the two pages before the address is noted
involve parodies of artists associated with the building. John had purchased
the loft "from a rich young lady with red hair who, for a couple of years, had

the notion she was born to dabble in watercolors and who'd remodeled the whole place, putting in hardwood floors, new bathroom, new kitchen, the works. John had the feeling she woke up every morning feeling as secure about herself and America and its dollars as a cherry tree feels about the ground it's planted in" (*One Flesh*, 8–9). When he talks to her about buying the space, her main concern is to demonstrate the superiority of her training to his. Interestingly, however, the narrator is careful in the exchange to give the full history of John's artistic education.

He follows this with a commentary on John's neighbor in the building, who is also an artist:

> Paul had come along in a trendier tradition than John. A write-up in *Art Digest* at age nineteen. Boston Institute of Contemporary Art. Andy Warhol film parties. Warhol influenced years of blow jobs, electric chairs, bosoms, soup cans, Draculas, Frankensteins, bike boys, Chelsea Girls, blue movies, harlots, lonesome cowboys. Paul claimed he had done hard drinking with the best of them at the Cedar Tavern. Paul also claimed to have met every-body—Truman Capote, Mick Jagger, Jacqueline Kennedy, Liza Minnelli, Robert Rauschenberg, Happy and Nelson Rockefeller, Elizabeth Taylor, Frank O'Hara, Frank Stella, Allen Ginsberg, Michael Jackson, Susan Sontag, Stephen Spender, Susan Rothenberg, Joan Mitchell, Larry Rivers, Gloria Vanderbilt. That some were long dead was of little importance. Paul called them by their first names and talked about them and other famous people like they were his close friends. (10–11)

We also learn that Paul simply adapts himself to the latest trends in art: "Art Deco, pop art, op art, the blotted-line technique, spray painting, photo-graphs, mopping, repetition, graphite, silk screen" (10).

These satiric portraits, one of artist as overeducated amateur and the other as unoriginal celebrity hunter, establish a contrast with John, who really cares about nothing but his art. He has relatively little interest in commercial success and supports himself by teaching in the local schools. His art is displayed and sold through the Greene Street Collective, rather than through a private gallery. Thus, he represents Major's ideal artist, com-mitted to developing his vision rather than responding to the marketplace. One irony, of course, is that his story is being told in a mass-market novel.

However, it would be a mistake to think of the protagonist as the suffer-ing artist living a life of sacrifice and deprivation. He has the loft because his father, a successful cardiologist, bought it for him. He keeps a car garaged near his apartment, though he seldom drives. While not well-off, he does not have to worry about making a living from his painting. He also has no doubts about his vocation. Like Manfred Banks of *Dirty Bird Blues*, he has confidence in his craft, regardless of what else is going on in his life. In the present time of the story, he is working on a large scale: the two paintings in the collective show are each seventy by one hundred inches. As John looks at them, the narrator reveals the self-protective satisfaction of the artist: "His pride, as he gazed at his own work, was like a covered wagon of the Old West, surrounded by a band of thugs on horseback shooting holes in its hide. In other words, pride was an emotion he felt he had to watch carefully. It wasn't very productive" (15). His isolation—from parents, friends, lovers—is the price he pays for his sense of artistic vision. Nothing else matters. Curiously, however, we see very little of the activity of creation in the narrative. John talks about art, some of his paintings are described, but we do not see him regularly at work on canvases. In one chapter, for example, there is a brief scene in which he applies color to a canvas until an image emerges, though it is abstract. He keeps shifting the color combinations and then, at the end, scrapes away all the paint.

Instead, we are given the everyday life of a young man in the city. We learn of the places he visits, the food he likes to eat, and the people he comes in contact with. The novel develops the themes of art, race, and romance, but John's engagement with them lacks intensity. We are told about, but seldom shown, anything like passion in the protagonist. The art theme, for example, is often shown through lists or name-dropping. As he waits on a street corner one day, John begins to notice the architectural features of a building nearby; these are rendered as a catalog. Later, he lists the primary hangouts in the area for artists in the 1960s. At various moments, he mentions the names of painters of the nineteenth and twentieth centuries. A curious example of the lack of engagement is in John and Susie's decision to go to Europe, primarily for the art; however, the trip itself does not become part of the narrative. They make the arrangements in one chapter; in the next, they have returned. Here the narrative itself seems to reflect indifference to John's vocation.

The most significant scene in terms of aesthetics is one that operates almost as a sermon on modern art. It is a rewriting of the scene from "Women in Love" discussed above. John, who defines himself as an abstractionist, begins a canvas but is soon aware of the presence of Gauguin watching him. The older painter encourages him to include a female nude, though one in the modernist tradition: "'Do a naked woman standing in a bathtub,' said Gauguin. 'I like naked women. The viewer should be looking at her from an angle at about mid-thigh. Let her appear to be an unmovable mass. You can use Susie, if you like. But make her bottom-heavy. I like them bottom-heavy. Make her one-sided too, about to fall out of the composition. I like a little danger'" (88). While John resists this advice, Gauguin launches into a discourse on perspective, similar to Major's own commentary in "Reaching and Leaving the Point." It insists on a rejection of Renaissance notions in favor of "heightened perception." John is advised to forget strict rules in favor of intuition. Moreover, the recommendation is also applied to his life: "'You don't need the plausible, measurable system. You paralyze yourself. Let your intuitive faculty fly. Do that in your life too. Susie will love you for it'" (89). At the same time that Major was working on this text, he was producing a series of nudes, including one leaning toward the edge of the painting. Thus, he is putting in the mouth of Gauguin his own ideas about what art should do.

John meets Susie at the collective show. She is the only person interested in his work. She sees the influence of Van Gogh in it, which pleases him. He gives her a tour of the show and introduces her to other artists. The relationship develops very rapidly. By the beginning of the next chapter, they have become a couple. Much of this early section of the book is devoted to explicating their backgrounds, Susie as an American-born Chinese and John as a biracial Catholic from the Midwest. They move in together, and Susie impulsively buys a dog from a woman on the street. Though John has no desire for a dog, his response tends to be passive-aggressive, a pattern displayed often in the text. By the next chapter, they have sold the dog, which proved too active for the loft. Susie immediately decides to get kittens, which they do despite John's claim that he is allergic. Interestingly, the difference between her impulsiveness and his caution never really becomes a significant tension in their relationship; in fact, though they have disagreements, there is no threat to the happy ending. Even at the end, when he discovers that she is bisexual and has had a liaison with her friend Mei Wong, it is resolved quickly, though it is not clear exactly how.

The primary source of conflict is with family, especially Susie's. It is here that Major develops the racial theme, as a displacement from black-white issues. In fact, while John records a few instances of racial problems, they have little to do either with his mixed-race parentage or his personal experiences. He does demonstrate some sensitivity to any racial implications in interactions, but these seem to operate primarily to demonstrate the pointlessness of racial consciousness. Where his race does enter significantly is in the attitudes of Susie's family. They are a traditional Chinese family who believe that their daughter is valuable only as a marriage partner for a Chinese man. Her desire for higher education and her interest in non-Chinese men are seen as insults to the family. When she goes off to UC Davis and later takes up with a black man, she is virtually disowned.

When she meets John, she has moved to New York and gotten a job in publishing. She also is a poet. In some ways she is more the representative of Major in the text than John is. She resents the narrowness of the life lived in San Francisco's Chinatown, just as the author felt the limitations of South Side Chicago. She struggles with the notion of a racialized identity, making use of it in her art but refusing to acknowledge it as essential to her sense of self. Whenever she talks to her parents, the conversations end in argument. Though she resists any simple ethnic identity, she is willing to introduce John to the world of New York's Chinatown. There they meet with her uncle Charlie, a black sheep in the family because of his gambling habit. He has some valued traits—hard work, frugal living, diligent saving to bring over his wife from China—but his practice of going regularly to Atlantic City casinos draws even Susie's condemnation.

A contrast in the representation of race comes during a brief episode in which John and Susie go with Mei Wong and her white date James to Bear Mountain to escape the city heat. At one point, James makes the observation, "'Hey! Think about it. We got all the races right here on one blanket'" (148). John sees the comment as both inappropriate and "innocent." But it seems to be deeply troubling for him: "John closed his eyes. A sense of dread swept through him. He hoped they were not going to get mired in a discussion of race. Better, at this moment, to plummet into the encoiled depths of a snowstorm." This thought is contrasted to his verbal efforts to neutralize the situation. The intensity of his thinking, however, suggests the extent to which Major reacts to the very idea of race; it recalls Klinkowitz's observation about Major's resentment of Sukenick's racial comment, mentioned earlier. Here that anxiety is reflected in the image of a vortex of whiteness.

The moment recalls an earlier point in the text where John also experiences powerful negative emotion. In this instance, a group of black teens are performing in front of the collective and have drawn a crowd:

> Six-feet-one, John could see over shoulders, and he saw the boys had a collection basket on the sidewalk in front of them. John reluctantly stood at the edge of the crowd and listened. The rap song was about getting "some

good pussy" and "not letting any bitch fuck over me" and "killing any motherfucker who gets in my way." The crowd was laughing and clapping, immensely pleased with the performance, while John felt a sudden and powerful sense of shame. Yet, strangely, he stood there as both the spirit of the crowd and the beat and rhythm of the voices infiltrated his emotions. (13)

The first question is why such an experience would be represented as shocking to John's sensibilities; it certainly would have been common in New York or any other large U.S. city in the 1990s. What is the source of shame here? Is John, like Ellison's invisible man, rendered abject by an encounter with the black vernacular, especially in the context of a white audience? Is he somehow implicated by race in what he might consider a minstrel show? Is it the language that he finds offensive, either for its obscenity or its objectification of women? In this sense, is this Major's opportunity to establish his womanist credentials? And why is John "strangely" fixed to the spot as the scene unfolds? Why does he feel "gratitude" when the police arrive to break up the show? A deep ambivalence pervades the character's engagement with race; he is both dismissive of it and profoundly troubled by it. But this awareness occurs at odd moments, almost as experiences of the uncanny, in which the unconscious makes an appearance in a life otherwise carefully regulated in terms of its emotions.

This point enters the relationship during the climax of the novel, when John and Susie go to San Francisco. She wants him to see the city but has no desire to see her parents. They stay at the Juliana Hotel, just a few blocks from Chinatown. At various moments, John imagines her as a subject for his art, but not as herself: "Yes, she could be his Saint Catherine. Or a factory girl. He could paint her worn out from long hours at a machine. Or as Joan of Arc! As Lady Godiva!" (211). As they visit galleries, he thinks about Van Gogh and about one Russian artist's use of the mobile axis. He makes a commitment to free his own art from any strict reliance on "Nature" and "more and more from his own intimate impressions of it" (212).

In the midst of these thoughts, they end up at the intersection of Bush and Grant, the lower end of Chinatown. Here John insists that they enter the enclave, though Susie claims that he promised they would not. The initial effort is marked by John's tourist-style observations: menu items, names of businesses, architecture. Soon they come close to her parents' restaurant. Again she resists continuing. John makes the point that, if she acts nervous, people are more likely to notice. But of course, it is his insistence on this path that is the problem. They walk past the business and, of course, are seen. What follows is a series of embarrassing and awkward scenes, during which John offers Susie no assistance. The result is that their relationship is rejected by the family and Susie is apparently formally disowned.

The reader's inevitable question is why John would put the woman he loves through such stress and humiliation. One answer is aesthetic; he creates a scenario using her as the primary figure in order to determine his "intimate impressions" of it and her, thereby engendering a work of art. His examples of roles for her include three figures who suffer—St. Catherine, Joan of Arc, and the factory girl—and one who is sensualized as a subject. Through the conflict he triggers, he constructs her as the suffering woman who is deracialized.

What he also does, however, is place her fully within his control by forcing the conflict with her family, thus bringing fully into the open their racism and close-mindedness and compelling her to choose him. Before this, there was always the possibility of reconciliation, as she would periodically speak to her mother. By pushing her into open rebellion, he forces her to cut her ties to them. In the process, he also pulls her into his way of thinking about race. It is a condition to be denied; those who insist on noticing it are to be shunned. While it is clear from the text that this assertion is more about repression than actual repudiation, it nonetheless is a way that John can *be* in the world and now that Susie can be too. Moreover, the control extends beyond race. John's accidental discovery of Susie's erotic photograph of Mei Wong and the resulting confrontation works to establish their relationship as heteronormative. He obsesses about it, and when he interrogates her, he finds unacceptable Susie's response that it was long ago, not serious, and irrelevant to their future. He must humiliate her and force her to destroy the picture, despite its obvious value to her: she had kept it in a drawer of her desk for years. His attitude seems related to his attack on the family; anything that involves her Chineseness has to be rejected. Like other aspects of the narrative, this element was not prepared for and has no consequences in the text. It is also noteworthy that the graphic description of Mei Wong's genital area is the only explicit sexual material in the novel. In this sense, it is connected to John's shame at the rap lyrics. In both cases, racial identity is tied to sexual expression, and his repudiation of both is tied to his uncomfortable fascination.

John's lack of affect in much of the novel, interrupted by sudden outbursts of abject feeling, voyeuristic tendencies, and demands for control, suggests a complex portrait of the artist and perhaps of Major himself. It is noteworthy that John has the initials J.C. and is thirty-three at the time of the story. The artist is Christlike in having two natures, one that experiences the world intensely and the other that distances himself in a godlike way in order to render that world in his own terms. He cannot be concerned too much in the details of life or he will lose perspective, a term essential to John and Major's vision. At the same time, he must have a depth of experience to draw on as material. He must not be caught up in determining categories of race, class, or gender because they will limit his individuality. But he must also be aware of them if he is to sell his vision to the world. There is also a hint of posturing in the story, that John must repress so much and yet control so thoroughly; the implication is that he may not be all he wants to believe he is. He may be no more than a version of the street rapper pleasing his white audience; he may attack other artists because he is uncertain of his own ability. After all, we are not given in the book any outside assessment of his work. He may humiliate Susie because he doubts his own sexuality. He may resent his father, not because of the parents' divorce, but because he hates his own blackness, whatever that word might mean. In a character such as John, Major seems to be working out these issues yet again. The discontinuities in the plot, the moments of strangeness, and the lack of passion in the romance would suggest that he has not yet completed that quest.

## TWENTY-FIRST-CENTURY PAINTING

Major's visual work since 2000 has been characterized by large scale (somewhat similar to that of his *One Flesh* protagonist, John Canoe), bright colors, and a return to a Postimpressionist aesthetic. Its principal subject is the female figure, though he has also done a number of landscapes. Many of them are local to the Davis area, including a number of the figures, since he returned to working in studio settings with models. In addition, some suggest nostalgia, such as a series based on a view of Twelfth Street on the Lower East Side, including one called *East 12th St., NYC, Between 1st and Avenue A. 1968*. The painting is dated 2008. In the foreground are two figures, with their backs to the viewer, who by their skin tones and dress could easily be Major and Sheila, who were living in the area before they went to Mexico. Another is titled *Rebecca, My Great-Grandmother* (2005), though clearly it is a modern image (plate 12). Given the notoriety of the original Rebecca in Major's telling of her story, it is noteworthy that the dominant color is red and that the concentric lines of her loose-fitting dress draw the eye toward her womb. The red around her eyes and the yellow tint of her skin tone suggest the pain and difficulty of her life.

The landscapes, some of which are large, emphasize what might be called the geometry of geography. *Blue City*, for example, an acrylic from 1999 (plate 13), works with a pattern of rich blue rectangles bordered by streaks of white and yellow. It is, in effect, an impressionist rendering of a city at night that is nearly abstract. Another effect is generated in *Tracks between Davis and Woodland* (2004). Here, because of the effects of perspective, a series of parallel lines (the railroad tracks, the rows of trees, and the green space between) form a series of elongated triangles that lead to the vanishing point. The painting is almost a deliberate illustration of his essay on perspective written a few years earlier.

Most of the work he produced in the first decade of the new century involves the female figure. He has made two important points about this material. The first is that such work is the great tradition of Western art, and the second is that his women are deliberately racially ambiguous.[15] This work includes nudes, some in the style of Gauguin, a series of seated figures in which he experiments with the position and size of one of the feet, group compositions, single figures who fill up the canvas, and several in which the figure is small in relation to the background. Most are influenced by post-impressionism, with short, thick brushstrokes. They range in palette from monochromatic to sharply contrasting colors.

Some are narrative in nature, even if only implicitly. *The Woman Who Danced Once with Dustin Hoffman* (2004, plate 14), for example, would appear to be a relatively simple composition using large blocks of color and geometrical devices to form the image of a young woman. But the title suggests a history, a narrative of being touched by celebrity and still caught in that moment. Elements of the work can then be interpreted differently. Unlike many of his figures, this one looks, not at the viewer, but off at an angle of the frame. Her stringy hair, short dress, and spread legs become erotic aspects associated with that past. She becomes, in effect, a character in a story rather than simply a figure in a painting.

A second narrative work is *Two Sisters* (2009, plate 15). Here the background is radically simplified, as is the palette. Its lines are all straight, with blocks of red, green, and yellow in rectangles and triangles. Light appears to be coming from both the back, casting a shadow from the "background" figure, and from the front, reflected on the skin of the foreground figure. Perspective is distorted, both in terms of the figures and the lines of the background. The result is for the viewer's eyes to keep shifting between the sisters. The technique creates a sense of distance between them; their postures imply hostility. While the one in red has no features, her aggressiveness is indicated by her akimbo stance with feet wide apart. The foreground figure has features that are constructed mostly of straight lines, and her elongated limbs are drawn almost into knots. The emptiness of the room, except for the red chair in which the foreground one sits with her back to the other, suggests a vacuum in their lives.

Others of his female figures do not clearly offer stories as part of the work. In some instances, they are part of technical experiments, such as a series involving women with crossed arms or posed in front of plain versus patterned backgrounds. A few seem to have been done primarily to produce sensual effects. Among the most striking of these are *Before the Interview* (2006) and *Joan* (2010). *Before the Interview* seems to be influenced somewhat by Toulouse-Lautrec, though it is less finished than his work. It features a figure in a short red dress, bent at the waist, adjusting her thigh-high black stockings. Though her body is turned away, her head faces the viewer, as though she had been surprised in the moment. The viewer, in effect, becomes a voyeur, drawn to the prominence of her buttocks, which are positioned in the center of the frame.

*Joan*, in contrast, is an almost-classical figure adapted to a contemporary setting (plate 16). It is traditional in its use of light and shadow to create subtle chiaroscuro effects. The light coming from the right adds volume to her nightgown and definition to the body. Her face suggests the Madonna, perhaps echoing the Byzantine and Renaissance art of his early trips to European museums. What makes it contemporary in terms of composition is the lack of balance in competition with the calm of the image. The figure leans to the left, with her elbow and whatever supports her body outside the frame. This positioning reflects Gauguin's comments in "Reaching and Leaving the Point" about the need in modern art to disrupt the viewer's expectations. The play with background also breaks the illusion of representation. What appears to be wallpaper, with its blending of yellow tones connected to the gown and hair and red-orange associated with the skin, in fact has an irregular design not likely in actual wall treatments. The sensuality of the painting is apparent in the careful attention to the folds of the gown and the texture of the hair as well as the tone of the muscles. It is the visual equivalent of an aubade, though the figure displays elements of androgyny in the Roman nose and jutting jaw.

THE POETRY OF ART

Major's last two books of poetry, *Waiting for Sweet Betty* (2002) and *Myself Painting* (2008), concern themselves with the life and work of the artist. As Megan Harlan observed in a *San Francisco Chronicle* review, *Waiting for Sweet Betty* is in the form of a triptych, with sections on California, travel (especially Paris), and notions of home. But it is also the poetry of a visual artist; it concerns itself with the ways perspective and light can be rendered through words. While several of the pieces make reference to earlier artists, the interest here is not so much in responding to their work or in imagining their worlds as it is seeing the speaker's world through their eyes. So, "San Diego and Matisse" plays with color and point of view; both parts include the word "perspective " in the title, both limit themselves to the colors pink and blue, and both play with the blending of interior and exterior:

> 1. *Inside from the Perspective of a Tree*
> Beautiful women in smoky blue culottes
> lying around on fluffy pink pillows
> beneath windows onto charming views,
> sea views, seasonal leaves and trees.
> Inside is outside and outside inside.
> Smell of saltwater in the room
>
> 2. *Outside from the Perspective of a Rocking Chair*
> Shadow of a lighthouse along the beach
> Whales spotted every day lately
> though winter's two months yet.
> The evening is as warm as an interior.
> Silverlight lagoonlight, snorkeling light,
> And a line of joggers against last light.
> Blue smoke snaking up the pink sky. (*Waiting*, 5)

Elements in the two parts are balanced. Not only do the same colors appear, and interior-exterior space blend, but the interior is made a natural space and the exterior is filled with human constructions (lighthouse, snorkeling, joggers). In each part there is also a single reference to a sense other than sight, but it is the visual, both in terms of images and the repetition of first "views," then "light," that predominates. The transparency of space here even suggests that Major wants to go beyond Matisse in imagining the fluidity of inside-outside.

Many of the poems in the opening section explore the vistas of northern California, especially Cambria and Half Moon Bay, between Los Angeles and San Francisco. Here Major does with words what he did with some of his paintings of the Italian coast: try to capture a sense of the vastness of space. In "Habitat: Time and Place," nature comes across as impertinent because it will not be contained for the artist's use:

> I'm suspicious of this open land laid out and out.
> It's friendly but
> unsympathetic—or maybe it's me. maybe it's just me.
> I keep framing it anyway
> but it goes beyond frame
> while staying the same, immodest and lippy. (15)

The anthropomorphizing implies a human relationship that the speaker seeks to have with nature, in part, of course, so that it can be brought under imaginative control. He tries insults: "chickweed clumsy and enchanting, / pink powder puff scraggly and skuzzy." He tries communication:

> Black codes: he [a condor] sends me his hot signals.
> I receive them openheartedly.
> Am I sending them back openly? (16)

But the world is what it is, regardless of his presence or desires:

> Nature is taking care of itself and all that matters.
> Nature goes.
> My presence is a flyspeck on a leaf.
> It keeps me down to size. (16)

He has no sense of despair or frustration. The speaker acknowledges his limits in this environment and does not attempt mastery of it.

If "Habitat" teaches the artist humility, "Purple California Mountains—Near Half Moon Bay" teaches the usefulness of boundaries. Wherever the speaker looks he sees frames for the views: "Pale blue lake nesting in a crevice," "Red pony chewing blue grass / in the yard, boundaries set by split joint," "The naked eyes— / that's a boundary, too" (20). If he turns the other direction, toward the water, there is not only the sea but also "This reminder, this reassurance, this bridge." In this poem, he values the human-built environment at least as much as the natural one; there is the solidity of the massive chimney in the rented house, and the bridge "affords necessary passage from one unmarked place to another" (21). In all of this, the poet-artist finds serenity; his conclusion is:

> I see
> the limits of what I can or will ever.
> These boundaries were always. (21)

Here there is no contention between the human and the natural; from the viewer's perspective, they are complementary. Some measure of what this means for Major is in his reference to the inlet of the bay:

> The inlet letting fishing boats in, way
> the other way, in a distance too close to distinguish
> from what is at hand. (21)

It is this play of perspective—the "distance too close"—that nails down his understanding about his own limits and possibilities of the final lines. "Inlet," of course, was the name of the town in *Emergency Exit*, a name selected in part to suggest narrowness and restriction in modern human society. In the poem, however, "inlet" enables safe passage and human commerce (in several senses) by "letting in" the fishing boats. The boundary that was before a problem now makes possible a secure harbor.

In part 2, consisting mostly but not exclusively of pieces about Paris, the first point to note is that very little material from the notebook of the 1998 trip is incorporated into the writing. The poems are also different from *Inside Diameter* in that there is less self-consciousness about links to other artists or the artistic possibilities of landscapes. For example, the opening poem of the section, "Van Gogh's Death," says nothing about the suicide or the agonies of art. It is, instead, about life:

> We climbed the steep stairway
> to the tiny attic death-room,
> more alive for doing so. (31)

Even what might be taken as the world's rejection of him is turned to something else:

> On the news the oldest woman said,
> He was the ugliest man I ever saw.
> And I hear him saying to her, Your beauty
> like a cypress by the road
> more than makes up for what I lack. (31)

What interests Major here is not the romantic notion of the suffering genius or the neglect endured by a true innovator or even the possibilities for the speaker's own work; rather it is the sense of Van Gogh's common humanity and his love of life: "And we came down with his life / all around us out there in the fields" (31). What the poem suggest for Major is that the artist must make peace with the world, regardless of how he has been treated and that, moreover, it is necessary to be modest and even humble about what one does. What is also evident is recognition of the value of ordinary life. Van Gogh's imagined soft answer to the old woman is accompanied by an awareness of a shared sense of mortality: "Everywhere people feel deeply / and look closely at last things" (31). It is no longer only artists who take life seriously; they simply offer their own perspective on it.

This recognition, however, does not mean that Major has given up on social critique. "An Eighteenth-Century Moment" offers a commentary on wealth, poverty, and art. The poem opens in the home of a rich young couple, who live expensively but without taste; they are "A waste of money and music" (34). Their steward, who is described as "snobbish," has no respect for them:

> He will tell you about the smell
> of the meat market, how both can't stand
> fruit or lute music for that matter,
> Macedonia or Haydn quiet or loud. (35)

The speaker, apparently a visitor in the house, looks out the window and sees a "midget with stumps / for arm and no thumbs" crossing the piazza to enter a church. The speaker imagines that, in the cathedral, this man kneels near a girl

> with a broken weedy heart,
> sitting in an unholy unladylike manner,
> knees apart, tears zigzagging down her face. (36)

Despite his apparent sympathy for these two, the speaker leaves them there, without telling us if they found any comfort.

He returns instead to the bowl of fruit that the steward had been carrying. Here he finds his true subject:

> Anyway, apples in an orange bowl
> Apples in an orange bowl.
> See the light coming from inside each apple

as though holiday candles were glowing
from inside a house?
And on the path of candlelight a band
of noble white mares
galloping out through the red skin,
filling the world with their thunderous music. (36)

Clearly, it is the artist who is the heroic figure. He can find not only the beauty the wealthy know nothing about but also an "inner light" not available to either the midget or the sorrowing girl. Moreover, he adds to this the grandeur of the white horses and the power of music. It is not money or suffering but the imagination that gives life its nobility. In a rather simple still-life—apples in an orange bowl—he finds all he needs. Of course, it is not the fruit itself but the painter's ability that makes this possible. It is the artist who knows how to bring forth the light, make audible the music, and show us the horses. In this sense, the painter has a godlike transformative power. In an interview in 2000, Major commented on his desire to discover the inner illumination of objects: "I've found that the hardest kind of painting to do is to find the terms on which an object can come to life *without* that process of light and shadow: with its own illuminosity, with its own inner integrity that gives it a position without a composition. It's very difficult" (Bunge, *Conversations*, 175). This move beyond "what the Impressionists had taught me" is a heroic effort. And behind this assertion, we have the poet who constructs the world in which the couple, the steward, the midget, the girl, and the bowl of apples exist. The humility of the previous poems must be accommodated to the divinity and heroism of this one. Importantly, there is no suggestion that the speaker in the poem assumes any moral superiority based on his creativity; rather, he simply leaves us with the image he has generated.

The last poem in this section, in fact, brings the speaker down to earth. "Wanderer in a Foreign Country" is a prose poem that tells the story of someone who has been "robbed of everything" (56). He wanders the city, checking in daily with the American Express office. He achieves a kind of invisibility that allows him to learn something of the lives of the poor, though he refuses to identify with them. What is most important to him is that "I hadn't fallen out of my own composition, though I'd lost the frame" (56). Later he recalls a woman he once loved as falling, though "She'd been suspended from a mobile axis" (56). The notion of the self as artwork suggests both the constructedness of identity and, by analogy, the organic nature of art, as "Painting after Lunch" in the next section shows. To be able to fall out of a composition implies that one has a place as a subject, a context with which one coheres. To keep that means that one can survive, even under distressing circumstances such as those of the narrator; to lose it means that, like the beloved, one ceases to exist.

While there is little sense of time in the poem, we are told that he becomes dirty and smelly, so much so that even the priests turn away from him. And now his view of the poor is turned against him: "They would not have accepted me" (57). Near the end, we do learn how long the situation lasted: "I wandered in that distant country for forty days and forty nights total" (57). The time period, of course, gives the narrative biblical dimensions: it is the period of Noah's flood, of Moses's meeting with God on the mountain, and of Jesus's time in the wilderness. "Forty Days and Forty Nights" was, interestingly, also a best-selling blues song by Muddy Waters when Major was a teenager in Chicago, where Waters was based. Thus, while the speaker has been brought low by his experience, having been made alien not only by his nationality but also by a status that even the poor look down upon, he nonetheless has achieved a heroic position through his endurance. The situation is such that, once the check arrives, the alienation is so deep that the speaker must bid himself farewell: "And I cashed it, and outside to myself said: I'm sorry for the duress you've felt these forty days and forty nights, goodbye lonely stranger, we loved having you among us, go home in peace" (57). The statement can only be understood as sarcastic, given the indifference of the local population to his troubles. In this sense, the poem echoes "Stranger in the Village," in which James Baldwin traces the responses of a small Swiss community to his presence. The difference is that Baldwin uses the experience explicitly to discuss matters of race; Major's work never mentions race. Instead, he maps the inner workings of the mind of a man in isolation, as he moves through a world in which he temporarily has no home. That literal condition does not become, however, the human condition. He waits and observes and then, at the end, moves on. This combination would seem more to be Major's notion of the life of the artist.

The third part of *Waiting for Sweet Betty* is about the possible meanings of home, not exile. "Rumors: A Family Matter," another prose poem, offers what might be considered a joint character study. It concerns Wilbur and Thelma, the speaker's aunt and uncle; they are similar to what readers of *Come by Here* learn about Wilbur and Carrie, Inez's brother and sister-in-law. While the poem speaks of rumors concerning the marriage, what is remembered is character: "Not a day in life did my uncle tolerate lawyers or funerals or fakers, crude women or insurance. . . . They said he never lied to anybody" (*Waiting*, 91). Though he suffered from throat cancer, there was from him "not a tear, not a complaint." Thelma was similar, though somewhat more vulnerable: "slim as a butcher knife, and though made of firmness itself, made sure he made out a Will to relieve her of fear" (91). While we are told little about their shared emotional life, the speaker says at both the beginning and end that "Aunt Thelma lived on in grief." The closing asks us to remember this "in kindness." What is important is not only the grief as a marker of their love but also the living on, as indicative of endurance and integrity. One kind of home, then, is made of strong personalities defining themselves through absolute principles and devotion. Major's admiration for it may come in part from the fact that it was never a part of his own early life, though it may be an emblem for the life he feels he has built over the past thirty years with Pam.

A version of the artist's home can be found in "The Painting after Lunch." It is a short, humorous prose-poem about the difficulties of painting. Because the composition is not coming together, the speaker steps away from the work into his yard. When he returns, it has become something different. To describe that difference, he brings together all the senses, linked to the natural world, in part the world of his yard: "After lunch, I saw it in a different light, like a thing emerging from behind a fever bush, something reaching the senses with the smell of seaweed boiling, and as visible as yellow snowdrops on black earth. Tasted it too, on the tongue Jamaica pepper. To the touch, a velvet flower" (92).

In effect, he domesticates his vision, though the references are somewhat exotic. Rather than merely imagine it or visualize it, he has a complete sensory experience of it. Then he tries to realize it on the canvas: "Dragging and scumming, I gave myself to it stroke after stroke. It kept coming in bits and fits, fragments and snags" (92). What he offers us is a version of the artistic process that in many ways is the opposite of both the romantic notion of inspiration and the modernist idea of careful, conscious construction. The work seems to have an existence of its own, as the ending asserts: "I even heard it singing but in the wrong key like a deranged bird in wild cherries, having the time of its life" (92). The painting is an organic thing that the painter must discover, but he must do so primarily through hard work. It is a kind of wild thing that the artist must tame without destroying.

The problem for the creator, then, is not to master the creation but to bring it into his world without losing its sensual power. The artist's home, in this sense, is the space in which the domestic and the untamed merge.

In "Thomas Eakins's Delaware River Paintings," Major explores another artist's sense of home, though this time with racial implications. In the 1870s, Eakins did a number of hunting images set on the Delaware River near his family home in Philadelphia. In the specific ones Major refers to, the hunter is identified as Will Schuster, a neighbor, along with a black man, whom the Yale Art Gallery identifies as Dave Wright.[16] In the poem, intimacy exists in conjunction with otherness. The opening and closing lines are nearly identical: "Land and water make love all night all day" (97). The reference here is to the marshlands in which the hunt takes place, where the tide rises and falls, and boundaries are fluid. The hunt depends on this intercourse, since it is easiest to maneuver the boats during high tide. The birds, known as rails, also have fewer hiding places during this period.[17]

The otherness has to do with Major's emphasis on the black man. First, he focuses attention on this particular figure, ignoring the white man altogether:

This one poleman, a black man—lean and strong—
stands barefoot on the back end pushing,
and suddenly distracted by a noise in the underbrush,
he looks this way,
motionlessly,
as if shot by a camera.
They say he is from farther south. (97)

As he has done in other poems, Major enters the painting, constructing a narrative that leads us to the moment of art. He even gives his subject an abbreviated history by suggesting origins. The line, "as if shot by a camera," has multiple connotations. It reveals his knowledge of Eakins, who used photography for some of his work and was also, of course, part of the realist movement of the late nineteenth century and thus attentive to accurate details of representation. Since the painting is about hunting, the line also carries an association with violence; a black man aiding in the hunt suddenly himself becomes the prey; the similarity of the description to Mark Twain's portrayal of Jim in *Huckleberry Finn* reinforces links to the escaping slave. Finally, the shot of the camera also can be linked to beliefs about photography as a means of stealing the soul of the subject. The black man, who is never named in the titles of the paintings, becomes the generic other rather than an individual.

The final section strengthens this sense of difference. First, we have mention of the group of paintings:

> Shooters, white men all,
> standing in their boats quietly.
> Polemen, black men all,
> all pushing them quietly along the river. (98)

Here Major notes a failure of the imagination; Eakins can never conceive of reversing the roles, no matter how many times he takes up the subject. One could argue that in doing so, his artistic realism is simply following the social realities of the time. But that is precisely how his imagination fails. The man who could set up an academy in which women students could work with nude male models could not conceive of white men being subordinate to black ones, even in art. Major drives home the point with the next lines: "Will Schuster and the nameless black man come here often. / Will Schuster shoots and the black man rows" (98). Since it is possible to know the name of the black man, the poet has chosen to insist on anonymity as part of the subject's social condition. He constructs the world that is the home of Eakins, Schuster, and Dave Wright as one in which racial hierarchy is fundamental to interactions. This "realism" then makes ironic the last line's repetition of the opening: "Land and water make love all day all night." Such intimacy may be possible in nature, but not in human relationships if they involve race.

Finally, the title poem is about how the world can be home for the patient self. The dominant word in the poem is *wait*; it appears in many of the fifty-nine lines. The "Sweet Betty" of the title is a medicinal herb more commonly known as soapwort (saponaria officinalis). It is a perennial that grows to 30 inches and has pink flowers and is said to aid in the treatment of bronchitis and skin disorders.[18] The speaker first takes different perspectives on the flower itself:

> Bird's-eye view
> sees a blanket of shimmering pink and white
> with green pods in sharp brightness.
> Down beneath in the flower's cool shade,
> in scattered shadows so dark, I wait
> in uneasy restfulness,
> waiting through sun and snow. (94)

This "ant's-eye" view offers a contrast both in terms of what is seen and in the effects of light. As in the paintings, we get both darkness and brightness, which allows a fuller sense of the plant as visual subject. We then shift to the various circumstances of waiting in a life. These include race: "I wait for the unmistakable black in white people to show. / I wait for black people to catch windflowers" (94). Each line suggests a desire for the breakdown of difference. While "unmistakable black" implies an essential quality, the speaker clearly believes that it is not limited to one group. His desire for blacks is what might be thought of as whimsy, the splashes of color associated with delicate springtime flowers.

He then begins a long series of lines opening with "I wait" that express the experiences of everyday life: "I wait for payday and I wait for the lottery. / I wait at the lake for the boat" (95). These include aspects of nature and of normal human interaction. In the process, he takes on different roles: a teacher, an actor, a believer in witch doctors, a patient. At the end of this grouping, he shifts to autobiography:

> I wait in Georgia sad on a base and in Illinois with a dime.
> I wait in New York with a subway token and a briefcase,
> Now we are recounting personal history.
> I wait in fatigues in line in Texas, waiting and waiting.
> I wait in the airport in Ghana and Liberia.
> I wait in France for my identity papers.
> I wait in the train station in Germany and in Holland.
> I wait in Colorado and California without skis.
> I await a Nebraska driving test and fail. (95–96)

All of these locations can be associated with specific periods in Major's life; many of them were unpleasant or merely tiresome. For example, the Georgia reference is to his military experience in Valdosta, not to his childhood in Atlanta and Lexington. What he suggests through this catalog is a definition of his life as anticipatory, as an endless process of waiting. More precisely, it asserts the idea that all lives, even those, like his, so given over to activity, are also filled with nothingness. He is, in effect, rendering in experiential terms the aesthetic notion of negative space. If this is so, then, as in art, the emptiness that is waiting gives shape and meaning to the activity that comes before or after.

But waiting also has an anticipatory quality associated with the imagination and with hope. It is to this that he returns at the end of the poem. First,

there is an unlikely change in nature: "I wait for Skunk Bush to stop smelling." He moves from this simple desire to a more extravagant image:

> I wait for Wandering Jenny to stop climbing the house,
> to stop flying around and around the clouds
> trying to kiss the upside-down boy. I wait for her
> to move in another direction, to rest on a rock. (96)

What he waits for is Wandering Jenny to wait, to stop the impulse to grow
and to change constantly. With this we return to the opening image:

> I wait the sweetest waiting of all—
> I wait for Sweet Betty and she won't bloom till next year,
> but she *will* bloom next year. (96)

What emerges from the poem and the book as a whole is a faith in the
processes of nature and art. Waiting can be emptiness, as it was in much
of his life, or it can be the space and time needed for creation. After all,
Sweet Betty needs a dormant stage in order to bloom again. While much
of society fails miserably to meet human needs, and those failures must be
recorded, it is the case that even such flaws can be the material of art.

The cover of the book shows a young black man sitting backward on
a chair. It is one of several similar works by Major and is titled *Waiting*.
He stares straight at the viewer, with brows that are slightly upturned, perhaps expectantly, but eyes that are sad. His arms are placed awkwardly, one
across the back of the chair, the other raised across his face with the fingers stretched down to the other arm. Is he in the process of raising his
hand to greet us or lowering it more firmly because we are not what he
expected? The ambiguity of the image reflects Major's blending of critique
and acceptance.

The back-cover publisher's summary of *Myself Painting* (2008) asserts
that the poems in it "speak not of painting itself but of its underlying process." Certainly, the last four pieces in the book concern the social processes, as they focus on the community of painters and on their relationships with models in their everyday practice. To a large extent, however, the
book is about experiences that might lend themselves to visual representation; for example, "That Face" seeks to interpret the facial expression of a
man who has a habitual scowl. The speaker imagines a history that would
help explain the present appearance. He calls forth a wife who loves the
man and decides also that "What seems troubled produces no howl" (21). It

is its difference that makes it a possible subject: "The otherness of it, in an odd way, is a thrill. / That's what's left and that's what's good" (21).

Around this time Major did a series of portraits of men, all of which could easily fit the pattern of this poem. It also suggests why he found those subjects of interest; he could imaginatively enter the life of such a man. In the poem, we find his career-long commitment to bringing his reading of experience into the art. Whether poetry, painting, or fiction, it must incorporate his feeling and sensibility in order to be a valid artistic expression. It is not enough to represent the figure or explore the technical issues of his craft; he must impose himself on it and make it his. Interestingly, by the time we get to this, his thirteenth book of poetry, he seems to have gained full control of his various subjects; there is little sign of the struggle that marked earlier works.

"Self Portrait" would seem to be a natural site for the struggles of the artist. As it opens, the difficulty is stated:

At the wedding of myself
and the mirror,
You, my best man, say nothing is more dishonest
than a self-portrait done out of love. (47)

The artist accepts the challenge: "So, I *will* to be what I will not be. / I will not shock myself." He then lists all the things he will not be: St. Dominic, "a lover on a white horse," the Minotaur, a pimp, biblical subjects, or "an old man in a dirty smock," among other things. Instead of working through to an image, he chooses nothing: "I will leave the canvas empty till I know / for sure. The empty canvas is about possibility." In a review of the book, Ron Slate finds the ending of this poem particularly troubling. He says that the "final adage about the empty canvas sounds like a desperate way out. . . . But poems reach their potential through tension and strange fulfillments that compel our attention while discouraging us from understanding too well."[19] What appears to Slate as desperation can also be read as a form of waiting. But such patience can also be a form of complacency, an unwillingness to strive for an answer.

Major's actual self-portrait, *The Mirror*, a 1984 watercolor, is a very stark image, with much of the canvas white (plate 17). Although painted in Venice, it suggests nothing of that environment. In the background is only a painting that itself contains nothing but two female figures, associated with Carnival. In the foreground, the artist holds a large white pad in one arm while drawing with the other something we cannot see. The composition draws the eye primarily to the artist's face and secondarily to his hand, both in sharp contrast to the overall whiteness. The head and face are haloed by black hair, which tends to extend out, similar to an Afro, though straighter. It may be intended to echo the representation in one of Van Gogh's self-portraits. It is presented very carefully, so that individual hairs are visible through the effects of lighting and background. The eyebrows also extend upward and outward. The effect is to make the head large in proportion to the body. The wide-open eyes stare directly at the viewer with intensity. The lips are given classical shape, and again suggest concentration on the matter at hand. The visible hand is similarly detailed. The fingers are elongated, with the forefinger pointing toward the background painting. He wears a wedding band and a wristwatch with the hands evident (set at 8:25). The light is carefully handled, coming in from the left front so that sharp contrast is seen in the color of the shirt and the skin. He plays with the effect so that the eye away from the light source is more visible than the other one. He also draws a brown-colored square around the image, creating the effect of a painting within a painting.

In contrast to the claims of the poem, here Major defines the artist as creating something out of nothing. He is almost entirely alone. It is his head and his hands that make a world. It also presents him as diligently doing that work, rather than sitting quietly among the things in a studio or house. At the same time, he is connected to the larger world; he is not the isolato. The watch and ring give him connections to social reality. If this is not exactly an image of self-love, as suggested in the poem, it is certainly one of self-validation. He stands firm in his commitment to what he does and challenges us to think otherwise.

Other poems in the book offer commentary on the practice and theory of art. "Trees," for example, talks about the "Sunday painters" who are "Genteel American women" (5). "Bad Nudes" describes a many-sided discussion among painters about art that goes nowhere. "Copying" involves a conversation about copying the great masters and learning the "rules" for painting. It ends with a dog barking, which reflects the poet's attitude about the issue. At the same time, he asserts some very definite ideas about artistic expression. "Song of Chance" takes a position:

Against all dissent, I take a chance
at the game. The rest is talk.
But no matter. This is what I stand for:

random chance. And it's a tight squeeze.

But I stand firm in my effort. (15)

This stance is consistent with certain of the pieces in the collection, in which a variety of images are offered, held together only by the fact of the speaker offering them. "All of Us" joins together a group of black women in an elevator, a nurse's aide singing opera, a trolley to the zoo, dancing to "angel icons, to gurus," white people having or not having fun, and Russian peasants cleaning the streets (20). Most of the poems, however, do not take such chances; they rather clearly define their subject and the attitude we are expected to take of it.

Perhaps the most important work in the book in regard to this issue and to the relationship of *Myself Painting* to Major's visual art is "In Search of a Motif for Expressive Female Figuration." The title both implies a quest, with the possibility of failure, and mocks itself with academic jargon. The poem opens with the phrase "She, the many," implying multiple facets of a single entity and thus perhaps a version of the mobile axis, a concept Major has played with at various points in recent years to suggest the flexibility of perspective. What he presents in the work are different ways of presenting "she," different poses as it were. Some of these are classical:

As she fixed her hair she crossed her legs
and raised her arms
so that her armpits showed hairless,
Beginning blackness. That unbearably lovely arm
extended, color of Tibet sunset,
in a thoughtless Degas gesture. She belongs
to a quiet moment, arabesque all of its seconds. (7)

Some are part of the contemporary suburban world:

Her station wagon stands in my driveway,
shadow directly beneath,
and two dogs or call it America,
with a red kitchen table. She bakes, suns,
runs, and rests. Women dancing
on the beach. The girl twins
in a burlap sack together hopping across the sand. (6–7)

Each is a possible compositional moment, often inflected with the feeling of the speaker-artist.

In the various ages, attitudes, conditions. and actions of the women we can see Major's interest in the potential of the female figure as a subject. But in his attraction to it, which has been part of his work from the beginning, we see also a traditional sense of the meaning of "woman." She is consistently depicted as daughter, mother, wife, lover. Her body defines her being:

> Everything cut to the bone,
> with hands folded in front of her,
> just below the belly like an answer
> to an unasked question. (6)

Moreover, her competence seems limited:

> And she could not swim
> across the lake of her life
> to save her life. (7)

Finally, she is always the model and never the artist; her attraction is in part her willingness to adopt the pose he desires, to be what he wants her to be. The poem reflects a deep commitment to the idea and image of woman as the great subject of art, both visual and literary. But this appreciation is clearly tied to traditional notions of gender roles. In this sense, Major's last community is that of women, but women under his control: it is models, characters in his fiction, and figures in his poetry. It is, in a way, a return to mother and protective sister, but now he is in charge.

# Returning to the Beginning

In 2002, Major published *Come by Here: My Mother's Life.* In the book, he intersperses narrative in her voice with his commentaries about how things have changed over several decades. He also incorporates genealogical information, such as birth and death dates and family histories that are not typically found in memoirs. Much of this information, verified through other sources, has been used in the present work. While the reviews of this work have focused on the story of Inez, as Major intended, the more important concern for this analysis is her son as author and covert subject. He notes in the preface that his relationship to her is split into son and observer. In addition to being his mother, she is a good artist's subject: "Inez's life, in its complexity and richness, is ideal raw material. It's a writer's dream" (*Come by Here*, x). A number of themes suggest the complex nature of the narrative. Race operates throughout as an arbitrary but important signifier of identity and condition. Art is a practice passed down through the generations, often with an emphasis on its technical and financial aspects. Relationships are often difficult, and there are a number of broken or troubled marriages. Women tend to be strong, independent, and highly social, but sometimes psychologically troubled. Finally, the book offers a variation on Richard Wright's *Black Boy* in its story of a young person's move from the Deep South to Chicago's South Side. The differences can be explained in part by time and gender; Inez moves in the 1940s rather than the 1920s, and as a woman she had distinct issues in employment and living arrangements. Nonetheless, the two books share a concern for finding social, economic, and political opportunities in a less oppressive environment that turns out to be less than ideal. What is particularly significant here is that Major sees his mother's story as "raw material," meaning that it is his task to turn it into a finished artistic product. He claims sole authorship of the text; it is *his* book, even if it is her story. It reflects his sense of theme, character, and structure, like all his other artistic efforts. I would also suggest that, in some sense, Inez's life is a metaphor for his career.

The matter of race is central to the narrative, but it goes well beyond her personal experience. Several of the reviews note the theme of passing and Inez's double life made possible because of her light skin. The first chapter opens with her sudden awareness that Jim Crow laws are not applied to her unless she in some way draws attention to her race. But the family history she relates is replete with racial mixing. Her maternal grandfather was "two-thirds" Cherokee, while her legal father, William Henry Hull in the book, was the son of a prominent judge in Wilkes County, Georgia. Inez herself, of course, was the daughter of a local planter, whose family was well established in the area. We later learn that her first husband's grandmother was a white woman who gave up her child by a black man and then that her second husband was of Chinese and African American ancestry.

But race goes beyond genetics in this narrative; it also involves social practices and attitudes. While the book offers some instances of racial insult and hostility, such behavior is not determined by the race or location of the perpetrator, and bad behavior is more than balanced by instances of generous actions. In parallel narratives about auto accidents, one in Georgia and one in Illinois, it is whites who assist her at the scene and white doctors who care for her. During her adult years, she learns from her mother that the relationship with Inez's biological father was one of love, not exploitation. These instances are noteworthy precisely because they stand out in a general atmosphere of racial oppression, if not outright violence; after all, this is a memoir of passing because Inez could not get good jobs if her race were known. On the other side of the color line, the young Inez, because of her skin color, is treated so badly by the local black children that she is sent first to Athens and then to Atlanta to go to school. Much later, her own son and daughter face hostility from their classmates because of their "white" mother. Adults have similar responses. In 1968, after the assassination of Martin Luther King Jr., young black men rampage through the streets of Chicago's South Side, attacking not only white but also black businesses, including her own. In the most important example, she is told by several people that Clarence Sr. does not love her but sees her as a trophy that gains him status in the black community. These negative experiences, like the positive ones above, must be contextualized by the encouragement and assistance she receives from family and members of her South Side community.

So it is that, in the world as Major represents it, race is an arbitrary signifier that cannot be trusted to define community or identity, insiders or outsiders, friends or enemies. It is a factor to be used strategically, if one is in a position to do so. Thus, Major can justify moving in and out of self-definition as "black writer," setting it aside whenever the available community or publishing possibilities offer the option of "experimentalist" or "postmodernist," and taking it up when blackness is in vogue. He can do so precisely because, for him, race is an artificial distinction and thus not a matter of personal or social integrity. As an individual, he is not obligated to act according to socially imposed rules built on such a fictional difference; as an artist, he has no responsibility to create work that in any way is linked to race. Trouble in *Come by Here* is generally tied to beliefs and practices that assume the reality of race. Freedom and opportunity follow when the individual is seen as an individual. The text validates Major's rejection of a racial binary in favor of an individualist path for both his life and his career. It also helps explain his sensitivity to being defined in racial terms. As seen in this study, he consistently and deliberately challenged racial expectations in the texts he created, in the publishers he worked with, and in the statements he made about his art. In addition, he seemed acutely aware of any intimations that he could be personally defined in racial terms. From his early identification with white movie cowboys to his apprentice days in literary venues on Chicago's North Side to the Fiction Collective to his angry response to Ron Sukenick's assumption that he would have performed jazz, he has resisted any essentialist notion of self based on race.

Similarly, *Come by Here* offers justification for the nature of relationships in his life and work. A maternal great-grandmother, Lucy Dupree, was married three times, as was Major's paternal grandmother, Anna. That grandmother herself was the product of an illicit relationship between a white woman and a black man: Inez was sired by a white man while her mother was separated from her black husband, Henry Huff. Clarence Sr. was raised in a fatherless home. Inez left him after experiencing abuse and later mar-

ried Halbert Ming, from whom she was also eventually separated. Relationships in the text are fragile and often temporary. Both men and women are
driven by desire and even love, but individual needs and impulses disrupt
a sense of permanence. It is also important to note, however, that connections are maintained despite the problems. Ada remained married to Henry
Huff, and he raised Inez as his own daughter. Anna called Inez to report
that her own daughter had beaten Clarence Jr.; it was this call that led Inez
to finally bring the children to Chicago.

Applying this pattern to Major enables us to see that he was psychologically prepared to enter and leave relationships based on personal compul-
sions rather than on commitment to institutional norms. He could marry
Joyce Sparrow after his air force stint because that was expected of a young
man returning home presumably to live and work in the community for
the rest of his life. Then, in his view, he could leave her with the children
when he realized that such a life would preclude the self-expression that
he needed. He could go to Omaha and set up a liaison with Olympia Leak
because he needed to have a sexual partner. This choice also proved disas-
trous, so he moved on again, apparently with little compunction about
leaving her with four children. Sheila in New York became a muse who
helped him get through the first novel, but their disparate needs soon drove
them apart. Sharyn Skeeter becomes the sophisticated wife for an up-and-
coming writer, one who linked him to both established black communities
and to the publishing world. They were a good match in that, for each, self-
fashioning is key to identity. But his career designs took them away from
the world of her future (New York) when he accepted a position in Boulder
to be at the new center of experimental writing. So they broke up, though
they remain in contact even now. Each fed the ego of the other until ambition drove them apart. Finally, in middle age, having achieved a narrow but
respected reputation, he found Pam Ritter, who left a marriage to be with
him. It is this thirty-year relationship that enables his settled life as established and productive artist in California. In all of this, we see the needs of
the self as most important, just as was true with the characters of *Come by
Here*. It is sometimes necessary to violate social conventions in order to be
true to that self; the family history shows that this is the reality regardless of
time period, gender, race, or status. One does what one has to do in order
to be who one is. The path must be followed regardless of consequences.

The fiction follows a similar pattern. From Eli Bolton's compulsive sexuality in *All-Night Visitors* to John Canoe's resistance in *One Flesh* to relation-

ships until he finds someone who will not interfere with his work, Major's protagonists move repeatedly toward and away from human connections. Eli is obsessed with Cathy, but his need to demonstrate his prowess leads him to other women. He needs relationships, but primarily to affirm his masculinity; therefore, devotion to one person is nonsensical in his world. Cora, in *Reflex and Bone Structure*, moves from one to another of the three men in the novel. The narrator needs her desperately but also talks of killing her off. In *Dirty Bird Blues*, Man cannot have Cleo, his music, and his whiskey, but spends the book deciding what combination to commit to. John Canoe seems to be passionate only about his art; his affair and eventual marriage, while supposedly central to the story, seem almost an afterthought.

The painting and poetry can also be thought of in these terms. Major's recent work focuses on individuals, even when there is an implied other, as indicated in such titles as *Waiting* and *Before the Interview*. From some of the early expressionist works that appeared in *Emergency Exit*, where there is an inversion of one of a pair of figures to newer pieces, such as *Two Sisters*, where the emphasis is on distance, the visual disjunction implies psychological separation. Even in a group work such as *Saturday Afternoon*, the figures are presented in small groups or by themselves. Isolation is further indicated by the revisions, which put masks on their faces. In some more recent paintings, where the pair of figures might be considered lovers, they are turned away from the viewer, so that we do not see their expressions. Much of the poetry throughout the career focuses on a troubled individual, such as Van Gogh, or on the speaker alone in nature seeking, perhaps, inspiration. He functions more as an observer than as a participant in either a relationship or a community.

If relationships are complex and difficult in Major's life and work as well as in *Come by Here*, it is because gender is complicated for him. It is the women who are the strong, active agents in the memoir. There is great-grandmother Rebecca Lankford, who, though the daughter of a Confederate soldier and apparently racist, nonetheless took a black lover and committed perjury to protect him from lynching. We meet the maternal great-grandmother Lucy Dupree and paternal grandmother Anna Major, both thrice-married; Anna also worked as a traveling preacher. Maternal grandmother Ada Bonner Huff had an affair with a local white man, then returned to her black husband with her child. Inez herself took up with Clarence, a man she knew her family would not approve of, and then moved far away when he became abusive; she retrospectively castigated herself for tolerating his abuse. In Chicago, she associated with socially active women, some of whom ran their own businesses. These women did not fit the model of the proper black woman concerned to repudiate racial and gender stereotypes of promiscuity, at least as that model was presented in the black literature of the late nineteenth and early twentieth centuries. They transgressed social conventions in pursuit of what they needed and desired for themselves and those they cared about.

In contrast, the male characters tend to be passive and somewhat feminized. Inez's biological father is seen as simply sitting around the local store, though he had a cotton farm to run. Her legal father seems to be accepting of his wife's infidelity, though with some signs of passive-aggressive behavior; he also adored Inez. While Clarence Sr. was assertive, he is also said to have soft hands and to be hostile to manual labor. His violence against his wife, of course, implies a profound insecurity about his masculinity. On occasions when Inez temporarily left, he came to visit her in the company of his mother. Unlike his father-in-law, he was clearly a man of little substance. Clarence Jr., though the oldest child, was protected by his mother and his younger but bigger sister once they arrived in Chicago. What Inez remembered of him was his interest in art and reading, not in his activities with other children.

We can see in Major's early adult life the playing out of these gender dynamics. He joined the military but spent his free time reading literature and philosophy, instead of socializing with other soldiers. After his military service, he took on, then gave up, the role of husband and father. He returned to Chicago, married, quickly had two children, but resented the time spent at the labor needed to provide for them. Instead, he focused on his writing and little magazine. He soon left Joyce and the children for Omaha, where he took up with Olympia, produced four more children, but again dissatisfied with his responsibilities, left them for the literary mecca of New York. The production of offspring could be considered the proof of his masculinity that is challenged by the "soft-hands" work of literary production. After that period, he made connections with women with strong personalities, such as Sheila Silverstone, Sheri Martinelli, and Sharyn Skeeter, all of whom served as muses in some sense. All provided assistance in one form or another. Each of the relationships lasted for a relatively short time, though he maintained ties of some kind with all of them over the years.

Out of that period came *All-Night Visitors*, the narrative of a hypersexu-alized young man who must constantly demonstrate his manhood. Later, we get Moses Westby of *NO*, who is emasculated, and the narrator of *Reflex and Bone Structure*, who fantasizes intercourse with his literary creation. Still later, in *Dirty Bird Blues*, we have Man Banks, who is obsessed with Cleo and finally chooses her over the male-oriented life of whiskey drink-ing and womanizing. The women of these novels are strong enough to be obsessions for the men, but they are ultimately the object of the male gaze and the male word. What is named love in the texts also has to do with their usefulness, much like the women of Major's own life.

Finally, out of *Come by Here* we gain a sense of one important value of art, which is that it empowers people. It is his skill as a designer of public and private buildings that gives Henry Hull respect in Dublinville among both blacks and whites. It was Clarence Sr.'s creativity in business that allowed him to start over again and again, even when his own addictions led to financial problems; like few black men of his time, he was able to keep his "soft hands." It was Inez's talent as a dress designer and maker that helped her support herself and her children. It was Major's literary and artistic skills that enabled him to define black masculinity in a different way, to turn away from the materialist expectations of both Atlanta and Chicago and devote himself to a career that lacked significant financial rewards, but that gave him the freedom to express himself in ways few others would or could. That commitment and skill brought him into communities that would otherwise have been closed to him and put him at the cutting edge of U.S. culture.

The price for this opportunity was high. Major left behind a trail of es-tranged family and friends and never achieved the recognition that came to others whose paths were at least somewhat more conventional. He re-mained productive even in the most difficult of circumstances; like his blues protagonist in *Dirty Bird Blues*, his art seemed inextricably linked to the complex circumstances of his life. It is a life and career that some-times deliberately and sometimes instinctively broke the rules. But he had a personality that allowed him to find and reach out to those who also were transgressors. Time after time, he found fellow outlaws. He has always been able to move on, to find new ways to do what he wants to do, new allies to appreciate his efforts. If the place he has come to in the new century seems less risky, less experimental, it is perhaps because his truest self has always been the combination of craftsman and gambler that is in his blood. He

always sought to be a respected and rewarded outsider, an American individualist recognized for his talent, even if it was hard to understand. In his
case, it meant trying to master many forms rather than only one. It is only
now that we can begin to see the fullness of that achievement.

Some readers might question why a long study of a lesser-known African
American artist such as Clarence Major is needed. After all, among his
cohort of writers born during or shortly after the Depression—Toni Morrison, Ernest Gaines, John Edgar Wideman—Major has received the least
public and critical attention. For such readers, the beginnings of an answer
might be found in *Come by Here*. His story, like that of his mother, reveals
much about the complexities of identity and expression in a racialized U.S.
society. Both figures display qualities of will, persistence, and individualism
in the face of racial and gendered constraints. Each comes out of a family
history that they knew involved breaking a number of social rules; both the
Major family and the Huff family included members who were either the
products of or the participants in racial mixing. Both of them attempted
to live conventional lives but discovered that they had low tolerance for
social rules when those restrictions challenged their senses of self. Inez left
her husband when his abusive behavior crossed that threshold, leaving her
children for years in order to establish the kind of life she wanted for herself
and for them. The young Clarence married twice but found that the price
of supporting a family was too high: it would cost him a career as an artist.
Like his mother, he left family behind to pursue that life. Both had essentially found that the place where they started provided too narrow a scope
for their ambitions. They risked social and familial opprobrium to bring
those ambitions into reality.

Both also were determined to achieve their goals, whatever the odds.
Inez took whatever work was available to provide for herself and then her
children. She passed for white in order to earn higher wages, even enduring the racist comments of fellow workers who were unaware of her background. She turned down opportunities for personal relationships because
she did not want to end up in a situation like that of her first marriage. She
limited her opportunities to move in important circles of black Chicago
because that social life interfered with her personal objectives. At the same
time, it took her much longer to bring the children north than she had
planned, perhaps in part because she enjoyed her newfound freedom and
social networks. However, when her son was harmed, creating a crisis, she
moved quickly and decisively.

That son himself pursued painting and writing even when he risked being called a sissy by schoolmates. He received enough recognition that he gained confidence in his own talent, even if many around him did not understand it. He sent out material and was not deterred by rejection. With only thin resources, he started his own little magazine and got well-known writers to submit their material. He moved from place to place in search of an intellectual and artistic community that could support his efforts. He took whatever jobs he could find in order to make possible his version of the artist's life; never once did he consider any of those jobs his true career, even when they were at major universities. And he still endlessly writes and paints, because that is both his career and his identity. What is different from the story of his mother is that his persistence is not in the service of security or family. His first novel came from a publisher of erotica and all of his fiction or poetry were done by small, specialized houses. Of his generation of African American writers, he is the only one not to have a conventional commercial publisher. Nonetheless, he is the most prolific of all of them. This situation results from a refusal to produce work that can be easily marketed.

Like his mother, he has dealt with the world on his own terms. His version of individualism has consisted in openly defying the expected behaviors of young black men, in repudiating not only the mainstream standards for painting and writing but also the ideological ones used to define race literature, and in maintaining an outsider position even within the networks and communities he so desired. He persists in a painting style very close to that of the Postimpressionists, even though the world of visual art has gone through multiple paradigm shifts since his career began. He sometimes calls himself an experimentalist and sometimes a traditionalist, but he wants to define these terms for himself. Thus, he can say that *Such Was the Season* is an experimental novel. Or that he is a traditionalist in painting, even when the work itself literally involves some kind of experiment. Ultimately, such labels are only conveniences, ways to speak to others about his work. But the truth is that he does what he wants to do and always has.

What we have, then, in the narratives of mother and son are variations on a basic American story: the individual who does not fit in and so moves on to find a different (and perhaps better) way of being. They can do this in part because they are themselves the products of earlier transgressors, whose stories they retain and pass on. They are tales deeply inflected with race, but not in the simple binary form that is so often told. Major recently commented on his definition of tradition: "Courbet in his Realist Manifesto stresses the importance of an artist turning intelligently to past art as the foundation for his or her own originality. This study of the past becomes my foundation."[1] What he has stated about art I would suggest also applies to the story he has told of his mother. She is the past that has been a foundation for him. From that foundation, which goes back generations, he has been able to build a transgressive, experimental, and very American life and career.

# Notes

CHAPTER 1. Breaking Boundaries: A Family History

1. Unpublished family tree, Clarence Major personal papers; e-mail, Clarence Major to author, 10 August 2006.

2. E-mail, Major to author, 10 August 2006.


CHAPTER 2. Becoming an Artist

1. See Bearden and Henderson, *History of African-American Artists*, 147–56.

2. This dynamic is evident, for example, in Zora Neale Hurston's *Their Eyes Were Watching God* (1937), when Tea Cake beats Janie because he must demonstrate to the community his control.

3. See the History page at the College of Complexes: A Weekly Free Speech Forum website, accessed 18 February 2011 at http://collegeofcomplexes.homestead.com/History.html, for the history of the "college."

4. E-mail, Major to author, 7 January 2010.

5. S. Moore, *Beerspit Night and Cursing*, 170.

6. Ibid., 173–74.

7. Ibid., 177.


CHAPTER 3. Making It in New York

1. E-mail, Clarence Major to author, 15 May 2009.

2. Clarence Major Archives, Books, box 3.

3. Ibid.

4. Ibid.

5. See De St. Jorre, *Venus Bound*, 93–111 and 281–90, for the story of legal battles with J. P. Donleavy, for example.

6. Clarence Major Archives, Books, box 3.

7. Lehmann-Haupt, "Books of the Times."

8. Clarence Major Archives, Books, box 3.

9. For additional commentary on the novel, see Coleman, "Clarence Major's *All-Night Visitors*."

10. For information on Umbra, see Dent, "Umbra Days"; Thomas, "Shadow World"; and Hernton, "Umbra."

11. See Baraka, "Black Art," in *LeRoi Jones/Amiri Baraka Reader*, 219-20.

12. Clarence Major, "Making Up Reality," unpublished manuscript, Clarence Major Archives, Nonfiction, box 3.

13. Review of *The New Black Poetry*.

14. Walter Lowenfels to Clarence Major, 15 November 1966, Clarence Major Archives, Correspondence, box 12; Major to William Meredith, 13 September 1967, Clarence Major Archives, Correspondence, box 7.

15. See Clarence Major Archives, Books, box 7, for the series of letters.

16. Major, "From Chicago to Yugoslavia," 113.

17. Ibid., 133.

18. Ibid., 135.

19. Joyce, *Gatekeepers of Black Culture*, 101.

20. Clarence Major Archives, Nonfiction, box 3.


CHAPTER 4. Beginning a Professional Career, 1975–1980

1. E-mail, Major to author, 15 January 2010.

2. Kostelanetz, "Alternative Book Publishers."

3. Clarence Major Archives, Books, box 14.

4. E-mail, Major to author, 22 January 2010.

5. Ibid., 11 January 2011.

6. Ibid., 23 January 2010.

7. "Queen Anne, Pamunkey (ca. 1650–1725)," AAA Native Arts website, accessed 3 August 2011, http://www.aaanativearts.com/article1125.html.

8. Bert Williams quoted in Brooks, *Lost Sounds*, 174.

9. MacLeish, "Ars Poetica," *Collected Poems*, 106.

10. On the origin of *cakewalk*, see Salzman, Smith, and West, *Encyclopedia of African-American Culture and History*, 1:175.

11. Clarence Major Archives, Correspondence, University of the State of New York (Albany), box 29.

12. David Bates, "A Brief History of the Union Institute and University," 2002, accessed 3 August 2011, http://people.umass.edu/~hendra/Briefhis.html.

13. E-mail, Major to author, 8 February 2010

14. Clarence Major Archives, Correspondence, Union Graduate School, box 28.

15. Clarence Major to Russell Banks, 12 June 1976, Russell Banks Papers, box 62.

16. See "Struga Poetry Readings," Struga website, accessed 3 August 2011, www.svp .org.mk/en/history.html, for a brief history of the poetry festival.

17. Weedon, *Post-War Women's Writing in German*, 58.

CHAPTER 5. The Machinery of Postmodernism

1. See Joyce, *Gatekeepers of Black Culture*, 92–94.

2. O'Brien, "Is Black Literature beyond Criticism?"

3. Major to Sukenick, 26 April 1978, Clarence Major Archives, Correspondence, box 28.

4. Major to Banks, 4 December 1978, and Major to Banks, 2 January 1980, Russell Banks Papers, box 62.

5. Quoted at Maud Newton, "The Other Side of the Window: Novelist Jonathan Baumbach on Independent Publishing," Maud Newton blog, accessed 25 May 2011, http://maudnewton.com/blog/?p=9125.

6. McCaffery, *Contemporary Literature*, 99–100.

7. Sukenick, "Guest Word."

8. Jeffrey DeShell, R. M. Berry, Lance Olsen, and Matthew Kirkpatrick, "The Fiction Collective Story," Fiction Collective Two website, accessed 3 August 2011, http:// fc2.org/about_us.aspx.

9. Baumbach to Sukenick, 24 December 1974, Ronald Sukenick Papers, box 60.

10. See various materials in Ronald Sukenick Papers, boxes 59 and 60.

11. E-mail, Major to author, 17 May 2010.

12. Baumbach to Sukenick, 10 January 1974, Ronald Sukenick Papers, box 60.

CHAPTER 6. The Art of Postmodernism

1. Major to Sukenick, 3 September 1974, Ronald Sukenick Papers, box 61.

2. Baumbach to Sukenick, 11 November 1974, Ronald Sukenick Papers, box 61.

3. Baumbach to Sukenick, 24 December 1974, Ronald Sukenick Papers, box 61.

4. Major to Sukenick, 19 February 1975, Ronald Sukenick Papers, box 61.

5. Ibid.

6. Klinkowitz, *Keeping Literary Company*, 185.

7. Major to Baumbach, 19 January 1975, Clarence Major Archives, Correspondence, box 22.

8. Major to Sukenick, 19 February 1975, Ronald Sukenick Papers, box 61.

9. Baumbach to Major, 4 June 1977, Clarence Major Archives, Correspondence, box 3.

10. Major to Baumbach, 13 June 1978, Clarence Major Archives, Correspondence, box 22.

11. Robert Minkoff to Sue Dillingham, Clarence Major Archives, Correspondence, 25 March 1978, box 22.

12. Major to Sukenick 14 August 1979, Ronald Sukenick Papers, box 66.

13. Major to Glynn, 18 October 1980, Clarence Major Archives, Correspondence, box 22.

14. Clarence Major Archives, Correspondence, box 29, p. 30.

15. See Simosko and Tepperman, *Eric Dolphy*.

16. Klinkowitz, *Keeping Literary Company*, 184.

17. *Black American Literature Forum*, 55.

18. Klinkowitz, "Notes on a Novel-in-Progress," 48.

19. "Outline of a Program of Work Leading to the Doctor of Philosophy Degree," Clarence Major Archives, Correspondence, box 29, "Union Graduate School."

20. Roney, "Double Vision of Clarence Major, Painter and Writer," 67.

21. Quoted in ibid., 67.

22. Klinkowitz, *Keeping Literary Company*, 185.

23. E-mail, Major to author, 27 June 2011.

24. Quartermain, "Trusting the Reader," 69.

25. Weixlmann, "African American Deconstruction of the Novel in the Work of Ishmael Reed and Clarence Major," 69.

26. Clarence Major, unpublished interview by the author, May 2007.


CHAPTER 7. Finding a New Life

1. Major to Banks, 5 January 1981, Russell Banks Papers, box 43.

2. Couturier, *Representation and Performance and Representation in Postmodern Fiction*, 163.

3. Fabre, *From Harlem to Paris*, 293–96.

4. Accessed 30 September 2011, http://www.permanentpress.co.uk/publications .html. As of this writing, the site indicates that copies are still available.

5. Fabre, *From Harlem to Paris*, 293.

6. "On the Trail of Cézanne: Modern Art in the South of France," *Guardian*, 14 January 2006, accessed 30 September 2011, http://www.independent.co.uk/news/world/ europe/on-the-trail-of-ceacutezanne-modern-art-in-the-south-of-france-522905 .html.

7. Halevi, *Way of the Kabbalah*, 112.

8. Haftmann, *Gouaches, Drawings, Watercolors*, 96.

9. Henri Matisse, The Personal Life of Henri Matisse, accessed 30 September 2011, www.henri-matisse.net/biography.html.

10. Weixlmann, "African American Deconstruction of the Novel in the Work of Ishmael Reed and Clarence Major," 73.

11. Major to Banks, 18 June 1983, Russell Banks Papers, box 45.

12. "Friends (and foes)," Clarence Major Archives, Books, box 3.

13. Weixlmann, "African American Deconstruction of the Novel in the Work of Ishmael Reed and Clarence Major," 73.

14. See Major's version of this in *Juba to Jive*, 57.

15. Klawans, "I Was a Weird Example of Art," 82.

16. Ibid., 82–83.

17. Klinkowitz, *Keeping Literary Company*, 181.

18. Ibid.


CHAPTER 8. Back to America, Back to Europe

1. E-mail, Major to author, 23 July 2010.

2. Selzer, "Clarence Major and Mark Twain Abroad," 71.

3. Wright, 67–75.

4. See especially Nancy Mairs, "Where a Zuni's Soul Dies," and Susan Lowell, "Song of the Turtle."

5. "Major's Passion for Writing Transcends Life's Hazards."

6. E-mail, Major to author, 20 August 2010.


CHAPTER 9. Consolidating a Career

1. E-mail, Major to author, 18 August 2010.

2. Ibid., 31 August 2010.

3. *The Long Road* is the name of Major's version of *The Scream*, discussed in chapter 3.

4. Colescott and Dove, *Progressive Printmakers*, 101–13.

5. Unpublished interview with author.

6. Klinkowitz, *Keeping Literary Company*, 182.

7. Clarence Major Archives, "Mexico Journals," n.d., Miscellaneous, box 3.

8. E-mail, Major to author, 15 November 2010.

9. Review of *Dirty Bird Blues*.

10. Quamme, "'Bird' Speaks Language of Blues."

11. Selzer, "Reading the Painterly Text."

12. "Paris Journal," 23 July 1998. Photocopy in author's personal collection.

13. Burns, "In the Spotlight."

14. E-mail, Major to author, 22 August 2010.

15. Major, unpublished interview with the author, 30 May 2010.

16. See page for Thomas Eakins's *Rail Shooting* at Yale Art Gallery website, accessed 3 August 2011, http://artgallery.yale.edu/pages/collection/popups/pc_amerps/details16 .html.

17. Ibid.

18. See "Soapwort," Purple Sage Botanicals website, last modified 12 June 2011, accessed 3 August 2011, http://www.purplesage.org.uk/profiles/soapwort.htm.

19. "On *Myself Painting*, Poems by Clarence Major (LSU Press), and *Present Vanishing*, Poems by Dick Allen (Sarabande Books)," *On the Seawall* (Ron Slate's blog), 23 January 2009, http://www.ronslate.com/myself_painting_poems_clarence_major _lsu_press_and_present_vanishing_poems_dick_allen_sarabande_book.

CONCLUSION. Returning to the Beginning

1. E-mail, Major to author, 8 February 2011.

# Bibliography

PRIMARY SOURCES

*Archives*

Clarence Major Archives. Archie Givens Sr. Collection of African American
　Literature, University of Minnesota Library
Fiction Collective 2 Archive. Harry Ransom Center, University of Texas, Austin
Ronald Sukenick Papers. Harry Ransom Center, University of Texas, Austin
Russell Banks Papers. Harry Ransom Center, University of Texas, Austin

*Publications by Clarence Major (Chronological)*

All citations are to the first edition of the publication listed in the bibliography.

Novels

*All-Night Visitors.* New York: Olympia Press, 1969. Reprint Boston: Northeastern
　University Press, 1998. As *I Visitatori della Notta*, trans. Antonio Tronti, Milan:
　Olympia Press Milano, 1969. As *Damonen*, trans. O. P. Wilck, Frankfurt: Olympia
　Press Sonderreiche am Main, 1970.
*NO.* New York: Emerson Hall, 1973
*Reflex and Bone Structure.* New York: Fiction Collective, 1975. Reprint San Francisco:
　Mercury House, 1996. As *Reflexe et Ossature*, trans. Maurice Couturier, Lausanne:
　Cistre, Lettres Differentes; Éditions L' Age D' Homme, 1982.
*Emergency Exit.* New York: Fiction Collective, 1979.
*My Amputations.* New York: Fiction Collective, 1986.
*Such Was The Season.* San Francisco: Mercury House, 1987. Reprint Voices of the
　South, Baton Rouge: Louisiana State University Press, 2003.
*Painted Turtle: Woman with Guitar.* Los Angeles: Sun and Moon Press, 1988.

*Dirty Bird Blues*. San Francisco: Mercury House, 1996. Reprint New York: Berkley Signature Edition, 1997.
*One Flesh*. New York: Kensington Books, 2003.

Short Stories

"Ulysses, Who Slept Across from Me." *Olivant* 1 (1957): 53–56.
*Fun and Games*. Duluth, Minn.: Holy Cow! Press, 1990.

Poetry

*The Fires That Burn in Heaven*. Chicago: n.p., 1954.
*The New Black Poetry*. Editor. New York: International Publishers, 1969.
*Swallow the Lake*. Middletown, Conn.: Wesleyan University Press, 1970.
*Private Line*. London: Paul Breman, 1971.
*Symptoms and Madness*. New York: Corinth Books, 1971.
*The Cotton Club*. Detroit: Broadside Press, 1972.
*The Syncopated Cakewalk*. New York: Barlenmir House, 1974.
*Inside Diameter: The France Poems*. London: Permanent Press, 1985.
*Surfaces and Masks*. Minneapolis, Minn.: Coffee House Press, 1988.
*Some Observations of a Stranger at Zuni in the Latter Part of the Century*. Los Angeles: Sun and Moon Press, 1989.
*Parking Lots*. Mount Horeb, Wis.: Perishable Press, 1992.
"The Slave Trade: View from the Middle Passage." *African American Review* 28, no. 1 (1994): 11–22. Reprinted in *Configurations*, 300–319, and Bell, 13–26.
*Configurations: New and Selected Poems 1958–1998*. Washington, D.C.: Copper Canyon Press, 1999.
*Waiting for Sweet Betty*. Washington:, D.C.: Copper Canyon Press, 2002.
*Myself Painting*. Baton Rouge: Louisiana State University Press, 2008.

Nonfiction

Editor. *The Writers Workshop Anthology*. New York: Harlem Education Program, n.d.
Review of *Flower, Fist and Bestial Wall* by Charles Bukowski, *Ceremonies in Mind* by Tram Combs, *Her* by Lawrence Ferlinghetti. *Anagogic and Paideumic Review*, no. 6 (1961): n.p.
"How *All-Night Visitors* Was Made." *Nickel Review* 3, no. 1 (April 1969): 11.
*Dictionary of Afro-American Slang*. Editor. New York: International Publishers, 1970. As *Black Slang: A Dictionary of Afro-American Talk*, London: Routledge and Kegan Paul, 1971.
*The Dark and Feeling: Black American Writers and Their Work*. New York: Third Press, 1974.
"Clarence Major Interviews Jacob Lawrence, the Expressionist." *Black Scholar* 9, no. 3 (1979): 14–25.

"Licking Stamps, Taking Chances." In *Contemporary Authors Autobiography Series.*
6:175–204. Detroit: Gale Research, 1988.

"Reaching and Leaving the Point." *High Plains Literary Review* 4, no. 2 (1989): 28–43.

Editor. *Juba to Jive: A Dictionary of African-American Slang.* New York: Viking, 1994.

*Necessary Distance: Essays and Criticism.* St. Paul, Minn.: Coffee House Press, 2000.

*Come by Here: My Mother's Life.* New York: John Wiley, 2002.

*Painting Exhibitions by Clarence Major (Chronological, list courtesy of
Clarence Major)*

Solo Exhibitions

Twenty Oil Paintings. Sarah Lawrence College Library, Bronxville, N.Y., Spring 1974.

New Works on Paper. First National Bank Gallery, Boulder, Colo., 3–17 January 1986.

Double Consciousness: The Paintings of Clarence Major. Kresge Art Museum, East
Lansing, Mich., 4 September–28 October 2001.

Figures in Full. 35 paintings on a five-at-a-time rotating display for a year,
previewport.com, 2002.

It's Raining Art. Schacknow Museum of Fine Art, Plantation, Fla., April–May 2003.

A Festival of Figures. Exploding Head Gallery, Sacramento, Calif., April 2003.

Impressions of Yolo County. Main Street Gallery, Winters, Calif., 5–31 August 2004.

Golden Valley Financial, Sacramento, Calif., February–March 2006.

Hamilton Club Gallery, Paterson, N.J., October–November 2006.

*Morning Light, Looking toward Winters #1,* and *Interior #2.* Permanent Contemporary
Art Collection, Hamilton Club Gallery, Paterson, N.J., 2007.

Ca. 50 paintings. Rominger West Winery, Davis, Calif., 6 May–3 June 2008.

Twenty-two paintings. Phoenix Gallery, Sacramento, Calif., November–December
2008.

Configurations. Pierre Menard Gallery, Cambridge, Mass., 6 August–3 September
2010.

Myself Painting. Center for the Performing and Fine Arts, Indiana State University,
Terre Haute, Ind., 24 February–25 March 2011.

Group Exhibitions

Oil painting entry. Carnegie Institute Gallery, Pittsburgh, Pa., 1950. (National
exhibition of the best works by high school art students.)

Oil painting entry. Montgomery Ward Department Store Gallery, Chicago, Ill., 1952.
(National exhibition of the best works by high school art students.)

Two paintings. Gayle Gallery, Chicago, Ill., 1957.

Three paintings. Gayle Galley, Chicago, Ill., 1958.

Two paintings. Gayle Gallery, Chicago, Ill., 1959.

Winds Over the Rockies Exhibition. National Center for Atmospheric Research,
Boulder, Colo., 1979.

Five paintings: *Banjo, Five Figures, Four Figures, Rest*, and *Gas Station*. In Poet Jazz Paint Exhibition, Porter Troupe Gallery, San Diego, Calif., April 2001.

Five paintings. In Spirit Made Visible. John Natsoulas Gallery, Davis, Calif., 9 May– 7 June 1992. Show also curated by Clarence Major, included works by Robert Colescott, Raymond Saunders, Oliver Jackson, and Mary Lovelace O'Neal.

*Birds*. In Families First Exhibit. Davis, Calif., July 1992. (A John Natsoulas-sponsored exhibition.)

All Creatures Great and Small. John Natsoulas Gallery, Davis, Calif., 1993.

Five paintings. Kiln Theo Studio and Gallery, Winters, Calif., 1999. (Paintings on display for a year.)

Three paintings: *Baseball, Blue Vase*, and *Two Figures*. Charles Rowell Collection Exhibition, Texas A&M University Art Museum, College Station, Tex., June 2002.

*Sweet Betty*. John Natsoulas Gallery, Davis, Calif., October 2002.

Eight paintings. In Figuratively Speaking. Exploding Head Gallery, Sacramento, Calif., August 2004.

Twenty-two paintings. In Small Works, Small Prices. Main Street Gallery, Winters, Calif., November–December 2004.

*Waiting* and *The Mirror*. In Poetry and its Arts: Bay Area Interactions 1954–2004. California Historical Society Museum, San Francisco, 11 December 2004–16 April 2005.

Landscapes. Blue Hills Gallery, Winters, Calif., April–June 2005.

New Artists Show. Phoenix Gallery, Sacramento, Calif., March 2006.

Art by Writers. Paterson Art Museum, Paterson, N.J., April–May 2006.

Group Show. Phoenix Gallery, Sacramento, Calif., July 2006.

Urban Landscape. Exploding Head Gallery, Sacramento, Calif., July 2006.

*The Interview*. Exploding Head Gallery special exhibition. Sacramento Court House, Calif. 2006.

*Interior*. In From Harlem to Paris: The Art and Travels of Herbert Gentry. Library Gallery, University of Rochester, Rochester, N.Y., October 2007.

Three paintings in a traveling show, 2007–8: Denenberg Fine Arts Gallery, La.; Anita Shapolsky Gallery, New York, N.Y.; Pierre Menard Gallery, Cambridge, Mass.

*Waiting*. 40 Acres Gallery, Sacramento, Calif., July 2008.

Four paintings. Phoenix Gallery, Sacramento, Calif., March 2009.

SECONDARY SOURCES

Allen, Bruce. Review of *Reflex and Bone Structure*. *Library Journal*, 15 January 1976: 667.

"American Author Speaks." *Daily Observer*, 7 June 1982, 9.

Bamberger, Bill. Review of *Inside Diameter*. *New Pages* 12:11.

Baraka, Amiri. *The LeRoi Jones/Amiri Baraka Reader.* Ed. William J. Harris. New York: Thunder's Mouth Press, 1991.

Bates, David. "A Brief History of the Union Institute and University, with References and a Guide to Sources." 2002. Accessed 30 June 2010, http://www-unix.oit.umass .edu/~hendra/Briefhis.html.

Baumbach, Jonathan. "Who Do They Think They Are? A Personal History of the Fiction Collective." *TriQuarterly* 43 (1978): 625–34.

Bearden, Romare, and Harry Henderson. *A History of African-American Artists: From 1792 to the Present.* New York: Pantheon, 1993.

Bell, Bernard, ed. *Clarence Major and His Art: Portraits of an African American Postmodernist.* Chapel Hill: University of North Carolina Press, 2001.

*Black American Literature Forum* 13, no. 2 (Summer 1979). Special Issue on Clarence Major.

Bradfield, Larry D. "Beyond Mimetic Exhaustion: The *Reflex and Bone Structure* Experiment." *Black American Literature Forum* 17, no. 3 (1983): 120–23.

Brettell, Richard. *Post-Impressionists.* New York: Harry N. Abrams, 1987.

Brooks, Tim. *Lost Sounds: Blacks and the Birth of the Recording Industry, 1890–1919.* Urbana: University of Illinois Press, 2004.

Bunge, Nancy, ed. *Conversations with Clarence Major.* Jackson: University Press of Mississippi, 2002.

Burns, Ann. "In the Spotlight: Dafina Books." *Library Journal,* 1 November 1996, accessed 15 November 2010, http://www.libraryjournal.com/lj/ljinprintcurrent issue/867267-403/story.csp.

Cabanne, Pierre. *Van Gogh.* Paris: Terrail Edigroup, 2006.

Cain, Michael Scott. "Three Novels from Writers, Not Publishing Houses." Review of *Reflex and Bone Structure. Baltimore Sun,* 9 November 1975.

"Clarence Major Issue." *African American Review* 28, no. 1 (Spring 1994).

Coleman, James W. "Clarence Major's *All-Night Visitors*: Calabanic Discourse and Black Male Expression." *African American Review* 28, no. 1 (1994): 95–108.

Colescott, Warrington, and Arthur Dove. *Progressive Printmakers: Wisconsin Artists and the Print Renaissance.* Madison: University of Wisconsin Press, 1999.

Couturier, Maurice. *Representation and Performance and Representation in Postmodern Fiction: Proceedings of the Nice Conference on Postmodern Fiction.* Montpellier, France: Delta, 1983.

Cushman, Jerome. Review of *Swallow the Lake. Library Journal* 15 November 1970, 3913.

Davis, George. "A Young Man Pursued by Demons." Review of *NO. New York Times Book Review,* 1 July 1973, 22.

De St. Jorre, John. *Venus Bound: The Erotic Voyage of the Olympia Press and Its Writers.* New York: Random House, 1996.

Dent, Tom. "Umbra Days." *Black American Literature Forum* 14, no. 3 (1980): 105–8.

Dunlop, Ian. *Edvard Munch*. New York: St. Martin's, 1977.

Fabre, Michel. *From Harlem to Paris: Black American Writers in France, 1840–1980.* Urbana: University of Illinois Press, 1991.

———. Review of *Emergency Exit. Afram Newsletter* 11 (November 1980).

Ferguson, SallyAnn. "Two Provocative New Books Illuminate the Black Experience." *Greensboro News and Record*, 28 August 1988.

Haftmann, Werner. *Gouaches, Drawings, Watercolors: Marc Chagall*. Trans. Robert Erich Wolf. New York: Harry N. Abrams, 1984.

Halevi, Z'ev ben Shimon. *The Way of the Kabbalah*. London: Rider, 1976.

Harlan, Megan. Review of *Waiting for Sweet Betty. San Francisco Chronicle*, 15 December 2002.

Harris, Michael. "The Struggles of a Black Everyman of the 1950s." *Los Angeles Times*, 29 July 1996.

Hayward, Steve. "Against Commodification: Zuni Culture in Clarence Major's Native American Texts." *African American Review* 28, no. 1 (1994): 109–20.

Hernton, Calvin. "Umbra: A Personal Recounting." *African American Review* 27, no. 4 (1993): 579–84.

Hill, Lodowick Johnson. *The Hills of Wilkes County, Georgia, and Allied Families*. Danielsville, Ga.: M. B. Warren, 1987.

Hogue, W. Lawrence. *The African American Male, Writing, and Difference: A Polycentric Approach to African American Literature, Criticism, and History*. Albany: State University of New York Press, 2003.

———. "Postmodernism, Traditional Cultural Forms, and the African American Narrative: Major's Reflex, Morrison's Jazz, and Reed's Mumbo Jumbo." *Novel: A Forum on Fiction* 35, nos. 2–3 (2002): 169–92.

Joyce, Donald F. *Gatekeepers of Black Culture: Black-Owned Publishing in the United States, 1817–1981*. Westport, Conn.: Greenwood, 1983.

"J.S.W." Review of *Reflex and Bone Structure. Kliatt Paperback Book Guide* 10, no. 1 (February 1976): 68.

Judd, Inge. Review of *Emergency Exit. Library Journal*, 15 November 1979: 2482.

Katz, Bill. Review of *Private Line. Library Journal*, 15 March 1972: 1021.

Klawans, Stuart. "All of Me." *Nation*, 24 January 1987, 90.

———. "'I Was a Weird Example of Art': *My Amputations* as Cubist Confession." *African American Review* 28, no. 1 (1994): 77–87.

Klinkowitz, Jerome. "Art as Life." Review of *My Amputations. American Book Review* 8, no. 5 (September/October 1986): 12.

———. *Keeping Literary Company: Working with Writers since the Sixties*. Albany: State University of New York Press, 1998.

———. *The Life of Fiction*. Urbana: University of Illinois Press, 1977.

————. *Literary Disruptions: The Making of a Post-Contemporary American Fiction.* 2nd ed. Urbana: University of Illinois Press, 1980.

————. "Notes on a Novel-in-Progress: Clarence Major's *Emergency Exit.*" *Black American Literature Forum* 13, no. 2 (1979): 46–50.

Kostelanetz, Richard. "Alternative Book Publishers," *Margins* 9 (Dec. 1973–Jan. 1974): 27–36. Accessed 23 December 2010, at http://www.richardkostelanetz.com/examples/altpub.php.

Lask, Thomas. Review of *Reflex and Bone Structure. New York Times Book Review,* 30 November 1975, 61.

Lauzen, Sarah E. "Surface, (Symbol), Loop." Review of *Emergency Exit. American Book Review* 4, no. 6 (September/October 1982): 8.

Lehmann-Haupt, Christopher. "Books of the Times: On Erotica," *New York Times,* 7 April 1969, 41.

Lewis, Samella. *African American Art and Artists.* Berkeley: University of California Press, 1994.

Lopate, Phillip, ed. *Journal of a Living Experiment: A Documentary History of the First Ten Years of Teachers Writers Collaborative.* New York: Teachers and Writers, 1979.

Lowell, Susan. "Song of the Turtle." *Los Angeles Times Book Review,* 18 December 1988, 2.

Lowenfels, Walter. *In a Time of Revolution: Poems from Our Third World.* New York: Random House, 1969.

Ludington, Townsend, ed. *A Modern Mosaic: Art and Modernism in the United States.* Chapel Hill: University of North Carolina Press, 2000.

Lyons, Gene. "Report on the Fiction Collective," *TriQuarterly* 43 (1978): 635–47.

MacLeish, Archibald. *Collected Poems, 1917 to 1982.* New York: Mariner Books, 1985.

Mairs, Nancy. "Where a Zuni's Soul Dies." Review of *Painted Turtle. New York Times Book Review,* 30 October 1988, 37.

"Major's Passion for Writing Transcends Life's Hazards." *Inside SUNY Binghamton,* 7 April 1988, 1.

McCaffery, Larry. "The Fiction Collective." *Contemporary Literature* 19, no. 1 (1978): 99–115.

————. "The Fiction Collective, 1974–1978." *Chicago Review* 30, no. 2 (1978): 107–26.

————. "Major's *Reflex and Bone Structure* and the Anti-Detective Tradition." *Black American Literature Forum* 13, no. 2 (1979): 39–45.

Mewshaw, Michael. Review of *Museum,* by B. H. Friedman. *New York Times Book Review,* 13 October 1974, 26–27.

Moore, Alexis. "A Risk-Taker Rises in Black Fiction." *Philadelphia Inquirer,* 6 December 1988.

Moore, Steven. "Sheri Martinelli: A Modernist Muse." Accessed 30 March 2010, http://www.gargoylemagazine. com/gargoyle/Issues/scanned/issue41/modern_muse.htm.

————, ed. *Beerspit Night and Cursing: The Correspondence of Charles Bukowski and Sheri Martinelli, 1960–1967.* Santa Rosa, Calif.: Black Sparrow Press, 2001.

Moore, Steven, and Lauri Ramey, eds. *Every Goodbye Ain't Gone: An Anthology of Innovative Poetry by African Americans.* Tuscaloosa: University of Alabama Press, 2006.

Nielsen, Aldon Lynn. *Black Chant: Languages of African-American Postmodernism.* Cambridge: Cambridge University Press, 1997.

O'Brien, John. "Is Black Literature beyond Criticism?" *Chicago Sunday Sun-Times,* 28 April 1974, 3:1.

Polk, James. "Outside the Mainstream: The Non-Narrative Novel." *Newsday,* 6 January 1980.

Quamme, Margaret. "'Bird' Speaks Language of Blues." *Columbus Dispatch,* 4 August 1996, 6F.

Quartermain, Peter. "Trusting the Reader." *Chicago Review* 32, no. 2 (1980): 65–74.

Review of *Dirty Bird Blues. Publishers Weekly* 243, no. 22 (27 May 1996): 67.

Review of *Emergency Exit. Publishers Weekly* 216, no. 14 (1 October 1979): 86.

Review of *Reflex and Bone Structure.* "Ebony Book Shelf." *Ebony* 31, no. 4 (February 1976): 26.

Review of *The New Black Poetry. Choice* 6 (October 1969): 1016.

Roney, Lisa C. "The Double Vision of Clarence Major, Painter and Writer." *African American Review* 28, no. 1 (1994) 65–75.

Rubin, Merle. "Mirrors in the Labyrinth." Review of *Fun and Games. Los Angeles Times Book Review,* 18 February 1990, 2.

Rushdy, Ashraf H. A. *Neo-Slave Narratives: Studies in the Social Logic of a Literary Form.* New York: Oxford University Press, 1999.

Salzman, Jack, David Lionel Smith, and Cornel West, eds. *Encyclopedia of African-American Culture and History.* 5 vols. New York: Macmillan, 1996.

Selzer, Linda Furgerson. "Clarence Major and Mark Twain Abroad." In *The Heritage Series of Black Poetry, 1962–1975: A Research Compendium,* edited by Lauri Ramey, 71–83. Burlington, Vt.: Ashgate, 2008.

————. "Reading the Painterly Text: Clarence Major's 'The Slave Trade: View from the Middle Passage.'" *African American Review* 33, no. 2 (1999): 209–29.

Simosko, Vladimir, and Barry Tepperman. *Eric Dolphy: A Musical Biography and Discography.* Washington, D.C.: Smithsonian, 1974.

Sukenick, Ronald. "Guest Word." *New York Times Book Review,* 15 September 1974, 56.

Thomas, Lorenzo. "The Shadow World: New York's Umbra Workshop and Origins of the Black Arts Movement." *Callaloo* 1, no. 4 (1978): 53–72.

Washington, Julie. "Heartwarming Tale of Black Tradition." *Cleveland Plain Dealer,* 3 December 1987.

Weedon, Chris. *Post-War Women's Writing in German: Feminist Critical Approaches.* Oxford, UK: Berghahn Books, 1997.

Weixlmann, Joe. "African American Deconstruction of the Novel in the Work of Ishmael Reed and Clarence Major." *Melus* 17, no. 4 (Winter 1991–92): 57–79.

Wright, Barton. *Clowns of the Hopi: Tradition Keepers and Delight Makers.* Flagstaff, Ariz.: Northland, 2004.

Young, Al. "God Never Drove Those Cadillacs." Review of *Such Was the Season. New York Times Book Review*, 13 December 1987.

# Index